RUSSIAN RESEARCH CENTER STUDIES
38

# National Consciousness in Eighteenth-Century Russia

# National Consciousness in Eighteenth-Century Russia

**BY HANS ROGGER**

**Harvard University Press, Cambridge, Massachusetts**

The Russian Research Center of Harvard University is supported by a grant from the Carnegie Corporation. The Center carries out interdisciplinary study of Russian institutions and behavior and related subjects.

This volume was prepared under a grant from the Carnegie Corporation of New York. That Corporation is not, however, the author, owner, publisher, or proprietor of this publication and is not to be understood as approving by virtue of its grant any of the statements made or views expressed therein.

Library of Congress Catalog Card Number 60–8450
SBN 674-60150-5
Printed in the United States of America

To My Parents

# Preface

My purpose in writing this book has been to determine the extent to which Russian life and letters in the eighteenth century were concerned with the problem of national identity and culture, and to discover in what terms that concern was expressed. In spite of the unusual readiness of Russia's upper classes to embrace all things Western, from fashions in dress to fashions in thought—and more often the former than the latter—the very depth of Western influence challenged and stimulated articulate Russians to look into their own past and culture for objects of pride and attachment. Indeed, the wish not to appear inferior in the eyes of a Europe of which they wished to be considered a part forced them to create that culture and the means for its expression. It is this process I have set out to describe, in the hope of contributing to our knowledge of a formative period of Russian history, in order to trace the origin of some of the central themes of Russian nationalism, and to discover how Russians began to define for themselves and for others the nature of their culture, their country and its people.

These goals, and the conclusions arrived at, require no fundamental revision of prevailing views about Russian history. They do, however, imply that a balanced picture of Russia in the eighteenth century, the century of Russia's Westernization, will have to take into account the themes and issues that are the subject of this book; and they suggest that the question of the origins of Russian nineteenth-century nationalism, which has been indicated here in the sketchiest fashion, stands in need of further study.

In acknowledging the various kinds of help and support I have received in the preparation of this book, I would first of all like to mention with deep gratitude the late Professor Michael Karpovich, who was a generous friend and wise teacher. I have had much help and kindness from Professor Robert L. Wolff, who read the manuscript at various stages. He, as well as Professor Richard Pipes, made many valuable suggestions and gave me much useful advice. I wish also to thank the Russian Research Center, and its former Director, Professor Clyde Kluckhohn, for encouragement and financial support while I was engaged in the research for the book. At the beginning of my work I had the benefit of a number of talks with Professors Roman Jakobson and Dmitry Cizevsky (now of the University of Heidelberg) which helped me to define the scope of my study. My wife, Claire Rogger, has assisted me in innumerable ways; whatever I might say here cannot do full justice to the extent and the value of her contribution.

I have employed the system of transliteration recommended by the Harvard University Press in its style sheet for the Russian Research Center series. It is a slightly simplified version of the table of transliteration in the *Sixth Report of the United States Geographic Board.*

Portions of Chapter II and Chapter VI have appeared previously in my contribution to volume IV of the Harvard Slavic Studies, *Russian Thought and Politics* (Cambridge, Mass., 1957); a portion of Chapter V has appeared previously in my article "The 'Nationalism' of Ivan Nikitich Boltin" in *For Roman Jakobson* (The Hague: Mouton & Co., 1956).

Hans Rogger

November 1959

# Contents

# National Consciousness in
# Eighteenth-Century Russia

# Introduction

Nationalism, most of its students are agreed, is a recent phenomenon, and any use of the term applied to events or attitudes before the eighteenth century unjustified.[1] Even then, only some favored few—the English, the French, perhaps the Dutch—could claim it as their own. The Russians, backward in this as in so many other things, did not, in the eighteenth century, have a nationalism worthy of that name, and "real" Russian nationalism did not make its appearance until the nineteenth century.[2] The first expressions of this nationalism have been attributed to the impact of the Napoleonic wars; the residence abroad of young Russian officers and students; the reception of German romanticism, of Herder, Schelling, and Hegel. It is out of these stimuli, and particularly out of the impetus furnished by German philosophy that the first distinctly nationalist school of thought, Slavophilism, is said to have arisen.[3]

There is no disagreement with the view that nationalism as a world-view, a system of values and beliefs—such as Slavophilism—was a late development in Russian life, as was belief in Russia as a distinct cultural entity, with guiding principles of her own and a unique role to play in the arena of world history. But it would be wrong to conclude that nationalism, or Slavophilism were sudden growths, foreign importations or mere translations of beliefs and attitudes developed elsewhere. This conclusion ignores the concern of much of Russian eighteenth-century thought with the issues of national identity and values, and neglects important sources of later thinking about the character and destiny of Russia.

The belief that nationalism was absent from the Russian scene before the nineteenth century has two sources. One of these is the theory, developed on the basis of the historical experience of Western Europe, that liberalism and nationalism grew together. Everywhere, in the words of Professor Carlton Hayes, "professed nationalists were leading apostles of popular sovereignty";[4] in every country, nationalism was stimulated by the demand for individual freedom and the desire for institutions reflecting the will of the national community. Where the apostles of popular sovereignty could not be found, nationalism was not likely to be present. Although Professor Hans Kohn does not explicitly link nationalism with the doctrines of liberalism or popular sovereignty, he too believes that "nationalism as an active force in history was confined in the eighteenth century to the shores of the North Atlantic. It expressed the spirit of the age in its emphasis upon the individual and his rights and in its participation in the humanitarian character of the enlightenment."[5] Russia, which has been called a country without an eighteenth century, was clearly deficient in all that went to make up the spirit of the age.

The other reason given for the late development of Russian nationalism is not the country's failure to participate in the Enlightenment, but the very depth of Russia's penetration by the West in the age of Peter and Catherine, her submersion in a flood of foreign influences. Cosmopolitanism and imitation, neglect or even contempt of their language, their history, and their native soil[6] supposedly characterized upper-class Russians when their French and English contemporaries were engaged in converting the dynastic into the national state, themselves from subjects into citizens.

Neither the dearth nor the excess of Western influence, neither too little Enlightenment nor too much French frivolity are adequate formulations of the question for Russia in the eighteenth century. Whether sensitive and thoughtful Russians embraced the spirit of the age or not, that spirit came to them from beyond the borders of their country and challenged them to evaluate its meaning for Russia and to define the character and validity of their own civilization. This was not perhaps nationalism—"a sentiment . . . molding all public and private life" [7]—but it was an act of national self-determination in personal and cultural terms; it was the development of an articulate national consciousness, a most important ingredient of nationalism. For Russians of the time, the problem of nationality was as much personal and cultural as it was political and social.

The term nationalism has been avoided in speaking of the events and ideas of the period from the death of Peter to the death of Catherine the Great, not because the absence of a liberal movement makes the term inapplicable; nor because the infatuation with another world kept Russians from developing an awareness of their own. It is because national consciousness and nationalism are each characteristic of a distinct period of Russian history. Although they share common features, they differ in their scope, their purpose, and their nature. The distinction between the two is central to this study.

National consciousness is here viewed as a striving for a common identity, character, and culture by the articulate members of a given community. It is the expression of that striving in art and social life, and characteristic, therefore, of a stage of development in which thinking individuals have been able to emerge from anonymity, to seek contact and communication with one another. National consciousness presupposes extensive exposure to alien ways; it presupposes a class or group of men capable of responding to that exposure; it requires, moreover, the existence of a secular cultural community or an attempt at its formation. In Russia, these conditions were met, could only be met, in the eighteenth century.

Nationalism goes beyond the search or the creation of a

national consciousness. In ninetenth-century Russia, as elsewhere, it is an inclusive system of thought, an ideology, which on the basis of a specific national experience attempts to provide answers to moral, social, and political questions. It is more than an awareness of national identity, more than a search for the bases of national being; it has found these and proclaimed their eternal validity. It is a philosophy, a value judgment, a metaphysic. Its basis is belief, not consciousness. However tolerant it may be of other beliefs, it usually values what is Russian more highly than that which is not. This form of nationalism, of national ideology, became increasingly common in the nineteenth century, playing a role that religious belief no longer filled for most thinking Europeans and one that the political ideologies of the twentieth century had not yet assumed.

Nationalism then is not the subject of this book. It is a phenomenon of a later age, yet it did receive themes, modes of thought, and symbols from the eighteenth century. There are some striking similarities in the thinking of the two periods about the relations between class and nationality, citizenship and morality; the national character and its attributes, Russia and the West. This recurrence of similar attitudes and language is no proof that eighteenth-century thought directly inspired specific positions of nineteenth-century nationalism. It does confirm that Russian nationalism, although nourished by German philosophy and encouraged by the Napoleonic wars, had native and earlier sources to draw upon.

If imitation and heedless borrowing did not exclusively dominate Russian life and thought in the eighteenth century, neither was a national or antiforeign orientation its outstanding characteristic. The age, in Russia as elsewhere, was singularly receptive to every current of ideas which emanated from Western Europe, and the growth of a national consciousness was, in fact, one of the elements and one of the signs of

Russia's Westernization. There was not so much a turning away from Europe, as there was an attempt on the part of educated Russians to develop a sense of their own character and culture—a national consciousness. The result was a synthesis of native and foreign elements, not simply another instance of xenophobia or a permanent distrust of the West. The creators of this synthesis were also the creators of modern Russia's secular culture, and their work was as novel as the role they were to play in Russian society.

The development of national consciousness was intimately and inextricably linked with the development of a national culture. The two processes constantly stimulated one another and at times they were identical. "The history of a higher, intellectual culture," wrote Otto Bauer, "of science, art, and poetry is a history of leisure. The peasant, tied to the labor of the soil, could not develop a higher intellectual culture." [8] Nor, for that matter, could the Russian landowning class which kept the peasant in subjection and was itself tied to the service of the state. Not until the emergence of the gentry as a distinct, privileged class, with corporate rights and a corporate consciousness, was the elaboration of a national culture and of an articulate national consciousness taken in hand. The privileged class of Russian society, increasingly free of state service, felt most strongly the need for a style, a culture of its own, particularly when it compared itself with the Russian peasantry or with the aristocracy of the West. A national language and a national literature, as well as an awareness of the national past—these were the creations of the most Westernized portion of the population. It is this fact which lent to the culture and national consciousness of eighteenth-century Russia its distinctive, European features.

The Russian experience in this regard was not an isolated one. The cosmopolitan eighteenth century, which was generally so inhospitable to specifically national or nationalist ideas,[9] promoted the interchange of ideas on a European scale. Frequent contacts between different cultures and nationalities made Europeans confront the question of their similarities and differences. The biographies of more than one European of cosmopolitan culture and outlook furnish instances of a newly awakened sense of nationality as a result of exposure to unfamiliar modes of life and thought. Goethe, perhaps the least provincial of German writers, was "deeply concerned to discover native and true principles of art and forms of life, particularly at Strasbourg, face to face with France."[10] August Ludwig Schloezer, the Goettingen historian who thought little of such notions as fatherland, and readily left his home to enter the service of another country, recalled that only in Russia, in a foreign and sometimes hostile environment, did he think of Germany as a single whole or fatherland, for the first and possibly the last time in his life.[11] And it was in reaction against Schloezer and his theories about the origins of the Russian state and the Russian language that Lomonosov, feeling his fatherland slighted, became more insistently Russian. The self, the specifically national, was determined and defined on contact with the other, the foreign, the nonnational.[12]

Contact with the foreigner, with his way of life, his thought and worship, was not new to Russia in the eighteenth century. What was new was Russian receptivity to such contact. This receptivity was born of the needs of the state and the desires of its servants, and it was more persistent and intense than it had ever been before. Exposure to foreign contacts came in a variety of ways: young men sent abroad to study; foreigners invited and welcomed as teachers; involvement in European wars which took Russian regiments deeper and deeper into Europe; increased travel and regular diplomatic relations with Western courts; an expansion of commerce and an unprecedented influx of foreign fashions in thought, letters, instruction, and social intercourse. In addition, some of Russia's monarchs of this century were themselves of foreign birth; others surrounded themselves with foreigners and made of the court and government a foreign enclave in the midst of Russian life. It was a result of the century's particular interest in all that was strange and novel that even those Russians who had never been abroad came to feel the impact of another world. Only after the Petrine reforms could literate Russians begin to judge critically the meaning of Europe for Russia, and only after critical evaluation could they begin to propose specifically national values to replace those of foreign origin which they found wanting or harmful. In this way, the first ingredients of a national ideology were developed.

## CHAPTER I

# The Government of Foreigners

Groups or individuals opposed to political or social innovation often denounce as alien those changes in the national life
of which they disapprove. It is not necessary that the object of
their protest be, in fact, foreign. By a process of extension and
displacement, discontent creates a wide variety of targets, some
of them symbolic, which are in their essence no more "foreign"
than the sources of discontent themselves are "national." In
the history of Russian nationalism, the importance of these
targets has always been great.

In the seventeenth century, changes introduced in prayer-
books and Church ritual by a Russian patriarch were fiercely
resisted as being of foreign, mainly Greek, origin. In the early
eighteenth century, resistance to the modernization and Westernization of political and social life expressed itself in opposition to the smoking and snuffing of tobacco, the drinking of
tea and coffee, the wearing of "German" dress, Italian singing
and painting, and the shaving of beards. The reign of Peter the
Great, with its influx of foreigners and foreign ways, was
widely regarded as a profound and radical change of heretofore familiar forms of life and was therefore resented and resisted by many.[1] When the monarch himself was not held
responsible for the introduction of new and evil ways, they
were attributed to the baneful influence of his foreign advisers.

It is today impossible to gauge the extent to which this
"national" opposition to the Petrine reforms found an echo
outside the circles of the Old Believers. It did, however, exist

and it is responsible for the creation of a set of readily available, readily recognizable targets of national protest which will recur throughout the century and beyond. The definition of these targets—St. Petersburg and the government of foreigners —arose out of a complex of personal, political, and social motives, out of a set of historical circumstances in which opposition to an individual, a class, or a course of policy could become identified as national opposition. Peter's forceful attempts to create a universal service state; the gentry's attempts after his death to free themselves of the burdens of state service; the uncertainties of dynastic succession, in which each change of rulers offered different groups the opportunity to advance their version of what the national interest and tradition demanded—these were the factors that in time made the invocation of the nation a necessity for government as well as public opinion.

St. Petersburg early became a symbol of all that was resisted and feared as strange, novel, and threatening to established interests and ways of life. The new capital of Peter became for many the "foreign" city, the home of an essentially non-Russian court, populated by ministers and courtiers whose interests were thought to be only rarely those of Russia. From it, there spread all over the country not only the "French kaftan," and the "German frack," the powdered wig, the mincing walk, the clean-shaven face, and the Prussian uniform, but also deceit, waste, and corruption. However naive and crudely expressed this feeling may have been, it was to have a lasting effect.

To Konstantin Aksakov, the outstanding theorist of the Slavophile school, the abandonment of Moscow, the ancient and revered capital of Muscovite Russia, and the transfer of the capital to the new city in the North, signified the abandonment of the true bases of national life. "It came to this, that we altogether renounced our history, our literature, even our language. A city with a foreign name became our capital, a city on foreign shores, not tied to Russia by any historical memories," while Moscow, the true heart of Russia, "the center of the national spirit," was left to become a provincial backwater.[2] St. Petersburg as a symbol of all that was non-Russian in Russian life had a central importance in the national teaching and philosophy of history of the Slavophiles. It was a symbol which they inherited from the eighteenth century, a century considered by them nonnational, imitative, and cosmopolitan.

As early as the year 1718 (and possibly before then) the opposition to Peter, looking to his son Aleksei as a rallying point, made the return of the capital to Moscow one of the central points of its program. If the report of the Hanoverian chargé d'affaires, F. C. Weber, is accurate, there was a move to place the Tsarevich on the throne by force, to make peace with Sweden, to surrender all Peter's conquests, to abandon St. Petersburg, and to burn the entire city to the ground. Peter's military and governmental reforms were to be undone, most of the army dismissed, all foreigners executed, and the entire constitution of the state returned to its old Muscovite foundations.[3]

Peter's death in 1725, before he had named a successor, created the first of many opportunities for conflicting elements within the ruling classes of Russian society to advance favorite candidates to the throne and to modify the government in their favor. Above all there was the wish, even among Peter's partisans, to slow the pace of reform and to limit the claims of autocracy over the lives and energies of its servants. This wish was strongest among the old nobility who had lost much of their status and power during Peter's reign and who supported the candidacy of his ten-year-old grandson, Peter.*

* The old nobility, composed of the descendants of princely and boyar families, proud of their family trees and jealous of the rights which these

In 1725 they lost out to Peter's widow Catherine, to the regiments of the guard, and to Alexander Menshikov, a man of obscure origins, now a prince and a field-marshal of the Russian empire. Though the brief reign of Catherine I (1725–1727) brought no modification of the principle of autocracy, the power of the monarch was limited in fact by Catherine's incompetence, by her subservience to Menshikov, and by the creation in 1726 of a six-member Supreme Secret Council which took precedence over all other organs of the central administration. It was this new institution which in February 1727, granted permission for a certain number of officers and men to retire to their estates.[4] This was the first of many measures which eventually freed the gentry from all service obligations.

Peter II acceded to the throne after Catherine's death in 1727. A minor and the son of the martyred Tsarevich Aleksei, he was favored by the conservative faction which hoped to make its influence dominant at his court. It seemed a good omen when he moved his court to Moscow in 1728 and ordered that whoever spoke of its return to St. Petersburg be

---

supposedly conferred, were the nearest approximation to an aristocracy in the Western sense that Russia possessed. In the creation of a numerous class of state servants, the gentry, the old nobility saw a serious threat to its claims to honors and preferment. Peter the Great's establishment of the Table of Ranks, making service to the monarchy the only road to social recognition and official favor, confirmed their fears. As a result, there was a good deal of hostility between the two main branches of what is commonly referred to as the Russian nobility—the landowning, military, and bureaucratic classes —whose attitude to the government was in large part determined by their fears, or hopes, of what a given monarch would do to, or for, them. The gentry, who were after all the creatures of the monarchy, tended to favor a strong ruler who would preserve and extend their rights, whereas the old nobility saw its best hope for a recovery of its status in a limitation of imperial power and a confirmation of its privileges. This contrast lost its political importance when both groups were freed of service obligations in 1762 and when Catherine's Charter of the Nobility (1785) created a privileged estate which embraced old nobility and upstart gentry. For an excellent discussion of this problem see the Introduction to Richard Pipes' *Karamzin's Memoir on Ancient and Modern Russia* (Cambridge, Mass., 1959), pp. 6–21.

put to the knout.[5] The young Tsar's decision to leave the northern capital was taken under the influence of his friend and confidant, Ivan Alekseevich Dolgoruki, a scion of the old aristocracy whose father was a member of the Supreme Secret Council and whose sister was the Tsar's fiancée. His advice was more than the expression of a private whim, for in the disputes and discussions which preceded the Empress Anna's acceptance of the Russian throne after Peter II's death in 1730, several groups of nobles expressed the wish that court and capital remain at Moscow.[6]

To the old nobility, as well as to many of the newer gentry, St. Petersburg was more then merely foreign. It was the seat of an absolutism which had kept them in attendance upon the court, the army, affairs of state—away from their ancestral estates and way of life. To be free of St. Petersburg meant, hopefully, to be free also of all those burdensome obligations of service which had characterized the rule of Peter. The resentment which the older landed families felt against the northern capital was only partially inspired by national feeling. The secretary of the Prussian legation, J. G. Vockerodt, who came to Russia during the last years of Peter the Great's reign, indicated in a memoir written in 1738, additional motives for the opposition to St. Petersburg ever since 1714.[7] For almost all their needs, Vockerodt pointed out, the gentry were dependent on what their estates could furnish in the way of food, services, and transport. In Moscow these things were readily available, and even the poorer of the nobility could spend a good part of the year on their estates and so save the expenses of life in the capital. St. Petersburg, however, was far from any readily available supplies. The gentry residing in the new capital could no longer live off their estates. They were forced to buy their supplies, which had been brought to St. Petersburg over great distances, in the open market and at exorbitant prices.[8] Neither European dress, comforts, the glitter of a Westernized court, nor even the glory of Russian arms could compensate for the economic burdens which the demands of the autocracy imposed. Some three years later the English ambassador echoed almost word for word the observations of his Prussian colleague:

There is no one among them [the nobility] who would not wish St. Petersburg at the bottom of the sea and all the conquered provinces at the devil, so that they could but remove to Moscow where, by being in the neighbourhood of their estates, they could all live in greater splendor and with less expense. Besides, they are persuaded that it would be much better for Russia in general to have nothing more to do with the affairs of Europe than it formerly had, but confine itself to the defense of its own ancient territories strictly called so . . . . All these gentlemen by consequence are utter enemies to the foreigners in their service; for though they may find the use of them in time of war, yet would they have them all discarded the moment after peace.[9]

An emotional attachment to their "tenderly beloved Moscow" and the "graves of their ancestors" (Vockerodt) was undoubtedly strengthened by economic calculations and the realization that every foreign servant of the Tsar was a charge upon their country and helped to strengthen the hold which the government had over its subjects. It was only too clear that the absolutist autocracy, with its seat at St. Petersburg, had been served and strengthened in power (as Dmitri Mikhailovich Golitsyn said on the death of Peter II) by a crowd of foreigners whom Peter the Great had called into the country. "Can't we live as our fathers and grandfathers did, who did not let in the foreigners?" [10] The answer was that one could not live in 1730 as one had lived in earlier generations, and that father and grandfather too had admitted foreigners. Now foreigners were no longer restricted to the periphery of Russian life as they had been under the Tsar Aleksei Mikhailovich, when the few Western experts and traders had lived in near isolation in the *Nemetskaya Sloboda* in Moscow. Foreigners now filled the highest posts at court, in the army, and the civil administration; they entered into the daily life of the country and influenced it deeply. Having few other ties to Russia than their service to the monarch, they became the whipping boys of absolutism, the Russian equivalent of the bourgeois officials against whom the Duc de St. Simon thundered with such venom in France. In Russia, however, this group was alien to the upper classes not only in a social but also in a national sense.

The return of the Empress Anna and her court to St. Petersburg towards the end of 1731, fixed the capital once and for all in the new city.[11] Nor was this arrangement upset by the Empress Elizabeth, the daughter of Peter and object of so many fond, patriotic hopes. She did, it is true, come to Moscow for an extended stay every three years until 1753, but made only one other important concession to the old capital during her reign—the foundation of a university. The decree providing for the establishment of Moscow University in 1755, specifically mentioned the city's central location; the new institution would be accessible to the gentry of the surrounding area who had "relatives or acquaintances there, from whom they may obtain quarters and food...."[12] Otherwise, the old capital was generally neglected, if not forgotten.

The Slavophiles were not the first to see in the abandonment of Moscow a departure from the true principles of Russian life. Prince Mikhail Shcherbatov (1733–1790), historian, man of letters, and public servant expressed this view in a number of his works. In his novel, "Journey to the Land of Ophir,"[13] written in 1787, Shcherbatov made little effort to conceal what were quite obvious references to Russian conditions. The major port of Ophir was called Peregab; founded on the Nevi by a ruler named Pereg, it replaced for a time the old capital, Kvamo, situated on a river of the same name. Shcherbatov, who was the most vocal and intellectual spokesman of the old aristocracy, made unmistakably plain why the new capital was in such disfavor. He gave full credit to the Tsar Pereg for his establishment of a well-ordered administration and for introducing the arts, the sciences, and modern military techniques into an unenlightened country. But he considered the removal of the old capital city from ancient Kvamo, at the center of the empire, to an uncomfortable and swampy place near its borders, "against the nature of things."[14] The building of the new capital had been costly in human and material terms and the city became the source of many evils for Ophir. In Peregab, the country's rulers had lost that intimate touch with their people that once characterized them. There, a new class of courtiers had sprung up; far removed from their villages, they had lost all awareness of the people's needs and had come to look upon the court alone as their fatherland. The best, the most important and patriotic families had remained in Kvamo; abandoned by their monarchs, they had lost love and respect for them. The remoteness of the capital kept the sighs of the people from reaching the throne, while its nearness to hostile borders caused suffering for the people, exhaustion to the state and disturbance to the throne.[15]

Peregab was foreign to the citizens of Ophir because its interests and policies, like those of Peter's city, seemed alien and harmful to the aristocracy which Prince Shcherbatov represented. The foundation of St. Petersburg at the very limits of Russia, facing Europe, had proclaimed Peter's intention of participating actively in European affairs. His determination to make Russia a factor in European politics, his call to glory and to power, evoked only a negative response from men who were content to run their estates, and wished only to rule their own country. Even after Peter's death, his city stood for a foreign policy which strained every resource of the country and was felt to be more of a burden than a promise, especially in Moscow and the provinces. The executors of that policy were the new service nobility whose primary loyalty, Shcherbatov felt, was to the state and to the ruler. In his view, they did not have the older nobility's independence, that deep attachment to the country as a whole which made the aristocracy the best spokesmen for the people. It was they who, by interposing themselves between the monarch and the natural leaders of Russia, kept the sighs of the people from reaching the throne and prevented a lightening of the country's burdens.

Here the national protest against the despotism of royal authority was not joined with an insistence on popular sovereignty, but with a demand for the reaffirmation of privilege. The government of Ophir, as described by Shcherbatov, was headed by a ruler whose power was limited only by that of the high nobility, the magnates. The remaining classes, even the rank and file of the gentry, had no access to the supreme power, no share in the government. The aristocracy of birth was the first estate of the kingdom. In contrast with Russia, admittance to this class in mythical Ophir was closed and could not be gained as a reward of service, a limitation which would automatically exclude foreign adventurers and specialists from social and political power.[16]

Although Petersburg lost some of its exclusive importance in Russian social and political life, reality never came close to the ideal pictured by Shcherbatov. The "great and happy change" which took place in Ophir when another great ruler (Elizabeth or Catherine?) gradually transferred the residence back to the old capital, while the new one remained only a factory or port town, was never realized as long as the monarchy itself lasted. Only with the coming of the Soviet regime did Moscow once again become the seat of Russia's government. With the gentry's release from state service in 1762 and the final confirmation of its corporate privileges by Catherine in 1785, Moscow did regain some of its former importance as

a center where the nobility conducted its social life with somewhat greater freedom than would have been possible directly
under the eyes of the court. Following the example Elizabeth
had set with the founding of Moscow University and the
establishment of a boarding school for young nobles, Catherine
also opened an institute for young gentlewomen at Moscow
and made a gift of the Dolgoruki mansion to the nobility for
its assemblies and balls.[17] But these were superficial concessions
which could in no way limit the power and importance of the
court and the imperial bureaucracy.

Catherine was sensitive to Moscow's mood—its stubborn
conservatism, its ill-concealed disdain for the upstart city and
its upstart ruler. She retaliated with satire. In one of her
comedies, two old gossips of Moscow society, Khanzhakina
and Vestnikova (roughly: hypocrite and talebearer), constantly lament the passing of the good old days, prophesy all
sorts of evils from the absurd measures of the government and
give currency to a wide variety of malicious rumors.[18] In spite
of occasional patriotic gestures in the direction of Moscow,
Catherine's preference for St. Petersburg was pronounced and
her suspicion and dislike of the older city deepseated. In her
"Reflections on Petersburg and Moscow," [19] the Empress admitted that St. Petersburg had been built at a frightful cost
in life and treasure; but she maintained that this had been more
than repaid by the economic benefits which the city had
brought to the empire during the forty years of its existence.
Moscow, for all its five-hundred years, had not been able to
match that record.

Even Prince Shcherbatov had been willing to concede the
advantage of Peter's city as a center of commerce and industry.
The real difference between his and Catherine's appraisal lay
in their divergent views of Moscow's mood and historical significance. To many Russians, the Empress reported in her
"Reflections," the removal of their capital to the northern

limits of the empire had been an unwonted disruption of historical continuity. They saw in Peter's act a repetition of the process by which the Emperor Constantine had shifted the seat of his administration from Rome to Byzantium and in doing so had removed the Romans from ancestral sites which inspired their patriotic zeal. This, Peter's critics believed, had been one of the causes for the decline of Roman virtue and greatness. For Catherine, the implied parallel with Russian history had no validity. To her the new capital's lack of historical associations was one of its greatest advantages. Moscow had altogether too much history, and far from inspiring patriotic zeal, the old town and its memories gave rise only to a spirit of rebellion, superstition, and indolence. "Never had a people before its eyes more objects of fanaticism, more wonder-working images . . . more churches, more of the clerical crew, more convents, more devout hypocrites, more beggars, more thieves . . . . "[20] Here was a city whose population was ready to oppose law and order at the slightest provocation, a custom in which it had engaged since time immemorial, cherishing the memory of past turbulence.

Catherine denied that it was a private prejudice in favor of the more modern, more European city that caused her dislike of Moscow. She claimed to be guided by reasons of state; Moscow, therefore, became impossible. It was disorderly, sprawling, and idle. The nobility might enjoy itself there, but what it enjoyed was an idleness and luxury which incapacitated it for the serious business of governing. In this indictment drawn against Moscow, Catherine revealed herself as a true child of the century and a true successor of Peter. Both the tempo and the temper of the city seemed to her too slow, too traditional, irrational. Reliance had to be placed, as before, on the courtiers and bureaucrats of St. Petersburg, the new men who had neither memories of past greatness nor vast estates nearby to which they could retire in silent opposition.

Time and habit might lessen hostility to the new city but they could not entirely extinguish the belief that it was not truly Russia's capital. The two foremost historians of the late eighteenth and early nineteenth centuries helped to keep alive their countrymen's affection and preference for Moscow, and passed these feelings on to succeeding generations. Major-General Ivan Boltin, author of a number of perceptive works on the history of Russia, found full justification for popular resistance to the change of capitals in the fact that it was "contrary to the natural conditions of the country."[21] Nikolai Karamzin, Russia's most widely-read historian in the first half of the nineteenth century, called the founding of St. Petersburg one of Peter's "glaring mistakes." As long as Riga and Reval were not in Russian hands, he felt there had been some justification for the city; it could usefully serve as a port of entry for foreign goods and give Russian exports an easier access to European trade. But the plan to make it the permanent residence of the country's rulers was harmful. Karamzin deplored the enormous cost at which the city had been built, on "foundations of tears and corpses," the enormous sacrifice at which it had now to be maintained amidst swamps and an unfavorable climate. St. Petersburg claimed new victims constantly and a century after its beginning still had a death rate which made depopulation a real possibility.[22] Given these conditions, it seemed sheer perversity to Karamzin to have placed the chief city of the empire where nature clearly had not meant it to be. The signs were there for all to see: "Man does not conquer nature," [23] Karamzin warned, indicating that good sense and obedience to God's will would have demanded retention of the capital at Moscow. In the very center of the country, amidst pleasant fields favored by nature, every foreign traveler, every reasonable man would expect to find Russia's capital.

By Karamzin's time, the old Muscovite opposition to St.

Petersburg had lost a good deal of the bitterness which Catherine recorded during her reign, and his critical remarks were
not inspired by the class interests of an aristocracy to which St.
Petersburg was the symbol of an upstart bureaucracy. Autocratic absolutism seemed to him a necessity of Russian history
and he expressed his gratification over the failure of the Dolgorukis and Golitsyns to restrict it in the time of Anna.
Karamzin, who in his youth had felt the temptations of the
West, was inspired by a purer historical vision in which
Moscow stood for the virtues and simplicity of an epoch which
had disappeared with the coming of Peter. St. Petersburg was
symbol and source of a cosmopolitanism from which Russians,
if they were once more to become Russians, had to retreat.
"We have become citizens of the world, and so have in some
ways ceased being citizens of Russia—it is the fault of Peter." [24]

While St. Petersburg continued for many to be the embodiment of a foreign despotism, it was not Peter's reign alone
which kept it fresh in Russian minds as a symbol of past
wrongs. In the period after his death (1725), foreigners continued to serve the Russian government in positions of power
and importance. St. Petersburg had been foreign to Peter's
subjects in the sense that it was alien to their interests and
traditions. It became foreign in a much more immediate sense
when non-Russians, no longer obedient executors of a determined monarch's will became themselves the directors of Russian policy. Such was the case during the reign of the Empress
Anna Ivanovna (1730–1740), Peter's niece and erstwhile
Duchess of Courland. It was the prominence of foreigners at
her court, even when they acted in the best interests of Russia,
that made the government and its policies ready targets of
national protest.

Anna, it must be remembered, had been called to the Russian
throne on the initiative of the *verkhovniki*, those members of

the Supreme Secret Council (in particular Vasili Lukich Dolgoruki and Dmitri Mikhailovich Golitsyn) who saw in the limitation of the imperial prerogative the precondition of their own return to power and importance, the restoration of the native aristocracy to its rightful place. The verkhovniki's attempt to impose a set of conditions on the ruler, by which she undertook to govern only with their advice and guidance, failed as a result of the opposition it met from the rank and file of the service nobility; the "Generality" (the four upper ranks of the service nobility created by Peter); and the guards' regiments, the strength of the gentry in the capital.[25] Although this combination of forces allowed her to tear up the verkhovniki's conditions which she had accepted before her departure from Courland, it was far from uniform in its demands and political complexion. During the heated discussions of the constitutional projects which preceded the Empress' arrival, a good many of the nobility and gentry assembled in the capital had been won over to at least part of the plans for governmental reform, as long as they too were to be represented in one or another organ of government.[26]

It was not unnatural that Anna should give her trust and important positions in her immediate entourage to a number of Balts and Germans. Under the peculiar circumstances of her accession, these appointments implied a distrust of native Russians who coveted the same jobs. Even the guards' regiments, whose loyalty had been the single most important factor in the Empress' support, did not long enjoy their position of undivided favor. In 1730 and 1731, three new ones were created—the Ismailovtsy, the Horse Guards, and a regiment of cuirassiers.[27] Loewenwoldes, Birons, Muennichs, Homburg princes, Freimanns, and von Lievens were given commands in the new as well as in the older regiments. Many of them were related by ties of family or country to other occupants of important and remunerative posts at court, in the army, and the government; they often received better pay and greater privileges than did their Russian colleagues.[28] To anyone disposed to see it, foreign dominance of the Russian state was a fact.[29]

In many branches of the government, foreigners, especially Germans, occupied positions of great importance. Andreas Ostermann, in Russian service since the beginning of the century and Vice-Chancellor of the newly created cabinet of three ministers, was undoubtedly one of the most important and capable members of Anna's government. Another was Burkhard Christoph Muennich, who had come to Russia as a young Hessian officer, and under Anna rose to the command of all Russian forces. But the man whose name became a byword for all that was detestable in the rule of foreigners, the man believed to be the real power behind Anna's throne, was Ernst Johann Biron (changed from Buehren), who did not occupy any official position in the government. Member of an insignificant family of Courland nobles, he had won Anna's favor, had become her secretary and chamberlain and had come with her to Russia as chief chamberlain of her court. Although the extent of Biron's interference in affairs of state has been exaggerated, a Prussian diplomat reflected the prevailing view when he called him the "greatest and most puissant Privatum in Europe." [30]

It is doubtful whether the number of foreigners in Russia during the period of the *Bironovshchina* was much greater than it was before or after Anna's reign; even more doubtful whether the foreign origin of the Empress' ministers and generals predisposed them to policies which could be called anti-Russian.[31] It was, however, natural that unpopular policies should be labelled foreign or traced to the evil influence of foreigners. This had been the case in earlier reigns, and now that a number of foreigners occupied positions of undoubted eminence and power, a national reaction was bound to set in. Muennich, for example, did not succeed in gaining popularity

among Russian officers, in spite of the fact that he brought
their pay up to a level which only non-Russians had previously
been paid. Nor did his many services to his adopted country
save him from the suspicion that his inclination for a Prussian
alliance had been bought,[32] while Ostermann's pro-Austrian
course failed equally to spare him the fate which was to over-
whelm them both. In the case of Biron, there is some evidence
that he let his judgment in matters of foreign policy be swayed
by gifts of money, titles, and the prospect of gaining the crown
of Courland.[33] Whether these facts were known at the time
is unimportant in view of the fact that they were widely believed about a man who was so generally feared and hated. It
is certain that almost every section of Russian society felt itself
aggrieved in some way by the Bironovshchina. The ease with
which the Biron regime was overthrown is the best testimony
to the general dislike in which it was held.*

Whether dislike of the new government was primarily
caused by the personal conduct of its members (Biron never
concealed his contempt for all things Russian and Muennich
was generally regarded as haughty and domineering), by its
rigorous tax policy, by the Lutheranism of many of its members, or by its persecution of the old nobility and the clergy—
its acts were from the very start looked upon as slights to the
nation's honor and injurious to its well-being. A report written
in September of 1732 by Lefort, a diplomat in the service of
the King of Poland and Saxony, made clear who was blamed
for the general discontent.

* In a "Re-Examination of the 'Dark Era' of Anna Ioannovna," *American
Slavic and East European Review*, 15, (1956), 477–488, Professor Alexander
Lipski has demonstrated that the reign of the Empress Anna was not nearly
as dark an epoch in Russian history as most of the country's historians have
assumed, and that the influence of Germans at her court was not exerted
against the national interests of their adopted country. But he, too, is led
to the conclusion that the prominence of Germans in the government offended national pride and caused resentments that led to uncritical though
unwarranted condemnation of the whole reign.

For some time now, the Russian nation has expressed dissatisfaction over the fact that it is being governed by foreigners. Libelous sheets have been disseminated in various places during the last few days; several prisoners have been brought to the fortress, not a few clerics among them; the day before, three boyars and eleven priests were brought from Moscow; all of this is being kept strictly secret. The most important cause of discontent is the forcible collection of back-taxes which the Empress Catherine as well as the Emperor Peter II had forgiven. Field Marshal Muennich is held responsible for the renewal of these collections. In short, the people are dissatisfied, and therefore the foreigners should prevail upon the Empress to take as husband a prince who through his conduct as well as his qualities can gain the love of the people and so support the foreigners who rule.[34]

Lefort's astute observations pointed accurately to those groups which the regime feared most: the three Moscow boyars were presumably members of the old aristocracy which had been opposed to Anna even before she came to Russia, and which was now made to pay for the role it had played in 1730. The Dolgorukis suffered most. They were banished from the capital with their families, condemned to hard labor, and deprived of rank and property. Four members of the family were executed as late as 1739. The Golitsyns fared not much better, and Prince Dmitri Mikhailovich was imprisoned in Schluesselburg fortress.[35] The priests must have been members of the higher clergy which suffered especially harsh treatment at the hands of a government with every intention of retaining state control over the church in the form of the synodal arrangement established by Peter the Great. Thus it came about that one after another of the bishops and metropolitans who had hoped for the downfall of Feofan Prokopovich, Peter's helper in matters of church policy, were themselves subjected to exile and imprisonment.[36] Two bishops, those of Vologda and Pskov, even went so far as to abandon (in secret, at least) the support which the higher clergy had traditionally given to the authority of the state.

Open opposition to the government was difficult, if not impossible, as the events of 1730 and the arrests of 1732 showed. The opposition also lacked a common basis, a program, and an opportunity such as a change of regime, which did not offer itself until the death of the Empress. For most of the decade from 1730 to 1740, resistance to the Biron regime remained a matter of words rather than deeds and was confined to private expressions of discontent and hostility among friends and confidants. The circle of Artemi Volynski,[37] which met towards the end of the thirties in St. Petersburg, grew out of such private confidences among friends and fellow-sufferers. It was a true microcosm of the opposition to the government. The bishops of Vologda and Pskov are known to have participated in the discussions, as did the chief procurator of the Senate, Soimonov; the president of the College of Commerce, Count Musin-Pushkin; and Lestocq, the Tsarevna Elizabeth's personal physician and prime mover of the forces supporting her candidacy to the throne.

Artemi Petrovich Volynski occupies an important place in Russian nationalist hagiography. Under any other circumstances than those of the Bironovshchina he would probably have been remembered, like so many of his contemporaries, as a man of ruthless ambition, restless energy, not inconsiderable talent, and rather doubtful standards of personal morality. The fact that his ambition and restlessness brought him into conflict with Biron, and that he gathered about himself a considerable number of malcontents who shared his dislike of the German court clique, let him appear to a posterity which stood in need of national heroes, as an "important fact in the history of the development of national consciousness in eighteenth-century Russian society."[38]

Volynski's rise to power was brilliant and meteoric. Entering Peter's service at the age of fifteen, a combination of ability and influence gained him constant advances in rank. He became governor of Astrakhan and under Catherine I was appointed governor of Kazan with the rank of major-general. It was at that post that news of the events of 1730 reached him and he was much disturbed by rumors of the verkhovniki's attempts to limit the imperial power. "We hear," he wrote to an acquaintance, "that you are about to create a republic in Russia. I have serious misgivings about this. God forbid that we do not get ten proud and powerful families instead of one autocratic emperor. If that is the case, we the *shliakhetstvo*\* will sink even lower and will have to seek the favors of others in even greater measure than before."[39] Volynski's championship of the imperial power was not inspired primarily by a dedication to the principles of absolutism. His real sympathy was with the projects formulated in 1730, which would give to the shliakhetstvo greater representation and power in government. This fact was not, however, known to the Empress and her entourage. For the moment, Volynski appeared as the defender of absolutism, and with the exception of a brief period of disfavor at the beginning of Anna's reign, his rise was uninterrupted. In 1738 he achieved the exalted position of cabinet minister; he hoped now to be able to execute his plans for a reform of the Russian state.

These plans had been ripening ever since a stay in Moscow in 1731. There Volynski had gathered about himself a number of people who shared his dislike of Germans and oligarchs alike. The members of the Moscow group were all of good family (though their genealogies could not, perhaps, compare with those of the oldest aristocracy); they were for the most part products of the Petrine period and considered themselves the leading members of the nobility of service, whose fear of oligarchic rule was greater than their fear of autocracy. The

---

\* A term of Polish origin which in the first half of the eighteenth century was most often used to refer to the nobility of service created by Peter. Its closest English equivalent is gentry.

presence in this group of Vasili Tatishchev, the historian, gives us a clue to its political orientation. As a counterproposal to that of the verkhovniki, Tatishchev, on behalf of the Senate and the generality, had submitted a project in 1730 which envisioned the abolition of the Supreme Secret Council and its replacement by two organs, a senate of twenty-one members and a lower house of one hundred, to represent the shliakhetstvo.

Tatishchev, moreover, had also come into conflict with Biron and Ostermann and was a more conscious patriot than Volynski.[40] In this group, Volynski's impassioned outbursts against the foreigners were given a more reasoned, theoretical basis. Tatishchev's rich knowledge of Russian history enabled him to see in it meaningful parallels with the present situation; others of the group acquainted Volynski with Machiavelli and Justus Lipsius; still others opened their libraries to him. During the next few years Volynski worked out a series of memoranda, among them a "General Project" for the reformation of the Russian state, from which he submitted excerpts to the Empress. Although it did not mention names, the memorandum was quite clearly directed against Ostermann; and Biron, perhaps sensing its antiforeign implications, perhaps jealous of Volynski's easy access to the Empress, helped bring about his downfall.

The "General Project"[41] envisioned the government of Russia as a monarchy with a broad participation of the shliakhetstvo in the sense of Tatishchev's proposal. The shliakhetstvo was to be the first estate of the empire. As was the custom in other European states, it was not only to furnish the chief functionaries of the government as well as the officer corps, but also the bureaucrats, and following the example of these other states, the gentry was to hold high clerical office also. But above all, the Russian government must consist of Russians, since "only harm can come from the foreigners, harm to the state and to the ruler." All ministers must be native Russians and of distinguished gentry families. In other parts of the project Volynski proposed ways of improving the economic position of the clergy, advocated a greater degree of autonomy for merchants (and prohibitions against their entering into trading companies together with foreigners, to prevent the export of capital), cautioned against excesses in the treatment of peasants and made other suggestions for judicial, financial, military, and educational reforms. Interesting among the latter two are the proposals for the founding of a university (which Elizabeth carried out in 1755), and the establishment of military settlements along the borders of the empire.

We do not know how far Volynski and his circle (which towards the end of the thirties began to meet in St. Petersburg with an enlarged number of participants) had gone in planning the overthrow of Anna's government, nor how many of its members had been taken into the minister's confidence if such a step was planned. But the composition of this group, and the reports of foreign diplomats suggest that at a favorable time he and his associates would have tried to remove Anna and her German advisers. It was perhaps the fear of such a step that brought about the arrest of Volynski on an insignificant pretext in April 1740, and finally led to his execution. Two members of his circle were also executed and there were widespread arrests, both in St. Petersburg and the provinces. Volynski's death "profoundly impressed his contemporaries as well as succeeding generations and bequeathed to the educated portion of Russian society the image of Volynski as a patriot and fighter against the Germans."[42]

Volynski's opposition to the Biron regime was inspired only partly by motives of patriotism. His "nationalism," if it can be called that, was of a pragmatic nature. Although he saw the enemy in the foreigner as the most visible and readily available target, he sought the reformation of the Russian state for the sake of greater efficiency, prosperity, and class advantage—not in the name of a national ideology or national uniqueness. His program did not insist that Russia's experience, tradition, or soul prescribed for her a way of life which must keep itself pure of foreign philosophies and techniques. He borrowed widely from Western authors, admired the corporate status and power of the Polish nobility, suggested that Russian officials be trained abroad, and included the Hanoverian Lestocq and other foreigners in his St. Petersburg circle. His opposition to the Germans in government was a tactic employed to gain a wider response for his critique of the Russian state. Volynski, it may be assumed, was not devoid of love of country or of true feelings of national pride, but his "nationalism" was not an ideology which informs its adherents about the nature of the state and society. In terms that were to be used in the nineteenth century, Volynski was a Westerner, in spite of his opposition to the Bironovshchina and German rule; his "nationalism" was utilitarian because it lacked the philosophical underpinning which let many nineteenth-century nationalists see Russia as a world apart.

Hostility to the German court clique was further deepened by the events which followed upon the death of Anna Ivanovna (17 October 1740). By naming a two-months-old boy as her successor—Ivan Antonovich, son of the Duke of Braunschweig-Mecklenburg and his wife Anna Leopoldovna—the German clique hoped to remove Peter the Great's daughter Elizabeth from the succesion and to strengthen its own position. It was, they felt, no longer enough to guide matters from behind the scenes; and with the agreement of Ostermann and Reinhold Loewenwolde, Biron himself took over the regency. His unpopularity, however, was such that even his friends thought it would go ill for all of them if he were to remain in power. During the night of November 8–9, Muennich, with the connivance of Ostermann, arrested Biron, proclaimed Anna Leopoldovna as regent, made himself "first minister," Ostermann admiral-in-chief, and the Duke of Braunschweig generalissimo of the Russian army.[43] Before long, Ostermann and Muennich quarreled; their rivalry created the opportunity for which Volynski and many others had waited. On November 25, 1741, Elizaveta Petrovna seized the throne with the help of the Preobrazhenski guards and put an end to what was felt to have been eleven years of foreign rule. Ostermann, Muennich, and Loewenwolde were sent to Siberia (Biron had already preceded them); Anna Leopoldovna, her husband, and the boy Tsar Ivan VI were imprisoned; other foreigners—Loewendahls, Keith, Manstein, the mathematician Euler—left Russian service.[44] Soldiers, bishops, and poets with one voice acclaimed the new Empress as their liberator from the foreign yoke, greeted her as Peter's daughter and in all the jubilation failed to notice that a German, a Frenchman, and a Swede had played major roles in the conspiracy which brought her to the throne. Neither the new Empress' refusal to countenance the excesses of xenophobia which demanded that all foreigners be dismissed from Russian service, nor her retention of the capital in St. Petersburg could dampen the ardor and joy of patriots.

Churchmen greeted the end of foreign rule and the restoration of the throne to the house of Peter with relief and jubilation. Archbishop Amvrosi of Novgorod preached a sermon in which he called the country's fallen masters men inspired in their evil deeds by crafty devils. They had offended piety and faith on the pretext of uprooting superstitions harmful to Christianity; not only men of God, but every Russian of learning and education had been persecuted, tortured, and destroyed. The foreigners' purpose had been to keep Russia in her state of tutelage: "They spared no means to convict a Russian experienced in the arts, as engineer, as architect, or soldier . . . to remove him by exile or execution, simply because he was an engineer or architect, a student of Peter the Great."[45] The ease with which foreigners entered Russian service and displaced native Russians from coveted positions remained a bitter memory. Amvrosi complained that special preferment was given them simply because they were foreign. He reminded his hearers of the Turkish campaign, of the sufferings and privations undergone by Russian soldiers so that their foreign commanders might gain glory and riches. "Their bodies, their shades may have been in Russia, but soul and heart remained abroad. . . . Thus they brought Russia to impotence, poverty and ruin."[46]

Kyrill Florinski, the archimandrite of the Zaikonospasski Monastery, described the evils of foreign rule and the sufferings visited on true believers by the emissaries of the devil in no less dramatic terms than had the Archbishop of Novgorod. But what in Amvrosi's sermon had been a relatively minor note became a point of great importance in the text of Florinski the apotheosis of Peter as the architect of Russia's greatness and as her teacher in the arts of war and peace. The Tsar, who during his lifetime had seemed to many of the clergy no less a foreign devil than Ostermann or Biron, began to take on the features of a national hero:

Peter himself, out of our coarseness and with his own hands, made us into beautifully fashioned statues. But while Peter's seed ripened, while the tree grew under whose branches we were to find shade and rest . . . . we were like unfeeling blocks of wood for more than ten years . . . slept while the foreign brood undermined the tree, slept till the seed itself called on us to awake.[47]

All of Russia seemed suddenly to have awakened, and to give voice to a grief felt for eleven long years. Pamphlets appeared in which the horrors of the Bironovshchina were once more recounted. They sounded the same themes as did the sermons of the clergy: the foreigners have undone the great work of Peter; they have ruined his armies and his fleet;

they have enriched themselves at Russia's expense; and have treated every true patriot as an inferior being. They have persecuted the true faith and have separated the shepherds from the flock. "But the Almighty brings the evil plans of the heathen to nought; the Holy Ghost has restored the great Peter's spirit to us in his daughter; He has helped her to wrest her father's scepter from foreign hands, and to free nobles and people from the iniquity which they have suffered at the hands of their German masters. . . ."[48]

The guards, who had played the most important role in Elizabeth's seizure of the throne, gave rather more forceful expression to their joy. They roamed the streets of the capital, looted, killed their German officers, or any other foreigners (and at times even Russians) they caught, mutinied in their camps and demanded that all non-Russian officers in the army be killed, "and then we will obey our own officers."[49] "All of us here," a foreign resident wrote in December 1741, "live constantly between fear and hope, since the soldiers, getting ever bolder, utter loud threats which, thanks only to Providence, they have not yet carried out. . . . We poor foreigners tremble for our lives. . . ."[50] Newspapers, academic speeches, theatrical performances, and poetic outpourings commemorated the great day. The poet Lomonosov returned to the theme of liberation from the foreign yoke by Peter's daughter in one after another of his stiffly grandiloquent odes, and as late as 1762 the memory of those great days could still inspire him to patriotic fervor. Elizabeth, Russia's savior, will usher in a golden age and save Russia from all fear.[51]

One of the most remarkable results of the period of the Bironovshchina was the change in attitude towards Peter the Great. From that time on, a protest against foreigners and their role in Russia was no longer automatically synonymous with the wish to undo the work of modernization and reform which Peter had begun. Instead, it could be made in his name

and in defense of his ideals. The foreigners were attacked now
not as innovators but as perpetuators of Russian dependence
and backwardness. It is perhaps the most striking testimony
to the general abhorrence in which Biron and his associates
were held by clergy, army, and people that Peter, whom
many of his subjects had seen as Anti-Christ in German dress,
could emerge as the founder of Russia's greatness and strength
only fifteen years after his death had been greeted with sighs
of relief. A folk song of the period has a young sergeant address the Tsar in the following words:

> Arise from your grave, oh noble Russian Tsar. Look on your
> guards, your regiments in ranks, how sorrowfully they hang their
> heads; for now they have no Tsar to rule them, no Russian prince
> gives command . . . but our commander is Biron, the evil tyrant
> from German lands. Arise, awake our Tsar, our sun.[52]

This elevation of Peter highlights the important role which
the conduct of the monarch was to play in the development
of Russian national feeling during the remainder of the century. Having established her claim as a Russian of Russians,
Elizabeth could surround herself with any number of foreigners and still enjoy her reputation as a patriot. If her accession seemed to her contemporaries a liberation from the
foreigner, the rest of her reign illustrated the completely
casual, not to say haphazard, nature of the nationalism of the
period. It is true that the highest posts in Elizabeth's government were occupied by Russians and that she was responsive
to the anti-German current in the opposition to her predecessors and utilized it, but she was far from being dominated
by it. Although native Russians once more came into their
own, the government chancelleries were nonetheless still occupied by men who bore such un-Russian names as Bevier,
Brevern, Sievers, Flueck, and Luberas. While Ostermann,
Muennich, and Biron remained either in exile or in oblivion,
a brother of the latter succeeded a Saltykov as grand-master

of the court, and a prince of Hesse-Homburg was second in command (after Elizabeth herself) of the newly named *Leib-Kompaniya*.[53]

Unlike Elizabeth, the daughter of Peter the Great, Catherine, an insignificant princess of German birth, had no claims to the loyalty of her subjects which were rooted in tradition or descent. She was acutely aware of the bitter memories which Anna's reign had left among Russians, and she tried from the start to strike a truly Russian pose, indicating the degree to which national feelings had to be taken into account. Her reign (1762–1796) also marked the emergence of what might be called "official nationalism," the conscious identification of governmental measures and goals with what were felt to be truly national aspirations. The erection of a monument to Peter I—Catherina secunda, Petro primo—signified her intention to appear as continuing a tradition to which most Russians could by now give their loyalty. The passage of time had removed the bitterest memories of Peter, and the more recent memories of foreign rule under Anna and Peter III had created the need for a heroic national figure to serve as rallying point and battle cry against foreign usurpation. Peter the Great, for the time being, became that figure, and Catherine, by paying demonstrative homage to his memory, tried to make it impossible for any opposition to claim him. By appearing as his historical legatee, the executor of his aims, she wanted to bolster her slender claims to the crown.

The brief reign of Catherine's husband, Peter III (December 1761 to June 1762) seemed to many Russians a revival of the hated Bironovshchina,[54] and it greatly facilitated acceptance of Catherine as the leader and standard bearer of a second national restoration. Neither the grant of freedom from service obligations to the gentry, nor any other concessions, such as the abolition of the secret chancellery, could reconcile Russian society to the excesses of stupidity committed by Peter III. Although he was the grandson of Peter the Great, he was hardly more of a Russian than his wife. Son of the Duke of Holstein, he assumed the role of Emperor of Russia without a real attachment to that country. It seemed as if every one of his acts were designed to underscore the deep distrust and contempt in which he held Russia and its people. He not only appointed foreigners to high posts, as had Anna and Biron before him; he himself became the instrument which executed, at least in the field of foreign policy, the wishes of his god and idol, the King of Prussia. He called to a sudden halt[55] the long and costly war which Russia had fought on the side of her allies Austria and France, at the moment when Frederick was willing to make important concessions. The campaigns which had carried Russian troops to Berlin had greatly increased Russia's pride in her arms and her prestige. A complete reversal took place in Russia's foreign policy, dictated by Peter's whims, by the influence of the Prussian Ambassador von der Goltz, and by vague promises of Prussian help in Peter's projected campaign against Denmark for the conquest of Schleswig and its incorporation into his duchy of Holstein.[56] Whatever approval Peter's ending of the war might have found among a war-weary people was dissipated and turned into hostility when the Emperor planned merely to substitute enemies. Peter ignored his Russian advisers—his chancellor and vice chancellor were often ignorant of his moves—and the direction of Russian foreign policy remained in Prussian hands. The influence of the Vorontsovs, the Golitsyns, the Shuvalovs, and Volkovs was constantly reduced, while that of von der Goltz, Schwerin, and Prince Georg of Holstein was on the ascendant.

The Tsar's total disregard of Russian national feeling was even more pronounced in his domestic policy. In measures affecting the Church, the guards, the army at large, Peter displayed his ignorance of Russian history and society. The lessons which 1741 had taught, and which his wife had mastered so well, were completely lost on him. Once again, national feeling manifested itself in a stubborn defense of accustomed forms of worship and of dress, symbols of national tradition which Peter had grievously outraged.

Church and clergy were struck by a series of measures which did not fail to raise the cry of "Lutheranism," echoed among the rest of the population. The monastic clergy was to have its landed holdings secularized and placed under a state administration, the secular clergy was ordered to register its sons for military service, and Dmitri Sechenov, Archbishop of Novgorod and Procurator of the Holy Synod, was personally instructed by Peter to see that Russian churches were cleared of all ikons, except those of the Savior and the Mother of God. Furthermore, the clergy were to shave off their beards and dress like foreign pastors. "Although these orders were not carried out," a contemporary recalled, "they caused strong dissatisfaction among the clergy, thus helping the Emperor's downfall." [57] Peter made no attempt whatever to conceal his dislike of Orthodoxy; he paraded it in public; stuck his tongue out at priests; and during church services talked loudly, walked about, received visitors, and once, at a particularly solemn moment in the ceremony, when the whole congregation was on its knees, left the church laughing loudly.[58]

One of the first acts of the new reign had been the dissolution of the Leib-Kompaniya founded by Elizabeth, which insured that a substantial portion of the guards, the instruments of every dynastic overturn since the death of Peter I, were added to the opposition. The rest of the guards and the army at large were embittered by the obvious preference of the Emperor for his Holstein guards, by his suspicion (which Biron had shared) of the whole system of permanent guards stationed in the capital, by his appointment of Prince Georg of Holstein to the post of Russian field-marshal, and by those senseless imitations of Prussian drill and dress which replaced the uniforms introduced by Peter I. As in 1741, the guards gave expression to their discontent by their direction and support of a plot which removed the occupant of the throne in favor of their candidate, Peter's wife.

Catherine knew how to strike a national note from the moment of her elevation to the Russian throne. On the evening of June 28, 1762, and on the next day, the Empress showed herself to her guards and her people in a uniform of Petrine cut, with long flowing hair, and a hat decorated with a cluster of oak leaves. "These dresses," wrote the Princess Dashkova, who rode by the Empress' side during these triumphant days, "were the ancient national uniform of the Preobrazhenski guards, and such as had been worn ever since the time of Peter I, until superseded by the Prussian uniform introduced by Peter III. And it is a circumstance worthy of notice that the Empress had on this morning scarcely entered the city, when the guards, as if by order, having thrown away their foreign costume, appeared to a man in the ancient uniform of their country." [59] Equally pleasing to Russian hearts seems to have been Catherine's appointment of a Russian to command a regiment of cuirassiers of which she was colonel, and which had previously been officered almost exclusively by Germans. [60]

The two manifestoes in which Catherine set forth the fact and the circumstances of Peter's deposition and her assumption of the crown, picture her, not her husband, as the true heir to the Russian throne, as the defender of faith and nation. The belief that Peter's Lutheran tendencies threatened the position of the Church was cleverly exploited in the accession manifestoes. "Our Orthodox Greek faith was . . . threatened with the destruction of its traditions . . . our Church . . . exposed to the extremity of a change in the old Russian faith and the acceptance of a foreign rite." Catherine also blamed Peter for the conduct of a foreign policy which debased Russia's hard-won glory by making peace with her most villainous enemy (Frederick the Great) and for planning another war which was not in Russia's interest. He had undermined the army by the imposition of new regulations and uniforms, "giving the regiments a foreign, at times even a perverse, appearance." In general, Peter had been guilty of hatred for Russia, of subverting the inherited order and wanting to place the fatherland in foreign hands.[61]

For the time being, Russia seemed willing to accept the image of Catherine as a second Elizabeth. The pulpits once more resounded to the triumphant notes of sermons which hailed Catherine as the savior of Church and country. Dmitri Sechenov, Archbishop of Novgorod, who had special cause to rejoice over the change of rulers, gave fulsome expression to his joy when he welcomed the new Empress to the Uspenski Cathedral in Moscow. He saw her entering into the city and its holy temple as into the hearts of her countrymen; addressed the Empress—who was a skeptic, and a synthetic Russian—as a devout and motherly defender of faith and fatherland from the heretics. Other dignitaries of Church and state followed the example set by their primate; medals were struck in honor of the great day, bearing the inscription: "Orthodoxy and the Russian fatherland saved from the evils threatening them by the heroic spirit of Her Imperial Majesty;" the Senate weighed the erection of a monument; Count Aleksei Bestuzhev-Ryumin suggested that the designation "Mother of the Fatherland" become part of the Empress' official title.[62]

The two foremost poets of the day welcomed the change with what seemed to be genuine relief. Alexander Sumarokov, the gentry poet *par excellence*, a man who was close to Nikita Panin, one of Catherine's fellow-conspirators, commemorated the day with an ode reviewing the dark days through which Russia had just passed and the dangers from which she was now freed. Before that happy turn of events, Russia had suffered from foreign oppression in every conceivable way; now all that was changed: "Their evil malice is defeated and Catherine's victory is assured. Gone now are mourning and despair, our sighs dispersed like lightest dust. . . ." [63]

An ode of Lomonosov's on the same theme also viewed Catherine's accession as Russia's liberation from foreign bondage. Recounting the mournful events of the last reign, Lomonosov invoked the spirit of Peter the Great to recall Russia to the glorious path on which he had set her, to rescue her from the parlous state to which Peter III had reduced the country. Ruled and exploited by foreigners, Russia had been lowered in power and esteem. Catherine's husband had undone the work of generations and made of St. Petersburg a citadel of enemies. He had loved neither the people over whom he ruled, nor their faith. Like Sumarokov, Lomonosov noted the ingratitude with which the foreigners had repaid Russian kindness: they had attacked the Church, abused their power, and debased the Russian people. And he warned Russia's enemies that any plans to enslave Russia were doomed to failure as they had now failed, thanks to an act of heroism on the throne. The reign of Catherine would assure victory over all Russia's foes.[64]

The general enthusiasm which greeted Catherine's accession and the high expectations held of her were marred by only a few minor demonstrations demanding the enthronement of Ivan VI, who had been in prison since 1741. Opposition to Catherine and her government was expressed only rarely in national terms, although the former princess of Anhalt-Zerbst was strictly speaking a usurper and would have presented an excellent target for such attacks.

There was, however, opposition of a silent kind, based not

alone on Catherine's Germanness. Prince Shcherbatov, in his "Corruption of Morals in Russia," saw in the fact that the former princess of a petty German state could occupy the throne of the Russian empire evidence of the general lowering of standards which he had traced since the time of Peter the Great. "A woman not born of our rulers' blood, a woman who rose against her husband in armed rebellion, has received crown and scepter of Russia as reward for such a virtuous deed and in addition the title 'most pious Empress' with which we include our rulers in our prayers." He feared that the morality of this most pious majesty rested on nothing firmer than the teaching of "the new philosophers, and not the . . . rock of divine law." [65]

This critic of despotic absolutism had raised the problem of foreigners in Russia's ruling family in an earlier work, "On the Marriage of Russian Princes." [66] It is a dialogue in which a minister of state and a private citizen weigh the advantages and disadvantages of marriage to members of foreign dynasties. All the arguments which the minister can marshal in favor of a foreign connection—reasons of state, alliances, superior education, royal blood—avail nothing against the citizen's insistence that a Russian is to be preferred in each case. His arguments obviously derive from the experience which the Russian monarchy itself had furnished: dynastic alliances are no more firm than any others; it is useless for a Russian prince to hope for assistance from a powerful relative since there are no European thrones occupied by Orthodox dynasties; marriage therefore is possible only with members of insignificant ruling houses, the only ones willing to change their faith, and allies gained in this fashion bring Russia more burdens and foreign involvements than benefits. A Russian not of royal blood is preferable to a German princess as the wife of a Russian ruler. If she has all the other qualities which make her worthy of a prince, she can be raised to princely dignity and rank. As far as the supposed advantages of a European education are concerned, the citizen finds that the German princesses have been vastly overrated in this respect. There is no reason to assume that the daughter of a Russian nobleman, educated in purity, virtue, and the spirit of the law, is in any way inferior to a foreigner. Even if the ruler should choose the daughter of an undistinguished Russian family, she would be preferable, for her family are sons of the fatherland and will strive for the well-being of the state, for their own glory's sake and for that of their posterity.

Shcherbatov's preference for Russians on the throne and in the civil and military services was not motivated by any deep-seated conviction that Russian birth *per se* conferred superiority of mind or heart. Nor did he believe that "Russian" could be automatically equated with virtuous. His tribute to the native Russian qualities of "purity, virtue, and spirit of the law," contrasted with the more fashionable and ephemeral learning of the German ladies, was grounded in practical considerations. He was too much the rationalist, too much of his century to believe that individual character could be derived from a fixed, a nationally determined pattern. Basically, his was an empirical preference, dictated by reason, by the experience of recent Russian history, and by what he understood to be the interests of his class. A foreign monarch, surrounded by a foreign bureaucracy, would not be *primus inter pares*, would not, as first and greatest noble of the land, share or even understand the concern of a native aristocracy of which he ought to regard himself a member. The foreigners and favorites who surrounded the throne and obscured the ruler's vision with their flattery, must be replaced by true and noble patriots who are not afraid to speak the truth on behalf of their country. "In a spirit of true nobility," Shcherbatov pleads elsewhere, "with steadfastness and love for the fatherland, let us . . . bring the truth which has been kept

from her, to the throne of the monarch. . . ." [67] The implication was that only the native aristocracy with its tradition
of powerful independence *vis-à-vis* the ruler could afford to
speak the truth.

The reign of Catherine stabilized for more than thirty years
the monarchical arrangements of the empire. By reaffirming the
gentry's freedom from compulsory state service and by defining its corporate privileges, the Empress had deprived this class
of its major. grievance against the state and its bureaucracy.
The benevolence of the crown, as well as the stability of throne
and succession, prevented a repetition of those antiforeign outbursts that had accompanied the reigns of the two Annas, of
Peter III, and the accessions of Elizabeth and Catherine. Opposition to Catherine, which appeared soon after her coronation,
might on occasion take on xenophobe shadings. But for the
most part, the connection of national with dynastic feeling or
with class resentment was broken. Manifestations of hostility
against foreigners in government and support of a candidate
to the throne under the aegis of a national restoration prac-
tically disappeared. Instances of a protest against Catherine's
government in the name of patriotism are strikingly few. Not
even Pugachev, who proclaimed himself Russia's rightful
ruler, made mention in his proclamation of the "foreign"
Empress. Only one of his pamphlets, dated August 1774,[68]
and obviously designed to attract the Old Believers, spoke of
the shaving of beards and other "German" customs as out-
rages to the Christian faith. An unknown peasant poet of the
period, in the "Serfs' Lament" [69] also pointed to the foreigners
surrounding the throne, those who had been called to enlighten
Russia and improve her government, as a source of peasant
suffering. Two examples of popular xenophobia, *pasquilles*
against the "foreign government" and its foreign ministers
appeared in 1764 and 1785 resepectively,[70] but they appear to

be the only evidence of such sentiment directed specifically against government and bureaucracy.

The short reign of Paul (1796–1801) who seemed to have inherited Peter III's fondness for the Prussian military and also insisted on the full subjection of all to his despotic will, resurrected that combination of patriotic and class resentment that had proved so effective in earlier years. Although protest was confined mainly to muted grumbling and the circulation of epigrams mocking the emperor's infatuation with Frederick the Great,[71] it resulted eventually in the conspiracy that led to Paul's assassination.

With this one exception, the last third of the century, dominated by Catherine, marks a change in the source and content of national feeling and national pride; the problem of nationality is shifted from politics to cultural matters. Now it was no longer Biron, Muennich, or a Holstein duke who were the prime targets of patriotic indignation; they had, after all, been phenomena whose nationality was more or less accidental; it was their social and political role that had rankled in Russian minds, the part they had played in enforcing the onerous demands of the state. Foreigners continued to be prominent in Russian service, but they were less obnoxious after the gentry had obtained its freedom. Now the French dancing master, the English carriage, the German tutor, the Russian Frenchmen, and some of the ideas they brought with them, became the despicable quintessence of the foreign as it appeared in Russia. And when in increasing measure the foreign seemed to corrupt the national essence, there occurred the first attempts to determine what that essence was.

What was challenged in the process of that determination was not a few foreign bureaucrats, but a foreign way of life. The eagerness with which the newly-liberated landowning class embraced the externals of Western culture deepened the gulf separating that class from a peasantry whose exploitation made the new style of life possible. Criticism of Western manners and mores, therefore, often came dangerously close to criticism of the established order. Catherine's emphatic nationalism, her stress on the native Russian virtues and her sponsorship of Russian culture, was in large part designed to forestall such criticism. For the former German princess who had read the lessons of Russian history well, there was, of course, double purpose in this: to demonstrate her attachment to Russia, and to foster among her subjects a pride in Russia and its achievements as a species of loyalty to herself and to her state. Her assertions of the nation's greatness and well-being were to minimize the evidence of the real state of Russian society which was appearing in increasing measure. Beginning with Catherine's reign there are two streams of national thought: the governmental and that belonging to public, i.e. critical, opinion. During the last third of the century, critical thought, no matter how antiforeign, did not automatically identify itself with Catherine's self-laudatory pride in Russia. There might have been agreement in specific instances and on specific issues, but "Russia," "Russian virtue," and the "national character" tended to mean different things to the government and to the critical part of public opinion.

## CHAPTER II

# Manners and Morals

When national feeling had expressed itself against the person of the monarch, his entourage, or the bureaucracy, it had necessarily taken on an antigovernmental character. It could find expression, therefore, only surreptitiously or with a change of regime. Any pretender to the Russian crown might utilize this feeling in the furtherance of his own aims, as both Elizabeth and Catherine had done, but could not encourage it consistently. Any permanent and publicly proclaimed dedication to the national principle might expose the monarch, members of his family or of the government to attacks in which patriotism might serve to conceal an opposition based on quite different grounds. This applied as much to Elizabeth as it did to Catherine, for although the former was a native Russian, foreigners, as we have seen, continued to be prominent at her court.

Moreover, by designating her nephew Peter, the young Duke of Holstein, as her successor and marrying him to a German princess, Elizabeth had conferred the imperial crown on a man who was in all his inclinations non-Russian, if not openly anti-Russian. In doing so, she created a perfect target for a nationalist opposition, one of the major reasons why she could not afford to lend continued support to the principle of nationality in government. For unless the Empress decided to change the order of succession, an attack on Peter would have been at the same time an attack against her person. There was always the fear, on the part of both Empresses, that opposition, no matter how motivated, might become indiscriminate, and challenge the very foundations of government. The quick and sharp suppression in 1743 of the Viborg mutiny of the guards' regiments, who clamored for the death of their foreign officers, left no doubt that a serious threat to the authority of the state would not be countenanced, not even from those who had helped it into power.[1]

After the fall of Biron, then of Muennich and Ostermann, there was always the possibility that this exposure of the holders of power to the rage and ridicule of the country might set a dangerous precedent. Men, who for ten or more years had exercised authority in the name of a Russian monarch, were stripped of their authority overnight. This meant exposing the authority of the state itself, undermining belief in its divine derivation. It was from such a precedent that the identification of *all* authority, foreign or not, as something alien and compulsive, unnatural in fact, could arise. Thus, in later generations, certain Russians could come to look upon the government and its apparatus of rule as a Swedish-German importation, grafted violently upon a reluctant nation.[2]

The stability of the two reigns—Elizabeth ruled for twenty years, Catherine for thirty-four—and the gentry's favored position after 1762 shifted national feeling from politics to the sphere of social life, morality, and culture. The shift was aided also by the changed nature of foreign influence. German regents, German ministers, German officers made way for French fashions, French books, French manners, and the French language. The French influence was much more pervasive than the German, and it found its most ardent representatives and propagandists among native Russians.

The gentry, as its service obligations became less onerous, discovered that the acquisition of French culture was a factor of social distinction welcomed at court and in society, and that it supplied those elements of *bon ton* which characterized most of the European nobility. To become French meant to become European. While the young *dvoriane* of Peter's time had been made to acquire a certain knowledge of mathematics, navigation, law or economics from their foreign teachers, with a view to their employment in government service, the young cadet of Anna's time was much more concerned with acquiring the polish of a young European gentleman than the rudiments of practical knowledge. Dancing, the French language, drawing, theatrical performances, and fencing occupied as important a place in the curricula of most educational institutions for the young gentry as did mathematics, history, political science, fortification, and other subjects useful in the military or civil service.[3]

Less frequent than the acquisition of the external accomplishments of a foreign culture, was a real penetration to its roots and sources. "People's walk has improved," Shcherbatov noted, "since they learned how to dance from the damn foreigners. . . . But that imparts neither morality nor convictions. The one comes from the heart and the understanding, and the other from the legs." [4] And his contemporary Golovkin complained that while the period of German predominance had replaced frankness of character with rudeness of manners, now the schools each year turned out a mass of *beaux esprits manqués* "who hardly know their own language, but sing, dance and rhyme endlessly . . . and value nothing more than social success." [5]

If Shcherbatov and Golovkin, in the manner of nostalgic men, overstated their case, if it is true that in addition to French perfumes, wines, dancing masters, and hairdressers, French books and ideas also made their appearance in Russia, these importations were much less frequent and in their immediate, visible impact on society much less influential. The number of men who had extensive libraries of French literature and a first-hand knowledge of French thought was not great. The number of those who dressed, curtsied and, in general, conducted their social intercourse *à la française* must have been considerable, judging from the frequency and intensity with which they were satirized and ridiculed.

The lack of balance, the wide gap between their real natures and their appearance and conduct, made the fashionplates of St. Petersburg and Moscow such ready targets for satire. In the absence of solid cultural foundations, the young gallants were little more than crude rustics dressed in the latest fashions. Their separation from the traditions and customs of Russian life, without first acquiring the foundations of another, created a cultural dilemma. In Klyuchevski's brilliant phrase, they tried eternally to be at home among foreigners and succeeded only in becoming foreigners at home. Taken in the West for Tatars dressed up to look like Europeans, they were considered by their countrymen Frenchmen born in Russia.[6] The position of the native foreigner, his "rootless cosmopolitanism," even his own subsequent realization of its ambivalence, furnished the impetus for the development of a new brand of national consciousness and necessitated a more discriminating attitude towards the manifestations of foreign culture.

By his thoughtless imitation of the externals of a foreign culture, the young dandy (*petimetr* in the language of the period, from the French *petit-maître*) had not only turned himself into a caricature; he had also forgotten or overlooked the concepts of honor, duty and, above all, service to society, which were as much a part of the ideal gentleman as his sword.[7] The castigation of the petimetr in the literature of the time clearly implied that by his contempt for Russia, by his separation from the native soil, by his neglect of service, he had put himself beyond the pale, had in a sense become a foreigner. Not only his chattering of French and the exotic nature of his dress stamped the young fop as antinational, but also the damage which his behavior inflicted on personal and social morality. Criticism of the native foreigner, of the "Russian Parisian," became at the same time criticism of a social class, or at least that part of it which believed that its release from formal state service released it also from all other obligations to the fatherland.

This dangerous proximity of foppery and indifference to duty and to the welfare of his fellow-man characterizes the very first *shchegol* (dandy or fop) of Russian literature. In the first satire of Prince Antiokh Dmitrievich Kantemir (1709–1744), the ignoramus Medor cares for European civilization only in the form of a new garment, hairdress, or powder, and would not trade a pound of it for all of Seneca. The first of a long line of ignoble types, Medor is joined in the second satire of Kantemir by another prototype. Evgeni, a do-nothing descendant of ancient nobility, thinks that his blue blood alone entitles him to the highest honors for which neither training nor talent have qualified him. Evgeni stands for the superficiality with which European models had been accepted, not only in matters of fashion, but also in the understanding of what constitutes nobility. His antagonist in the satire is Filaret, who proves to him that any right which he may have to an exceptional position in the state must be based on works and virtue; his own, not those of his ancestors.[8]

In these two early satires of Kantemir—their first versions date to 1729—it is not a nationalist but a moralist who speaks. Still, he anticipates a later notion that the senseless denationalization of custom and costume is in some measure also an uprooting of Russian virtues. One is struck by the frequency with which the coxcomb who adorns himself with foreign feathers becomes a symbol of the baneful effects of foreign influence, while service to the fatherland, rather than social position, becomes a distinguishing feature of the true patriot. "Always to marvel at foreign achievements, never to taste of

one's own strength, never to strive for one's own skills, is a
sign of ignorance and laziness," wrote the poet Tredyakovski
at about this time.[9]

The high point of Francomania was reached approximately
during those years, 1755–1775, in which it was most sharply
castigated in literature. Yet Kantemir had created his poetic
prototypes, the coxcomb and the noble do-nothing, some
thirty years earlier; and there is even more direct testimony
that the problem was not totally new. A Danish traveler who
visited Russia in the 1730s, described two Russians whose
numerous progeny will appear time and again in the pages of
the satirical journals and on the stage. First, the young Princess
Kurakina, the female dandy, the *shchegolikha* or *koketka*:

> She rides out with a coach and six, accompanied by two out-
> riders and four footmen, keeps two dozen maids and as many
> lackeys, eats luxuriously and always at odd hours, sleeps until
> noon, dresses like a singer of the St. Petersburg operetta, knows
> only Russian, but mixes it with so many French and Italian words
> with Russian endings, that native Russians have a harder time
> understanding her than foreigners. Her conversation consists for
> the most part of praises of French fashions and free behavior; she
> mocks pious women . . . and . . . tries to prove that amorous
> adventures are possible in Moscow no less than in Paris or
> London.[10]

All the basic features of the species are here outlined: laziness,
vanity, a contempt for piety and simple virtue, as well as for
the purity and beauty of the native language. These traits of
conscienceless dandyism did not, of course, characterize only
the *jeunesse dorée* of Russia. The young gentlemen and gentlewomen who, in Alexander Pope's phrase, "sauntered Europe
'round and gather'd every vice on Christian ground," to return home unrecognizable and incomprehensible to their
worthy and solid parents, were as much a phenomenon in
German or English life and letters as in Russia. Against the

Russian background they stood out in even sharper relief than
did their Western counterparts.

The Prince Cherkasski and his wife are the opposite of the
witless Kurakina in their willed and conscious Russianness:

The Prince asked if I understood Russian. I answered, yes, a
little. Then the Prince said that since in all his travels he was forced
to speak in the language of the country in which he found himself, he could not permit that anyone spoke any language other
than Russian in his own country. I should like to know, he continued, why the Russian language cannot be considered as being
on a level with French and German. I suggested that this might
in part be traced to the fact that learning had not yet flourished
in Russia, and that therefore the language had not evolved or
spread; but also for the reason that foreigners had only recently
begun to hold the Russian Empire in esteem, and that, of course,
the reputation of a language grew with the power of a state. The
Prince seemed satisfied with this, but then the Princess asked me
whether I were a German. When I denied this, she took off her
straw hat, which was made in the English fashion, and asked me
whether I thought that such things ought to be imported from
abroad. I replied that such a lapse was atoned for by the utility
of the article which Her Highness had been forced to buy. But
you see, the Princess said, this hat was made by my *muzhik* in
Moscow, and therefore we need neither the foreigners nor their
wares in Russia.[11]

We are confronted here by still other elements of the growing
national consciousness: the insistence that "we too" have a
language worthy of ranking with the foremost languages of
polite society, that "we too" have native artisans who can produce whatever is needed with skill and taste equal to that of
the fashionable hatters or dressmakers of London and Paris.
In a sense, the wish to establish Russia's equality with the rest
of Europe in human and intellectual resources implied the
acceptance of standards set by the foreigner and his culture.
The attempt to demonstrate Russian equality, this "compensatory nationalism," was in fact a recognition of the superiority

of the foreign model. For the time being, Russia's dialogue with Europe was conducted in terms that Europe had supplied.

Kantemir had outlined the basic character of the petimetr; other writers made his features more precise. In the comedies of Alexander Sumarokov (1718–1777), the petimetr's passionate interest in the latest fashions became specifically an interest in the latest French fashions, and his lazy indifference to the welfare of his country turned to contempt for all that reminded him of Russia. As a result the satire of the petimetr became more hostile, more of a protest in the name of national pride than mere moral didacticism. In two of his comedies, written in 1750, Sumarokov added to his gallery of pedants and petty bureaucrats the petimetr Dyulizh who complains of his fate: "Why was I born a Russian? Oh, Nature! Are you not ashamed to have given me a Russian father?" [12] Dyulizh finds it unbearable that his Russian birth and nationality put him in the same category with the rest of his countrymen for whom he has nothing but contempt, and he challenges one of his rivals in love to a duel for having called him a Russian and a brother.[13] His conception of service to the fatherland extends no further than mastering the arts of dressing, of gossip, and other adornments of polite society. The vice which Sumarokov held up to ridicule was the fatuous neglect by an entire generation of its duties to class and country. It was the performance of these duties that gave the gentry its right to privilege and position. Sumarokov repeatedly returned to this theme in his satires, his fables, and his comedies. Of all the virtues which grace the nobleman, "love for the fatherland is the first, the undoubted witness to our rectitude; not only is it impossible to be a hero without it, but also to be an honorable man." [14]

Observing the corruption of morality in his class, the loss of civic virtue and personal integrity caused by wasteful luxury and an infatuation with foreign fashions, Sumarokov sought in a purer and simpler period of Russian history the values which he wanted his contemporaries to follow and uphold. He found them in the reign of the Tsar Fedor Alekseevich (1676–1682), an age in which Russians had not yet learned to mistake extravagance of dress for nobility of character. The last of the Muscovite Tsars had "proscribed the usage of ruinous dress, which is the ornament of men without mind and character; he abolished the prerogatives of families who drew their pride from their ancient genealogies alone and not from services rendered to the fatherland. . . ." [15] In their language, their appearance, and their morals Russians had been purer and, therefore, more truly themselves, before they had accepted the curious notion that by changing their speech and their appearance they could also change their nationality.

The Russians of that time did not yet try to convert themselves into Frenchmen or Germans, but to improve their state and to enlighten themselves. They tried to be worthy originals, not weak, ridiculous, and wavering copies of foreigners who had only contempt for their own qualities. One did not then think, as so many do today, that by covering one's head with a certain wheat flour which we call powder, we would become like the rest of the Europeans. For the inhabitants of our continent do not differ from Asians, Africans, and Americans through the use of powder, but through learning. Those who proclaim that we were nothing but barbarians before Peter the Great . . . do not know what they are saying; our ancestors were in no way inferior to us, and this last Tsar was the worthy brother of Peter the Great.[16]

Those who do believe that Russia had been called to life and civilization with the coming of Peter had themselves been changed from "unpowdered men into powdered animals."

Here is an almost perfect illustration—the first as far as can be ascertained—of the mechanism in which the challenge posed by the inroads of a foreign culture almost forcibly leads to a reexamination of one's own. The search for native qualities and virtues, the rediscovery of the past, led Sumarokov, as it led others after him, to deny the assertion that only with

Peter, only with the external Europeanization of Russia, had Russians become civilized. To have admitted this charge would have meant to share in the belief that Russia had had no identity, no culture of her own, before Europe discovered and shaped her. It is the first statement of a theme which will be heard more than once from Russians who want to show that they are not mere *arrivistes* on the scene of history, that they do not exist merely by virtue of an act of discovery or recognition by the rest of Europe. It is the starting point for later assertions that the Muscovite period of Russian history was not inferior to the imperial period initiated by Peter the Great, that in its patriarchal simplicity, honesty, and religiosity, it had been vastly superior. In Sumarokov we do not find, as we do later in Karamzin, that the source of many evils is to be sought in the activities and the person of Peter the Great. Sumarokov wants merely to redress the balance in favor of Peter's predecessor, the last of the Muscovite Tsars, to claim for him worth at least equal to that of the reformer.

One of the first balanced appraisals of Peter's work, which viewed its impact in historical perspective, is to be found in the writings of Prince Shcherbatov. He did not question Peter's greatness or his services to Russia which were greater than those of the ruler of an enlightened country. Peter had had to build anew; his was a lonely and heroic figure, struggling against almost insuperable odds to raise his country out of ignorance and backwardness. Shcherbatov calculated that, but for Peter it would have taken seven generations, or 210 years (from 1682 to 1892) to accomplish what through his efforts was achieved by the end of the eighteenth century.[17] Shcherbatov likened his glory to a great river: the farther from the source, the more it grows.[18]

For all the glory and greatness which Peter had given to Russia, he had also set her out on the risky way of foreign borrowing. Once his own example was lacking, once the spirit of service and dedication to the state with which he had imbued his work disappeared, the shell alone remained. The evils which Shcherbatov traced to the waning of high purpose and strict discipline were the same evils which the satirists saw embodied in the petimetry.

Although ... the Russians were transformed from bearded men into clean-shaven ones, exchanged their long coats for short ones, and became more sociable and refined, true attachment to the faith began to disappear, the sacraments to fall into disrepute, firmness to weaken and to give way to barefaced flattery. Luxury and voluptuousness laid the foundations for their domination and greed began to enter the halls of justice, to the destruction of the laws and the harm of the citizens. Such is the condition of morals in which Russia was left after the death of this great ruler, in spite of all the barriers which he placed in the path of vice by his own exertions and example.[19]

To Shcherbatov, the most serious consequence of this weakening of the moral fiber was the dissolution of the ties of conscientious loyalty which had bound husband to wife, parents to children, friend to friend, and every Russian to Tsar and fatherland. Love of country and devotion to the sovereign had been replaced by flattery and favoritism. Hypocrisy became essential, for only the monarch could bestow the rewards that made indulgence in foreign pomp and luxury possible. Shcherbatov thus traced the decline of selfless patriotism directly to the taste for European elegance which Peter, with quite different goals, had introduced. He did not, however, call for an undoing of the reform and its effects, or for a return to the patriarchal simplicity of Muscovite Russia, but for the enactment of fundamental laws to protect the state from the consequences of the ruler's caprice, from favoritism and the blind flattery of courtiers.[20]

The comedies, comic operas, and satirical writings which after the beginning of the sixties belabored the theme of corruption through foreign influence with almost monotonous insistence, did not all share Shcherbatov's high moral tone, his fear of unlimited absolutism, or the complexity of his historically buttressed view. The very forms in which satirists and dramatists worked and the audiences for which they wrote made that impossible. They were forced, therefore, to paint with broad, almost crude strokes, to caricature, to overstate. Their purpose was quite as often to amuse or to entertain as it was to edify and preach, to reach a market which proved itself receptive to their wares. Much of the literature which satirized the Francomania of the day lacked that deep concern with the state of Russian society which characterized Shcherbatov's writings. The aping of all things French, the preoccupation with looks and pleasures and the strange jargon of the fashionable world were quite sharply drawn; but questions about the sources or the meaning of these phenomena were rarely asked. To treat manners and morals in this fashion, lightheartedly, was to treat them safely, without questioning the social order of which they were the products. Here was one vice which could be mercilessly flayed by every author without danger or fear of contradiction.

Vladimir Lukin (1737–1794), who had greeted a Russian version of Holberg's *Jean de France*[21] as a necessary medicine for the "weaning of many of our young fellows from the absurd and shameful imitation of French pranks," complained in the preface to his "Constancy Rewarded," that the public wanted only to be amused and did not care whether the plays it saw—many of which were thinly disguised translations—bore any relation to Russian reality.[22] He set out, therefore, to make the theater correspond more closely to what was familiar to his audiences by the quite superficial method of supplying the characters of his "adaptations" with Russian names and by placing them in situations and places appropriate to their supposed Russian origin. This method did not, of course, create a truly native or national comedy, but it brought home more closely vices and follies which earlier could have been shrugged off as nothing more than inventions of a foreign author's fantasy. Since it also lent a more didactic tone to the comedy, it was no longer quite so easy to dismiss this aspect of a pleasant evening's entertainment. Constant repetition of a number of basic themes also insured that their significance would not be entirely lost on the theatrical audience.

These themes, restated and made even more explicit in the satirical journals, implied that there was more than a casual connection between the young fop's infatuation with all things French and his inhuman treatment of his peasants, his carefree attitude towards family ties and his obligations as a citizen. Lukin, in "The Wastrel Reformed By Love," [23] introduced the young worldling Dobroserdov (Goodheart) who is rescued and returned to the path of virtue by a young woman who holds old-fashioned and high-minded views about the sanctity of marriage—views which are shared by her servant maid. Contrasted with these is the worldly *koketka*, a woman devoid of all shame and modesty. Morality, Lukin appeared to tell his audiences, is more easily found and preserved among those who have not accepted the fashionable and foreign-derived standards of behavior. The same point is made in his "Toy-Shop".[24] There Chistoserdov (Pureheart), his nephew, and an honorable ex-officer (the owner of the shop), are contrasted with a group of ten customers who represent a variety of vices and follies. They bear such names as Nimfodora, Pritvorov (Hypocrite), Vzdorolyubov (lover of trash), and Legkomyslov (Superficial), and typify the *haut-monde* of the capital. Lukin makes this clear by having Chistoserdov point out to his nephew, the artless, honest provincial, that he is showing him what people are truly like in the capital, so that he may beware of the snares set for him. The young man, who has been imbued with sound moral precepts by his father, is safe, however, from the blandishments of fashion and well able to profit from the lessons of the shopkeeper and his uncle. These include a warning not to mistake rank or position at court for intrinsic merit, to recognize such merit even in merchants or clerks, to respect the sanctity of the marriage vow, never to be ashamed to do a good deed, nor to corrupt the beauty of the native tongue by interlarding it with French words. Finally, and most importantly, the young man is urged to respect the humanity of his inferiors, especially that of his peasants.

With this last lesson, Lukin introduced the thought, subsequently more fully developed by other writers, that the excessive luxury of the frenchified young gallants was a direct cause of the peasants' ruin. In a preface to the play, he pointed specifically to the mania for foreign trinkets and amusements as being responsible for the squandering of estates and souls (i.e., peasants), and for the inhuman demands on the peasantry.*

Lukin did not explicitly identify evil with that which is foreign, or define virtue as purely a native quality. His characters, however, are early examples of highly stylized personifications of good and evil which, in the circumstances of the time, were evocative of patriotic feeling. "Good" was unmistakably on the side of those least corrupted by the fashionable life of court and capital. Faith, loyalty, steadfastness, and honesty were virtues which grew better in the provinces taught by an old-fashioned father than in St. Petersburg or Paris under the tutelage of some *monsieur*. Virtue was the heart of gold concealed under a rough Russian exterior, and no amount of European polish could compensate for its

---

* Lukin was aware of the dilemma posed by one of his positive characters, the shopowner, who continues to supply the petimetry with their ruinous trinkets. He resolves the dilemma by letting him announce that if he didn't overcharge them and take their money, even more unscrupulous foreigners would do so and remove the money from the country. He appeases conscience and patriotism by devoting a third of his earnings to the poor.

absence. In this confrontation of two spheres of life, the *rusak*, the coarse but honest Russian, stood for all that was good and true in the national character and way of life.

The two opposed positions were upheld by a variety of characters in N. P. Nikolev's "Vainglorious Poet" (1775). The infamous petimetr Modstrikh, whose speeches reveal the deep gulf which separates him from his countrymen, is the representative of a generation which considers Paris its capital. There they have surrendered their souls, to acquire in their place "only hot air." [25] All the young bloods are characterized by this absence of soul and an education of the heart. They have the appearance of human beings, but are in reality only artfully constructed dolls, animated by springs. "Such is the degree of perfection the arts have reached in Russia, that we make machines that are very much like people." [26] Modstrikh's views on life are in keeping with his character. He thinks it perfectly proper that the French should sacrifice decency and honor for the sake of elegance and beauty and cannot admit that they too have their share of blockheads and fools. To have been born in Russia is a disgrace; marriage vows, education, and love of country are matters of small moment to him. He has the utmost contempt for his native language, and although barely literate values Racine and Boileau because he knows them to be French.[27]

Only scorn for their homeland could, in the view of their critics, make the Modstrikhs believe that theirs was a mission of civilization, a presumption fed by their distorted notions of civilization. These critics did not doubt that such arrogance could arise only out of a total ignorance of human dignity and values. Where concern for one's soul had been replaced with concern for the figure one cut in the world, little better was to be expected. This is the point of Knyazhnin's comic opera "Misfortune from a Carriage" (1779).[28] Of all the works so far discussed, it is sharpest in its castigation of Francomania, viewing it as the source of the peasants' ruin and misery.

The worship of French fashions, the ignorance, emptiness, and viciousness of the young gallants came gradually to be looked upon as more than a ridiculous incongruity. Their representation on the stage and in the pages of the satirical journals turned into a protest not so much against the foreigner or his fashions, as against the effects these had in Russian life. A social protest made in the name of an oppressed class, whose deplorable situation was pictured as a direct consequence of its masters' xenomania, added a new and almost radical dimension to the statement of the national point of view.[29] The very fact of the peasant's appearance, the sharp contrast of his long-suffering figure to the foppish caricature of his master, was an invitation to audiences and readers to ask which of the two was the better Russian, which of the two did more for his fatherland, which of the two was more truly "national." With Ya. B. Knyazhnin (1742–1791) begins the conscious attempt to take the problem of Francomania out of the realm of broad comedy and to locate it in a social class. There is much that is tragic in his "comic opera," and it is the tragedy of the peasants' situation, abandoned to their masters' caprice, that directs sympathy to them as a group rather than to the figure of an abstractly personified virtue—Mr. Pureheart or Mr. Goodheart.

In showing the dissoluteness of a class which had divorced itself from its native soil, which had torn up its roots in the Russian countryside, Knyazhnin adumbrated the first note of a large and important theme of Russian nationalism: the true source of the national life and strength is the patriarchal village, where peasant and lord live in harmony, dedicating their lives to each other, to country, and to Tsar. It is still a far cry to what Turgenev called the mystical kneeling before the peasant's sheepskin, but the discovery of the gulf between the frenchified master, the *barin*, and his serf was an important first step.

Lukyan, the serf-hero of Knyazhnin's piece, is in love with the peasant girl Anyuta and wants to marry her. But the master's steward Kleman, making use of the barin's order to sell some of his peasants for recruits so that he may buy a new Parisian carriage, tries to get rid of Lukyan and to marry Anyuta himself. Kleman, once known by the "stupid and barbarous" Russian name Klementi, is only ostensibly the villain of the piece. There is little doubt who is really held responsible for the peasants' misfortunes. "Good God," Lukyan exclaims at one point, "how unhappy we are to have to drink, eat, and marry according to the whim of those whose joys are made of our agony, and who would die of hunger but for us." [30]

The Firyulins, master and mistress, are like all the other Russian Parisians except that they have carried their Francomania to a logical and horrible extreme. Not only are they ready to exchange good Russian gold for foreign trinkets; they are willing to barter "Russian trash," Russian "souls," for the shoes, caps, and carriages from Paris without which they cannot let themselves be seen in polite society. With these articles, as much as with the bits of French they speak and the French name by which they call their steward, they think they have contributed their mite to the enlightenment of Russia. "Barbaric nation! Savage country! What ignorance! What coarse names! How they offend the delicacy of my ear!" This is how Firyulin greets his homeland, and his wife remarks with horror that in their village, so close to the capital, no one speaks French, quite unlike France, where even at a hundred versts from the capital everyone does. [31]

The decline of the patriarchal principle and the dissolution of the familial bonds between lord and serf are most graphically illustrated by an incident at the end of the play. Anyuta's father, happy over the joyous resolution which has allowed his daughter to marry her beloved after all, gratefully addresses Firyulin as father, only to be interrupted impatiently by his master: "Creature! How dare you call me father? Perhaps my father was your father. I don't want to be father to such swine. Don't you dare call me that in future!" [32] The incident is almost identical with one reported in the satirical journal "The Drone," in which the village elder reports to the barin that he has carried out the orders for punishment of a peasant who dared call him father: "From Anthony, because he called you father, not Lord, in his petition: five rubles. He has also been publicly whipped. He said: 'I did it from stupidity,' and henceforth will no longer call you father." [33] From a protector and powerful friend of his peasants the master has become an absentee landowner who resides in the capital, a man indifferent to their interests, their way of life, a foreigner to the place which formerly was their joint sphere of activity. For the new-style landowner, the village is little more than foreign or conquered territory, to be exploited at will, without regard for the conservation of its human or natural resources. "You wrote that the harvest has not turned out well," Firyulin tells his steward. "That is not my affair, and it is not my fault that our soil is not as good as the French. I order and beg of you not to ruin me: find the money where you will. . . . Are there no men fit to be sold for recruits? Well, then, take them and sell them." [34]

Even the happy resolution of this "comic" opera does not soften the underlying tragedy. It is not a change of heart or character on the part of the Firyulins which saves Lukyan and Anyuta, but once again a whim, a whim which might just as easily have turned against them. When Lukyan finds out that he is to be sent off to the army, he attacks Kleman in his despair and is put in chains. He and Anyuta plead for mercy: "*Monseigneur*," cries Lukyan on his knees; "take pity on us." "*Madame*," Anyuta seconds him, "defend us." The Firyulins are horrified. "*Mon coeur*," says Madame, "he knows French and is in chains," and her husband who also finds this shocking

confesses his guilt before *"mon ami"* Lukyan. He has him
released, allows the two to marry and makes Lukyan his lackey
on condition that he never again speak Russian. "A trifle was
our undoing, and a trifle was our salvation," all sing at the
end. But the salvation is only for Lukyan and his bride, since
Firyulin still wants his carriage and announces that there are
other peasants he can sell.[35]

The frequency with which the young windbags, frenchified
fops, and falsely proud petimetry appear in the literature of
the period leads one to wonder whether this was not merely
the repeated exploitation of a literary formula which had
been found successful both in Western Europe and in Russia,
or whether it was, in fact, the accurate reflection of a widespread social phenomenon. The tastes of audiences and the
didactic purpose of authors probably demanded broad caricature and led to exaggeration. But the persistence of the
caricature indicates at least the presence of the original in real
life. In addition, there is the testimony of contemporaries that
the dandies were considered immoral outgrowths of Westernization, and not alone sham targets for ridicule with a moral-
istic intent. A foreigner's description of the prototype of all
the female dandies has already been cited. The commonsensical
and prosy Andrei Bolotov, whose memoirs are an important
eighteenth-century source, was moved to pity for the young
wastrels and for his fatherland, by the spectacle of a whole
generation losing itself in senseless pursuits, and implied that
they were no use to the fatherland.[36] Other memoirs of the
period confirm that the caricatured excesses of dandyism had
some basis in fact, and they point to the nihilistic disregard
of conventional morality flaunted by the young people
of this cosmopolitan generation.[37] Awareness of a relationship between the veneer of a foreign culture and the underlying immorality of its adherents was not uncommon and went
beyond the exploitation of a literary formula. This immorality

was traced to the abandonment of all inherited moral precepts and standards of behavior without replacing them with a new set of firm principles. In this sphere too, Russian gold, Russian substance, had been squandered for foreign trinkets. Shcherbatov was not alone in feeling that, although many of the superstitions of an antiquated religion had been uprooted, there had also taken place a loosening of the attachment to the true faith, a decrease in true religiosity, leaving a void which fashionable, imported philosophies could not fill.

What the acceptance of French example was thought to lead to in the sphere of sexual morality and filial piety was vividly portrayed by M. M. Kheraskov's comedy "The Hater" (performed in St. Petersburg in 1779). Stovid, imparting the lessons of fashion to a younger friend who is trying to win a young lady's favor, advises him "to confuse her principles, to convince her that there is nothing lower in the world than a child's love for parents and family, that such a thing is considered mean in Paris, natural only to Philistines." Pryataya, the young lady in question, has already shown herself receptive to the new teaching, and proudly Stovid relates how she applied it: "At first she babbled deliriously of Paris, and then told her father 'Stay away! In France, fathers do not keep the company of their children, and only merchants let their hands be kissed by them.' And then she spat at him. . . ." [38]

The contrast between a decent regard for one's elders, one's country and religion and a shameless Francomania, is unambiguously stated in Dmitri Khvostov's comedy "The Russian Parisian," where even the names of the main protagonists— Frankolyub (Francophile) and Rusalei—emphasize that more than abstract views, national traditions are in conflict. Much in the comedy is familiar, especially the character of Frankolyub and his contempt for Russia, her ignorance, superstition, and crudeness. A new element is the articulate and reasoned comparison of French and Russian reality, made by a character

whose name, Blagorazum (Wisdom), suggests the soundness
of his views.

Blagorazum is no blind defender of Russia's superiority.
His purpose is to recall Frankolyub, whom nothing in Russia
can please, who does not want to serve his fatherland or marry
a Russian girl, to a sense of balance about his own country. He
invites him to read the history of France in order to learn what
evils and misery that most enlightened country has caused
mankind. Comparing old Russia with France, he asks "how
can they reproach us for superstition when rivers of blood
have been spilled in France, when superstition paired with
ignorance destroyed the very bonds of government there?" [39]
Blagorazum is willing to give the French their due, to admit
that France has produced great minds; nonetheless, ignorance
and prejudice are general everywhere—in London and Paris as
well as in Moscow and St. Petersburg. Russians may still be
a bit ill-mannered, ignorant and superstitious, but they have
qualities which more than make up for these deficiencies.
Rusalei, as the possessor of these native Russian virtues becomes their embodiment, and when Blagorazum speaks of him,
he speaks also of the national character: "He is honest, just,
forgiving, charitable; a good brother and friend, firm in his
given word—all these are qualities of the true Russian." [40]

Rusalei's sterling qualities are less the results of any conscious effort of education than they are the products of the
soil in which he has grown to maturity, of the environment
which has shaped him. He was not sent abroad for his education, such as it was, but received it at home from mother and
nurse who instilled in him the deep wisdom of the people and
a healthy suspicion of foreigners. Frankolyub remains uncon-
vinced and unreformed. He wants only to return to France
for which his love is growing from day to day. Its very intensity is for Khvostov the measure of his estrangement from
Russia, and his creator abandons Frankolyub to let him return

to his real home. It is significant that abroad Frankolyub has learned not only to look down upon his country, but also upon its simple people.

These are more than isolated instances of the estrangement of a Westernized upper class not only from its country as such, but from the peasantry, the people, who by contrast assume some of the attributes of the folk, a concept which was to play such an important role in the nationalism of the romantics. The attitude of the eighteenth century to the people, the broad masses, was still beset by too many ambiguities to allow of their emergence as the idealized embodiment of the national virtues. For the most part, they appeared either as quite unreal rococo figures in a pastoral idyll or were ignored altogether as *chern* (rabble), so that it is an event of some importance when a peasant, or even a merchant, is made the spokesman of an author's views. Yet it seems that readers were being led gently and gradually away from courts, capitals, and the vagaries of fashion, by way of the sensible gentry of the provinces — the Starodums, Blagorazums, Chestons, and Rusaleis—to the peasant village itself where, far from the big world, simplicity, constancy, and honesty still rule.

Fashions of thought were held as responsible for the master's estrangement from his people and for their ruin as were fashions of dress. The *voltairianstvo* of some of the gentry, their absorption in intellectual abstractions to which the environment was hardly receptive, widened the gulf between them and the mass of the people as effectively as did more senseless pursuits of novelty. "He does not fear God," an old peasant is made to say of his barin, "and how can he? They say he is some kind of magician or *farmazon* [i.e., *franc-mason*]! You should see how many boxes of books we brought to him from the village. And they say that none of the books is in Russian! That's how he loves the Russians! And he never goes to confession! Our peasant brother is lower to him than a dog."

Another peasant in a contemporary novel censures those who have become willful foreign children instead of being responsible Russian masters. An education, he says, is best gotten at home. Abroad one learns only disdain for fatherland and fellow-citizens. These foreign-educated gentlemen treat their peasants little better than beasts and brutes.[41]

The attribution of godlessness and inhumanity to a non-Russian education and the reading of strange books, did not probe very deeply into the causes of the problem. The question remained unanswered as to what had caused this turning away from the fatherland, how it came about that so total a supremacy of French manners and modes of thought as was suggested by its critics could have been established. Those who posed it rarely asked what special conditions of Russian history and society favored this blind imitativeness, or why it was that the superficial aspects of French culture were so readily assimilated. They merely blamed foreign tutors and foreign travel as the source of the infection which returned soulless puppets to Russia.[42] Even those who went abroad for purposes of serious study were depicted as shaming the Russian name and bringing home little more than the knowledge of new vices and distractions. Where a trip abroad was impossible, a foreign tutor, for the most part a Frenchman, was imported to take its place and to instill in his charges that dissatisfaction with Russian life which was one of their distinguishing features. Whether the foreign tutor was called Chevalier Kokadu, or Chevalier de Mensonge, whether he was an erstwhile lackey or coachman, he was pictured as harmful in his effect on young Russian hearts and minds. The conclusion drawn from such an unflattering picture of the results of foreign instruction was that since Russians seemed so easily corruptible there had perhaps been good reason for the pre-Petrine prohibitions against foreign travel.

The historian Boltin, for example, fearing a quick and undiscriminating change in his country's morals and manners, saw in unrestricted travel the danger of such change, especially if the traveler lacked a mature mind and firm grounding in the laws and morals of his fatherland. Boltin talked of the young travelers as if they were children who had suddenly been confronted with a wide variety of new and shiny toys, only to abandon them shortly for still newer ones. The fault, he believed, was Peter's, who thought that merely to go abroad meant learning, while experience had justified the opinion of earlier generations that the benefits were few and the evils were many.

When we began to send our youth abroad and to entrust their education to foreigners, our morals entirely changed; together with the supposed enlightenment, there came into our hearts new prejudices, new passions, weaknesses, and desires which were unknown to our ancestors. These extinguished in us our love for the fatherland, destroyed our attachment to the faith of our fathers and to their ways. Thus we forgot the old, before mastering the new, and losing our identity, did not become what we wished to be. All this arose out of hastiness and impatience. We wanted to accomplish in a few years that which required centuries, and began to build the house of our enlightenment on sand, before having laid firm foundations.[43]

Boltin, although he is often considered an early Slavophile, was in no way an opponent of Western influence as such. Like Sumarokov and Shcherbatov before him, he deplored the loss of identity on the part of Russians who mistook imitation for Europeanization and as a result were neither Russians nor Europeans. The remedy was to become conscious of the values and the substance of one's own culture, to become imbued with it, to have that firm foundation of Russianness which alone could prevent the hastily adopted European façade from crumbling.

The events of French political history, especially after 1792, seemed to confirm many cherished prejudices about the harmful effects of a French education. The "giddy inconstancy" of that nation, which had so fully revealed itself in the private sphere, now demonstrated the lengths to which it could go in political life. Many more Russians than ever before now came quite readily to believe that the ease with which Frenchmen had overturned political arrangements held sacred for centuries, was only one more expression of the lightness of heart with which they approached most of life. A letter published in 1792 in a St. Petersburg review, and ascribed to the Princess Dashkova, stated that little better than the trampling underfoot of the most sacred laws of God and man could be expected from so flippant a people as the French. The lessons were obvious: Let us free ourselves from the foreign example and foreign teachers; let us return to the sources of the national life. "Let Russians be Russians," the letter demanded, "not copies of a vicious original; let us always be patriots; let us preserve the character of our ancestors who were always firm in the Christian faith and in their loyalty to their ruler. Let us love Russia and the Russians more than the foreigners." [44]

The example set by Catherine was one of sharp political reaction to the French Revolution, especially after the execution of Louis XVI. As early as 1790, she had ordered all Russians in France to return home; in 1791, French diplomatic representatives were no longer received at her court; on February 8, 1793, the Empress signed a decree breaking off diplomatic relations with France and ordering the exile of all French citizens in Russia who did not take an oath of loyalty to the French crown. Ships flying the French flag were barred from Russian ports and Russian citizens were forbidden to travel in France, to receive French newspapers, or to import French products. [45] The call for a return to Russian foundations and the rediscovery of the national heritage was hardly answered by these political measures. Nonetheless, the violence of the reaction to political events in France, especially when it expressed feelings of national pride and indignation which had existed before 1789 or 1793, served to reinforce a trend of opinion which asked Russians to be true to themselves and their country. But to be truly Russian once more, to return to the ancestral virtues, one had first to know what these virtues were, what elements there were in the national culture that were vital and unique.

In the search for the native Russian virtues, Catherine had led the way a good many years before the French Revolution seemed to make it necessary to protect Russians from the French fever. In the satirical journal *Vsyakaya Vsyachina* (Miscellany) published and in large measure written by Catherine in 1769, she sounded a call for a demonstration of the goodness, excellence, and uprightness of the Russian character. Unfortunately, contemporary evidence of these sterling qualities appeared to be lacking, and the demonstration was turned into an historical exercise which searched for the old Russian virtues in archives and ancient manuscripts. The publisher of "Miscellany" was confident that publication of these materials would bring a growing number of examples of Russian virtue to light and public notice. "Oh praiseworthy virtues of our ancestors, to you I address myself, show yourselves to the world; stop those who slander you and yet do not know you; spread your fame . . . and set an example which is worthier of imitation than a foreign one." [46] The impetus given by Catherine to the development of a set of national values found a wide response among her contemporaries. Their motivation however was not always the same as that of the Empress who wanted to prove to her subjects and to the world that her reign had brought untold blessings to Russia and that her government was not responsible for the dark sides of Russian life. Two of Catherine's subjects, the publicist N. I. Novikov (1744–1818) and the playwright D. I. Fonvizin (1745–1792) viewed their society in a more critical light. Both made important contributions to the elaboration of those values that came to be regarded as national because they were the opposite of the vices which imitation was thought to have produced. They were the simple virtues on which every nation thrown into contact with a more complex civilization tends to pride itself: possession of a generous heart and simple soul as guarantees of man's humanity which fashion denied; the preservation of a certain roughness of manner and appearance, which was the price paid for not resembling those dolls which move and talk but lack all character; the avoidance of luxury and a proper regard for probity, sincerity, friendship, and honest service.

Of all the satirical journals published as a result of the example set by Catherine's "Miscellany" none was concerned more persistently with the problem of Russia's cultural independence and the discovery of native values than those of Novikov: "The Drone" (1769); "The Painter" (1772–1773); "The Purse" (1774); and "The Tatler" (1770).[47] Remembered in the history of Russian social thought primarily for his humanitarian concerns, as a freemason of tender sensibilities, as publisher and editor whose activities brought him into collision with authority and made of him a symbol of free thought in conflict with despotism, Novikov was instrumental in recalling his contemporaries to a sense of their own national worth and past. The directness, not to say crudeness, with which he lashed out against the Gallomania of his environment comes as something of a surprise in a man whose main weapons in any struggle one would expect to be silent suffering and infinite goodness. When he dealt with the life of the peasantry and contrasted it with the worldly pursuits of society, he spared no colors, and drew with as bold and broad strokes as any of the playwrights and satirists already mentioned. When, not unlike Catherine, and possibly in response to her appeal, he tried to uncover the treasures of the Russian past, of a morality and style of life indigenous and unspoiled, he was less successful and remained caught in contradiction and inconclusiveness. Nonetheless, the impetus he gave to a critical attitude towards foreign borrowing, his sponsorship of a native literature, and the publication of a most valuable collection of historical source materials were events of first importance.

The first two of Novikov's journals are dominated by social protest against the oppression of the peasantry and by national protest, one deriving strength from the other. The targets of Novikov's not always very subtle satire are familiar: they are the young men and women of the capitals who have been blinded by their passion for all things foreign to the best in Russian life. There is young Narcissus, ignorant of his native language, unhappy to have been born in Russia where his talents—dancing, fencing, card-playing, and the other arts of worldly conduct—are not appreciated; there is the neglect of native arts and artists because they are Russians, or worse, Russian serfs. But above all, there is the renunciation of the Russian past, of the virtues and morals of earlier generations for the lightheartedness and superficiality of manners, morals, and learning introduced by the depraved French. Novikov described this unfavorable exchange with rather heavy irony in economic terms listing "the domestic trifles, such as hemp, iron, leather, tallow, candles, linen and others" which Russians were glad to exchange for such important and necessary foreign goods as "French swords of various kinds . . . snuffboxes . . . lace, fringes, cuffs, ribbons, stockings, buckles, hats, studs, and links. . . ." The vessels on which these items have been brought to Kronstadt, and on which the Russian "trifles" will be exported, are called *Trompeur* and *Vétilles*.[48]

The exchange of unfinished Russian goods, of coarse but valuable raw materials for luxury goods devoid of any intrinsic value was of more than economic significance to Novikov. It stood for the whole process by which Russians had irresponsibly abandoned true native values for the externals of a foreign culture and he deplored the tendency to consider even the foreigners' vices as positive qualities, to call French insolence a noble freedom of behavior and English rudeness a noble greatness of spirit. It is not, he insisted, the French or the English people themselves whom he was attacking, "for they both have much that is good," but only the harmful elements of their cultures as seen in Russia. How could these harmful elements strike such firm roots in Russian life? How could the blind passion of imitation—Novikov calls it a disease—afflict so many of his countrymen? How could the native virtues go down to such easy defeat? Novikov's answer is no more satisfactory than that of his contemporaries, and in a quite mechanical fashion he assigns to the foreign teachers responsibility for the general lowering of standards of decency and honesty. If the lie rules in contemporary life, if the old ideals of service and respect for one's fellow-man have gone out of fashion, the fault lies with the Chevaliers de Mensonge and the Monsieurs Fripon. The French ships bring to Russian ports not only trifles, but triflers and swindlers as well, the whole brood of French adventurers who call themselves barons, chevaliers, marquises, and counts, people whose main qualifications for teaching Russian youth were, in Novikov's eyes, their quarrels with the Paris police.[49]

Perhaps realizing the shortcomings of a purely negative approach Novikov set out in the last of his journals, "The Purse," to articulate and to determine what the "ancient native virtues" were, what there was that could be opposed to the teachings of men who saw "their paradise in hell," to combat the notion that Russians had to borrow everything abroad, "even their character." This conscious dedication of the journal to patriotic purposes and its almost total avoidance of any other issues, makes it the most nationalistic of his efforts in the field of journalism. But in spite of repeated references to the ancestral virtues, to the times when "our ancestors were a hundred times more virtuous than we are, and when our land did not give birth to children who lacked in goodness and love for the fatherland," no standard of the national virtues as they were supposedly revealed in Russian history was forthcoming. Novikov's attitude towards the Russian past was at best ambivalent and a letter, probably written by him, challenged his readers to produce the Russian virtues so highly recommended for imitation. Were they to be found in a past devoid of art and science, full of crudeness, brutality and ignorance; in the customs of the old Russian Tsars who, as part of the wedding ritual, pomaded their hair with honey, bathed together with their wives and limited their reading to the prayer books? Are those times, the letter continued, to serve as a model in which Russians married without first having seen their wives, in which they burned one another for making the cross in the wrong way? Where, indeed, would the Russians be today without the civilizing influence of the French? [50]

These questions, to which Novikov promised an early reply, went unanswered, and although it is unlikely that Novikov himself was ridiculing the Russian past, there is little doubt that he was unable to resolve the conflict between the desire to glorify his country and its history, and the inability to do so without reservation, as Catherine wished. It is this fact which makes his satire so much more effective and convincing than his attempts at praise. All he finds it possible to say is that Russia's backwardness is no sign of her inferiority, but an historical circumstance which time and the superior native talents of Russians will remedy.

Russians, in their approach to the arts and sciences . . . have as much keenness, understanding, and penetration as the French, but have vastly more firmness, endurance, and industry; the difference between the French and the Russians . . . is that the latter applied themselves much later to the sciences. France is indebted for the spread of the arts and sciences to the age of Louis XIV; but in Russia, fate reserved this glory for Catherine the Great. . . . If we look at the speedy successes which the Russians have made in the arts and sciences, then we shall have to conclude that they will be brought to perfection in a shorter time than in France.[51]

Novikov was willing to admit the possibility that Russia was less enlightened, less advanced in a formal and technical sense, than the West; but he felt this was no disadvantage since the absence of the superficial aspects of progress had preserved the more valuable human virtues. These would insure that when the time came and the need arose, Russia would prove her equality in every way.

The dilemma of Russian "nationalism" in the eighteenth century is summed up in the person of Novikov. Unwilling to return completely to a past which had not yet become romantically transformed, incapable of glorifying a present which was so manifestly inglorious in many ways, he yet wished passionately to demonstrate that Russia had dignity and greatness of her own. To make that demonstration concrete was difficult, for Novikov was as unwilling to become an uncritical defender of Russian reality (past or present) as he was unprepared to reject all that Europe had given her. He realized that Russia was not a world sufficient unto herself and that she could not yet live exclusively by her own cultural and intellectual heritage. This made his resistance to uncritical borrowing a call for self-awareness, a call for a more discriminating reception of the West, not its rejection.

The problem of wanting to believe in a fatherland in which there was too much that gave rise to doubt and loss of faith, also beset D. I. Fonvizin, the talented author of "The Brigadier" (1766), and "The Adolescent" (1782).[52] He too alternated between hostility to alien ways and the search for an autonomous culture and morality, between censure of a blind adoration for all things foreign and an attempt to reconstruct the virtues of the past. For all his sympathy for a simpler and purer age, Fonvizin, like Novikov, found it impossible to give the traditional way of life of the Russian gentry an entirely positive treatment. If Ivanushka in "The Brigadier" and his inamorata, the wife of the Councillor, were ridiculed for their childish Gallomania, the ways of the older generation also came in for their share of derision. The Brigadier himself, a man who is proud of having reached his rank through sweat and blood, is a coarse, blustering, illiterate trooper. His knowledge of literature is limited to the articles of war and he cannot imagine that God should be ignorant of the Table of ranks. His wife upholds the traditional view of old-Russian family life (a view which her creator would have found hard to share) by telling her son that it is the parents' job to select a wife for him, as has always been the custom. The figures of the Councillor and his wife are hardly more engaging, nor do they form a positive contrast to the superficial Europeanism of Ivanushka.

With the creation in "The Adolescent" of Starodum (the name suggests the wisdom of the older generation), Fonvizin came closest to the creation of a culture-hero, a character who personifies the purity and honesty of a less corrupted age. Starodum is first and foremost an old-timer, a man who says of himself that his father educated him in the old ways and who saw no need, therefore, to reeducate himself. To be an old-timer who lacked the barbarous and primitive features of Fonvinzin's other Russian types, to be a man whose morality was shaped at home, not subject to changes of fashion but eternally valid—this meant to be more truly Russian than those who believed that "education" could be gained from the instruction of unscrupulous foreign tutors. The foreign tutor, when he is not merely ignorant or incompetent, remains the symbol of an education which is preoccupied with externals and neglects the heart. The adornment of the reason or the mind with the latest pedagogical fashions is as little effective in creating a true human being as is the interlarding of one's speech with French words in creating a true gentleman. "Have a heart, have a soul," says Starodum, "and you shall be a human being always . . . ; all else is governed by fashion: mind and knowledge are as much subject to it as are buckles and buttons." [53]

The antithesis between training and education, thought and feeling, form and substance, with the latter of each being the more highly valued, was to become one of the basic and persistent ingredients of Russian nationalism. In the literature of the eighteenth century, it was most explicitly stated in Fonvizin's letters from Europe. They are the first significant attempt made by an educated Russian to come to terms with the problem of Russia *vis à vis* Europe at first hand. So far, European culture had been judged, if at all, at one remove, through its effects on Russian society. Not until the formulation of Slavophilism and Westernism was an attempt made to determine the essence of the two worlds. Nor did Fonvizin's comparison see them in their political and cultural totality, or arrive at any final conclusions about their essential and characteristic traits, but for the first time it posed critical questions about the life of the West itself without regard to the forms it took when transplanted to Russia. Inevitably, a critical appraisal of the phenomena of Western life led to a reappraisal of Russia and to the articulation of a set of antitheses which seem in retrospect an anticipation of many later debates between Russia and the West. In these debates, certain of Fonvizin's criticisms of European life became almost patterned responses for succeeding generations.

Fonvizin and his wife made altogether three extended journeys abroad, mostly for reasons of health which took them to

France, a number of the German states, Austria, Poland, and Italy. Each trip lasted for about a year, and it is from the first of these sojourns, spent for the most part in France (during 1777–1778), that the majority of the letters date. As a close associate of Count N. I. Panin, then in charge of Russian foreign policy, Fonvizin was received everywhere, by foreigners and Russians alike, with honors and attentions not usually given a private traveler. None of these attentions however could reconcile him to what he felt were the negative aspects of the environment in which he found himself. "That which is good here," he wrote to his sister, "you will find only by searching for it; that which is bad jumps to your eyes of itself." [54] The intrusion "of itself" of the bad on Fonvizin's perception has given rise to certain doubts about the autonomy of this process, leading to suppositions that the bad did not so much obtrude itself as it was sought out; or, at least, that Fonvinzin's rather jaundiced vision of Europe preceded firsthand acquaintance. Prince Vyazemski, his first biographer, denied Fonvizin's judgment any balance, and asserted that he approached Europe with a hostility and prejudice which were, moreover, actually drawn from European sources.[55] It is true that the critical element predominates in the correspondence, and that the praise which certain European intsitutions and customs can win from him does not entirely restore the balance. The explanation for this must be sought, however, not so much in European sources, nor in the bilious or melancholy disposition of an invalid, as in a conscious attempt not to become another Jean de France who is delighted by all he sees. As a man of education, Fonvizin reinforced his patriotic skepticism with the wish to demonstrate that he was unlike his coarse and ignorant Ivanushka, who felt constrained by a feeling of inadequacy about his own background to admire all that was placed before him. "I am very happy," Fonvizin wrote to his sister, "that I have traveled in foreign parts. At

least our Jeans de France cannot impress me . . . I don't deny
that there is much that is very good here, but believe me, that
which is truly good would escape these gentlemen." [56]

Unlike Ivanushka, Fonvizin was from the start determined
to look at Europe discerningly, not to join in the admiring
"ahs" and "ohs" of his countrymen who were in his view in
no position to judge. On balance, and when he reasoned calm-
ly, Fonvizin was committed to the proposition that good and
bad were everywhere found in equal measure, that people were
everywhere the same. Yet in his reaction against the xenomania
of his fellow-citizens, it was almost foreordained that a critical
note should prevail. It extended from the dirt in the streets to
the pedantry of German professors, from the dullness of Italian
social life to the poor quality of food or accommodations in
posthouses along the way. But above all, it was centered on
France, her institutions, customs, and philosophers, as the
microcosm of the European world, the model which had
always been held up to Russians.

The main task which Fonvizin set himself in his appraisal
of French society, was to distinguish myth from reality: to
discover not only whether the French reputation in the world
had any basis in fact, but also whether the image French
society had of itself, as expressed in its laws, institutions, and
literature corresponded to reality. The conclusion was foregone, but it is important for the study of Russian attitudes
towards Europe to discover where a Russian of the eighteenth
century found French reality to be deficient and in what terms
his criticism was formuated. The choice of target as well as
the language employed should furnish a clue to the claims that
would be made directly or by implication for Russian reality
by way of contrast with European pretensions.

In the much vaunted freedom of Frenchmen, Fonvizin
observed the first, perhaps the major, discrepancy between
claim and reality, between form and substance, that lay at the

basis of most of his descriptions of French society. Since he came from a country which was sensitive to the charge of slavish subjection to authority leveled at it by more enlightened Europeans, Fonvizin was especially keen to discover what the famous liberties of Frenchmen really amounted to. He did not fail to pay an impressive tribute to the formal and imposing structure of French laws and the system established to carry them out, but almost immediately reserved the right to question whether with all its corruption and excessive intricacy it really served to preserve and safeguard individual freedom:

> The first right of every Frenchman is freedom. But his true and present situation is slavery; for a poor man cannot gain his livelihood except by slavish labor; and if he wants to enjoy his precious freedom he must die of hunger. In a word, freedom is an empty name, and the right of the stronger remains a right which is above all laws.[57]

Having made this distinction between a freedom which was provided by law but not enjoyed in practice, Fonvizin was led to question the very efficacy of a formal legal system which lacked substance and meaning. To compare it with a situation in which individual rights were not, perhaps, prescribed, but nonetheless enjoyed on the basis of custom and tradition alone, was a logical next step. He had learned, Fonvizin himself said, to distinguish between "liberty by law and real liberty," and to deepen this distinction to one characteristic of France and Russia: "Our nation does not have the first [i.e. formal or legal freedoms], but enjoys the latter in many ways. By way of contrast the French, having the right of freedom, live in virtual slavery." [58] Human worth, human dignity, Fonvizin was saying, cannot be called into being by even the best of laws, just as the best-laid course of instruction will not furnish an education of the heart. What will the most ingeniously contrived laws avail man, if he lose his faith in his fellow-men, the only warrant of true freedom? "The best laws are meaningless if the first law, the first bond between men has left their hearts—good faith. We have little of it, but here there is not even a trace." [59]

However little there may have been of good faith in Russia, in comparison with France his native country seemed to Fonvizin to have at least the vestiges of it. To France, the supposed seat of European enlightenment and learning, the Russian traveler denied true religiosity and real learning. In learning and religion, as in government and law, all is appearance; every effort is made to put on a brilliant exterior, none to furnish real content. Whether it was the meeting of the Estates of Languedoc (who in a strange old ceremony vote a *don gratuit* to the King which would in any case be taken by force), or an overelaborate church service, the philosophy of the salons or the teachings of the priests, or yet the niceties of the *point d'honneur* among gentlemen—all these provoked his distaste because of their deceit and artificiality. Fonvizin was most disappointed by the ethics of a nation which, if it was not abandoned to the superstitions of the priests, had let itself be captivated by the cold and unlovely rationalism of the new philosophy. The priests perpetuated the slavery of minds to chimeras, while the philosophers of the Enlightenment led their charges to the new extreme of selfishness and impudence. To a skeptical outsider the differences between the two camps were not as significant as they might seem, for with Frenchmen it was not so much a question of what they said or believed, but how they said it. The fear of ridicule, of social censure, this inconstancy and lack of independence in mind and judgment explained for Fonvizin why there was only one truly learned man, one mathematician for two hundred mediocre poets of fashion in all of France. Small wonder then, that the *coryphées* of French intellectual life found as little favor in his eyes as the average Frenchman. Few of them, he complained, live what they preach. All, with few exceptions, are haughty, false, and

greedy. In their own way, Diderot and D'Alembert are char-
latans no less than the hawkers of the latest intellectual fashions along the boulevards. The God of the philosophers is the
same as that of all other Frenchmen—Money; and it is the
spirit of selfish materialism, not a humanity which has rid
itself of superstition, that has taken the place of the religion
of the priests. A virtue which was independent of religious
precept was inconceivable to Fonvizin, and those who believed
in nothing disproved in their very persons the possibility of
their system. "What wise man of this century, having conquered all his prejudices, has remained an honorable man?
Which of them, denying the existence of God, has not self-
interest as his sole deity, willing to sacrifice all his morality to
it?" The French "philosopher gentlemen" he had met or
heard about, made him shudder to think what man would be
like without religion and how durable human society would
be without it.[60]

"Prejudice" and "Superstition" which were to the enlightened mind of the eighteenth century terms of shame and
opprobrium began to lose some of their sinister connotations
for Russians. Men like Fonvizin discovered that the more
advanced thought of the West was not entirely free of them
and that their absence was not an unmitigated blessing. If the
abandonment of religion in the name of reason had led to the
superficiality and coldness of heart which characterized the
new philosophy and its practitioners, were not Russians, for
all their supposed backwardness more nearly human, more
likely to be happy than their more enlightened contemporaries
in the West? Fonvizin at least seemed to think so, and it was
a conviction which was only confirmed by subsequent trips
abroad. Italy was if anything worse than France; and the
Germans, whom at one time he had preferred to the French,
found little favor in his eyes at a later date. "In a word," he
concluded his observations about them in 1784, "everything

with us is better, and we are bigger people than the Germans."
(*my bolshe lyudi chem nemtsy*).[61] That is, we are more
human, have more feeling, more heart, a greater capacity for
love and happiness. Perhaps the "broad Russian soul" here was
first unveiled to the world.

Characteristic as the feeling that "we are bigger people"
was to become subsequently, in the eighteenth century it was,
at least on the level of full consciousness, a fairly exceptional
remark. The major conclusion that was to be drawn from a
comparison of Russia and Europe was that Russians had no
need to feel inferior, that they had no need to let themselves
be blinded by the glitter of foreign cultures, that as people,
as human beings, they were as good as anyone else. "I feel that
God created us no worse people than they are," and since
people are everywhere people, since the amount of reason or
stupidity is everywhere the same, "our nation is no worse than
any other, and we can enjoy a true happiness at home, without
having to go bounding about in foreign parts." [62] In spite of
his insistence on the full identity of the human situation everywhere, one cannot help sensing that in his inmost heart Fonvizin felt it easier to be more of a human being in Russia than
elsewhere. It is not merely happiness, but true happiness that
can be found there, and possibly there alone. The pomp and
show, vanity and greed of a sophisticated cosmopolitan society
are lacking in Russia. Is this not an assurance that a clear conscience, true humanity, and happiness were more likely to be
attained in its relative backwardness and isolation?

Fonvizin came close to an explicit answer twice. Once in
individual terms, in an autobiographical sketch wherein he
fondly remembered his old-fashioned father, a man possessed
of sound reason and the Christian virtues. Though lacking in
formal education, somewhat naive and rustic, this product of
a Russian environment was more truly human than all the
learned scoffers.[63] Another time the argument was stated in

historical terms as the belief that Russia's simplicity (her back-wardness), her youth, her freedom of the burdens of progress was a guarantee of future happiness. The letter containing the expression of this belief deserves to be quoted at length, for it is the first known statement of a thesis which was to become central to much of Russian thought during the nineteenth century and particularly to nationalist thought. It was the belief that the very backwardness of Russia was assurance not only of her equality with the rest of Europe, but possible token of her eventual superiority, of her ability to avoid the mistakes which those who preceded her had made and to bring youth and freshness to the task. The letter was dated Montpelier, January 25 / February 5, 1778.

I shall not tire you with a description of our voyage. I shall only say that it proved to me how true the proverb is—the grass is greener beyond the hills. True, sensible people are everywhere rare. If they began to live here before us, then at least we, beginning to live, can give ourselves such form as we wish and escape those defects and evils which have taken root here. *Nous commençons et ils finissent.* I believe that he who has just been born is happier than he who is about to die.[64]

The isolated and scattered remarks of a Fonvizin or Novikov should not be construed as a fully developed nationalist theory or a Slavophilism *avant le mot*. The prevailing mood of the century, in Russia as elsewhere in Europe, was decidedly cosmopolitan. There were, however, other statements of the antithesis between mind and heart, form and substance, youth and age, Russia and Europe. These make possible the assumption of a certain continuity in the Russian intellectual environment and an influence which men who grew up in the early years of the nineteenth century could hardly have escaped.

## CHAPTER III

# Towards A National Language

A concern with language has ever been intimately connected with a people's search for its identity. Where such identity has been in doubt, because of the absence of a common historical tradition or political cohesion, language has often been made to bear the main burden of proof of nationality. Down to the twentieth century, local dialects and archaic tongues have been cherished and resurrected to lend substance to political and cultural claims or to recreate memories of a shadowy and fading past. Zionists and Irish nationalists, Provençals and French Canadians, have each, with varying degrees of success, stressed language as a bulwark of defense against the inroads made by foreign, often hostile, culture groups.

In Russia, as elsewhere, the evolution of a national literary language was a phenomenon of growing national consciousness, as well as being a response to practical and cultural needs. The present chapter does not trace this development in philological or linguistic terms. It merely views the formation of a national, secular, literary language—and the negation of foreign intrusions in it—as a conscious act in the creation of a culture aware of itself and of its merits. Such was the case in Renaissance Italy, France of the *Grand Siècle*, Germany of the Reformation, and England in the Elizabethan period.

A look at the processes that are involved, and at the concern which Russians expressed for their language and its perfection, shows how fully comparable the Russian development in this regard is with that of the West. Richard Carew's *Epistle on the Excellencies of the English Tongue* (1723), Charpentier's *Défense de l'excellence de la langue française* (1683), the work of Justus Schottelius on the German "capital language" (1663), that of Thomasius, Leibniz, and Gottsched in defense or furtherance of their native tongue, the foundation of academies and societies—each found its counterpart in eighteenth-century Russia. The declarations of linguistic independence, like those made by other countries beginning to free themselves from French tutelage, were among the first signs of resistance to the unbounded sway which French civilization and literature had held.

Herder's remarks on language in the *Materials for the Philosophy of the History of Mankind* are the most striking example of the importance which the men of the eighteenth century attached to language as the microcosm of a people's culture. "Has a people anything dearer than the speech of its fathers? In its speech resides its whole thought-domain, its tradition, history, religion, and basis of life, all its heart and soul." It was only with language, Herder thought, that the national character, "the heart of a people," was created, and it seemed to him most natural that the creation of a national language should be a task of great importance among peoples with only dim memories of their past and uncertain expectations for their future. "With language is created the heart of a people; and is it not a high concern amongst so many peoples—Hungarians, Slavs, Rumanians, etc.—to plant seeds of well-being for the far future and in the way that is dearest and most appropriate to them?"[1] As one of the larger Slav peoples, and one which enjoyed independence, the Russians may not have been uppermost in Herder's mind. But his observations were fully applicable to them. They found confirmation in a variety of ways: as protests against the corruption of the native speech with foreignisms, as appeals for a return to purity, as demonstrations of the antiquity and wealth of the native tongue and of its equality with all others, or even of its superiority. The concern with language appeared also as a quest for uniformity and simplicity and as the wish to create a common literary standard for Russians which could serve as evidence of an autonomous national culture and a medium for its further development.

There were two underlying reasons for the century's absorption with the problem of language. The first had its origins in the tenth or eleventh century, when the Russians received, together with the sacred texts of Christianity, their first written language. Church-Slavonic, although it could be understood by the Russian Slavs, was from the very beginning different from the idiom of everyday speech. Yet in the course of time the spoken and the written languages grew closer to each other and Church-Slavonic, losing certain of its old-Bulgarian features, had by the fifteenth century yielded its exclusively bookish character and even its purity. It was at that time that the clergy purged literature of "vulgarisms" and as a result, Church-Slavonic changed less over the centuries than did the popular speech, and remained distinct and remote from it. Thus the early eighteenth century found Church-Slavonic, the only recognized literary language of the time, inadequate for the expression of the civic, secular, and technical aims animating Peter's work. The secularization and Europeanization of the written language, its transformation from a vehicle of rhetoric, theology, and divine service to one of general utility in governmental and private life paralleled the secularization and Europeanization of Russian life in general.

In this as in other spheres, Peter's personal interest furnished much of the motive force for the changes that were actually achieved. The primary objective was to make the written language a vehicle for the transmission of instructions and information directly related to the work of reformation, to make it generally accessible even to those who had no firm grounding in the Church-Slavonic tradition, to bring it closer to the speech of the government chancellery, the counting house, and the market place—in short, to effect modernization by some kind of synthesis between Russian, the colloquial speech of the majority of citizens, and Church-Slavonic as the literary language. The fortunes of these two linguistic elements, the discussions of their mutual relations and the role each was to play in a modernized literary language, constitute a major part of the history of the Russian language in the eighteenth century.[2]

An almost equally important role in that history, and the second reason for the preoccupation with language, was played by the century-long debate over the degree to which Russian could, or should, welcome foreign influences and foreign example. Such influences were no novelty; whether they came from the Greek East, the Polish-Latin area of the Southwest, or from Germany and France, style, syntax, and vocabulary had long revealed their nature and their impact. The influx of foreign linguistic elements had been continuous, but it reached a high point of intensity and a new depth of penetration at the time of Peter the Great. This was due in great measure to the large-scale recruitment of the gentry into permanent military and bureaucratic service. The level of literacy of the average Russian landowner was not far superior to that of his serfs, and his literary culture, shaped by archaic influences, was in any case inadequate to the new tasks he was called upon to perform in the service of the state. In the absence of a generally accepted and practiced literary language, the flood of foreign words and phrases which entered Russian, created a terrible confusion. The result was that in the first quarter of the century, Russian was a language devoid of a proper orthography, having only the most arbitrary grammar, and a vocabulary composed of the most diverse elements. After the middle part of the century, the gentry's increasing consciousness of its special social position, and its official recognition, also led it to develop a literary culture that was to give full expression to its separate identity as a class and a nation. It is against this background, and with the growing cultural nationalism of the period in mind, that one must view the search for a new, a national literary language, and with it the search for a national literature.

During the Petrine period, governmental goals for the language consisted primarily in its simplification and Westernization. They were expressed most clearly in the instructions which Peter and his collaborators issued for the guidance of translators. One of these, Fedor Polikarpov, was admonished to let himself be guided by the usage of his chancellery (the *posolski prikaz*), to make every effort to avoid "high Slavic words" and to render the foreign work into Russian "not with high words, but with simple Russian speech." [3] "Simple Russian speech" must not, of course, be understood in the sense of popular speech, but as the language which was in most common use among the functionaries of the government, in the army, the civil service, and at court—a mixture of bureaucratic, diplomatic, and military style. During the first quarter of the century, this was considered the best model for a common, national literary language, as distinct from the stylistic and lexical complexity of Church-Slavonic, which was inappropriate for the expression of new concerns, unwieldy and no longer quite comprehensible to the general public. "The simplification of the literary language," writes Vinogradov, "bringing its grammatical, lexical, and semantic structure closer to the understanding of wider circles of the Russian people, the comprehensibility of the language—these were the watchwords of the government and the vital necessity of society." [4] The language of everyday usage, the *Umgangssprache* (*obkhoditelnyi yazyk*), became the desired norm, the "average, civic speech" as Fedor Polikarpov called it.

Secularization was extended even to the letters of the printed alphabet, and in 1700 Peter introduced a new, civic or secular type, the *grazhdanskaya azbuka*, based on the written letters of everyday script.[5] The reform of the alphabet may have had only rather limited and practical ends—according to Peter's instructions, books dealing with historical, commercial, and military subjects were to be set in the new type—but its importance lies no less in the fact that it prepared the ground for a wider literacy which was entirely distinct from a study or a reading of sacred texts.

The priesthood itself became increasingly aware of the extent to which the language of the Church, its sermons and its literature, were retreating into a sphere which was no longer easily accessible to the majority of its flock. Feofan Prokopovich, Archbishop of Novgorod and Procurator of the Holy Synod, repeatedly warned against baroque intricacies in the sermon, against Polonisms and turns of phrase which might be incomprehensible to the majority of the faithful. His own "First Instruction for the Beginner in Writing and Style" (1722) and Gavriil Buzhinski's "Rules for the Confessional" (1723), set out to state their admonitions in clear and simple language, comprehensible to laymen and clergy alike. Even priests, the preface to Feofan's primer remarked, often lacked requisite guidance in the performance of their duties for want of a book written in simple speech rather than in high Slavic dialect, incomprehensible, apparently, even to them.[6]

Modernization and secularization of the language was thus a twofold process which undermined not only the hegemony of Church-Slavonic and led to its reformation in the direction of greater simplicity and comprehensibility; it also raised everyday speech to a higher level, made it more nearly a literary language and gave to it some of the prestige which heretofore only Church-Slavonic had enjoyed. It was an approximation, an accommodation which took place between the two linguistic patterns, as a response to changed social and cultural needs. Europeanization of the language, however, was most intensive in the colloquial speech, where it was reflected in syntax, style, and grammar, but above all in vocabulary. As the intellectual horizon widened, as familiarity with European thought and techniques spread, new concepts and terms came into being and had either to be created anew or to be borrowed from Western languages. German, for the most part, furnished the new administrative terminology, and such words as *rang, ampt, patent, kontrakt, politseimeister, shtraf,* and *sotsietet* began to appear. Holland and England supplied a naval terminology: *farvater, kil, shkiper, bot, fut, brig, michman* and others. The French influence, as yet less strong than others, was restricted to a fairly small number of diplomatic and military terms.

It was inevitable that the Western orientation of Peter's reign would express itself not alone in the borrowing of foreign terms which were necessary to designate new activities and concepts, but also in their use as fashionable adornments of speech, indications of the degree to which their user felt himself in step with the spirit of the monarch and the times. The result was that in language as in other areas the undiscriminating infatuation with the strange and the novel was responsible for the often undiscriminating violence of the patriotic reaction. Fashion alone, the wish to appear Europeanized, rather than any necessity, could explain the replacement of perfectly adequate Russian words with such barbarisms as *bataliya, fortetsiya, viktoriya, ambitsiya*. Peter himself was on occasion disturbed by the excesses to which this naive form of Westernism led, and he admonished one of his ambassadors, who had practiced it, to write in Russian. "In your correspondence you employ a great number of Polish and other foreign words and expressions, because of which it is impossible to understand the subject matter; in future, therefore, write . . .

to us entirely in Russian, not employing foreign words and terms." [7] This affectation of foreignisms led to rather ludicrous results at times, as when a subordinate officer reported to his commander that he could nowhere find a locality named "Avantazhny." There was also an element of social snobbery involved in the use of foreign words and the speaking of a foreign language. A guide for the good conduct of young gentlemen published in 1717 admonished its readers to converse in a foreign language, especially in the presence of servants, and so that they might be distinguished from ignorant dolts. [8]

The question might well be asked whether the development of Russian literature, social thought, and national consciousness in the latter half of the century would have been as speedy if general comprehensibility had not been first demanded in the time of Peter. As the literary language became more nearly like the language in which Russians spoke to one another, it became easier for a larger proportion of the population to take pride and interest in the monarch, the state, the nation, and its culture. As long as the literary language had remained stilted and remote from everyday speech, a wide communication of everyday concerns and feelings was as difficult as the expression of an interest in political and cultural matters of national scope. The new literary language made possible not only a worldly lyric poetry, but also the emergence of state and nation as objects of patriotic loyalty and fervor. The whole subsequent history of the language proves the close connection between the creation of a language generally accessible and usable, and the belief that it was a necessary prerequisite for the cultural and perhaps even political and economic autonomy of the nation.

Vasili Tatishchev (1686–1750) possessed this awareness to a high degree. A typical product of the Petrine period, historian and geographer, mining engineer and administrator, he combined each of his pursuits with high patriotic motive. The wish to see his country freed of foreign tutelage, involved Tatishchev, as we have seen, in the discussions and activities of the Volynski circle, and brought him into conflict with Russia's German rulers. That an interest in the national language, its history, uniqueness, and perfection should so greatly occupy a man who was neither a writer nor a literary scholar, indicates the importance which the age attached to questions of language.

Tatishchev was at one with Peter in the belief that the furtherance of a people's language could not be left to chance, that the government had actively to participate in it. The expansion of nations as well as of their languages, was the result, he believed, of the wise and careful policies of their governors, and he pointed to Greece, Rome, and France as worthy examples of such enterprise. France, above all, was to be followed in the care and support which her government had given to the institutions devoted to the spread and perfection of her language.[9] His enthusiasm for governmental sponsorship in the promotion of Russian was so great that he referred to the short-lived gatherings of a few members of the Academy of Sciences in St. Petersburg devoted to the "perfection of the Russian language, its purity and beauty," as a Russian Academy (*Rossiiskaya Akademiya*).[10] In that same year (1735) he submitted to the Empress Anna a project for the translation of mining terms into Russian. Practical considerations—the training of Russians would be facilitated—and the "honor and glory of the fatherland" demanded the change. The Russia of Biron's ascendancy, of the man who did not want to know Russian and insisted that all correspondence with him be conducted in German, was hardly the place in which to strike a blow for the native language. The project, although the Empress had approved it, foundered on Biron's opposition. In spite of this, and in spite of the fact that Biron came to look upon Tatishchev as a confirmed German-hater, the latter eventually introduced Russian terms into all the mines and plants directly under his authority.[11] It was a minor victory and hardly of significance in view of the continued predominance of German at court, in the army, and at educational institutions. Of 245 young Russians in the Corps of Cadets in 1733, to cite but one example, only eighteen studied their native language, with fifteen, fifty-one and 237 pursuing the study of Latin, French, and German respectively.[12]

Tatishchev, in advocating the use of Russian mining terms, did not extend this policy of Russification to a rejection of all language borrowing. To borrow was inevitable, but he warned against the custom of over-loading one's native speech with foreignisms. It was a custom characteristic of "conceited clerks and scribes who do not know any language . . . and consider their extreme stupidity as great cleverness, boasting when they should be ashamed." [13] In spite of the necessity of occasional borrowing, Russians had a language of their own which was rich and flexible enough to answer to any needs. It was richer than many others, as useful in philosophy and the sciences as French and German and, as demonstrated by the works of Lomonosov, Tredyakovski, and Sumarokov, capable of greater succinctness than either. The past of the Russian language appeared to Tatishchev to be at least as glorious as its future, and he took issue with those foreign writers who had asserted that a written language was a comparatively late development in the areas settled by the Slavs. They had had an alphabet even before the time of Christ, while the "Slavyanorussi" had used a written language even before the time of Vladimir. Many ancient writers, as well as the existence of a collection of laws, attest to the antiquity of Russian letters, a subject which Tatishchev deemed of such importance that he devoted to it an entire section of his history. He even seemed to consider the Slav language, the ancestor of the Russian of his time, as something of a *lingua franca* of antiquity, which was used as widely in Greece (i.e., Byzantium) as French in the Germany of his time, "for not only ministers and courtiers, but emperors too, did not disdain to speak it. . . ." [14]

For all his patriotic fervor, Tatishchev's linguistic interests necessarily had a somewhat casual character. It was not until the appearance of men who joined to their patriotism a scientific or creative interest in language that systematic efforts were made to unify and perfect its various elements into a normative whole. In these efforts, the problem of style continued to be paramount. Which was the better foundation for the new literary language? The language of the Church books, or the new, Europeanized style being formed out of the conversational language, secular narrative, and lyric poetry?

V. K. Tredyakovski (1703–1769), a translator and poet, later secretary and Professor of Rhetoric at the Academy of Sciences, decided in favor of bringing the literary language closer to the "simple Russian word, such as we speak amongst ourselves," and in the preface to his translation of Paul Talle-ment's *Voyage à l'île de l'amour* stated why he preferred simple speech to Slavonic dialect. The latter, he said, is the language of the Church, whereas the book he had translated was a worldly book. The second reason was that Slavonic had in the present century become "so very dark" that it was no longer understood by many who read it. And the third reason, he told his readers, "which you may consider of least impor-tance, is that the Slavonic language now has a savage sound to my ears. . . ." The goal was not alone the translation of a single work, but the creation of a secular literary language on the basis of "our native tongue." In orthography too Tredyakovski demanded a break with the Church-Slavonic tradition in favor of a reproduction of living speech. One must write, he de-clared, not according to the root or derivation of the word, but according to the sound. [15]

The task outlined by Tredyakovski would have exceeded the powers of any single individual, and in March 1735, the first institutional attack on the problem was made. In that year, the "Russian Conference" (*Rossiiskoe Sobranie*) was formed at the Academy of Sciences and Tredyakovski appointed its secretary. The ambitious program which he formulated for the new institution included the cultivation not only of language but of history, the creation of a grammar, and a complete dictionary. His "Discourse on the Purity of the Russian Tongue" which he delivered at the opening session of the Conference, reviewed all the difficulties which would have to be faced and overcome to make the Russian language more perfect. But he held that this was no impossible task.[16] The effort, though great, would find rich rewards in honors and fame. Russia, Tredyakovski implied, must not lag behind the rest of Europe, and he pointed to the French and Florentine Academies, as well as to the Learned Society of Leipzig, as models which Russia might well follow. Unfortunately, the Conference existed for only three years and none of the ambitious tasks which it had set for itself—grammar, lexicon, translations of old and new authors, rhetoric, and versification —was completed. Nonetheless, the direction for the future had been indicated, the tasks had been defined, the first organized attempt at their solution had been made. During its brief life, the Conference was the meeting ground for translators and authors, an important forum, the only one Russia possessed, for the exchange of views on language and literature. To it, Tredyakovski brought his theory of tonic verse; here, Lomonosov and Sumarokov, undoubtedly stimulated by their disagreements with Tredyakovski to work of their own, submitted their first poems.[17] It was, in its way, a forerunner of the Russian Academy founded in 1783.

Tredyakovski himself, in the year the Conference first met, furnished the work on Russian versification which he had set as one of its goals, the "New and Short Method of Russian Verse." [18] Its principle was that the new verse conform to the natural tone of the spoken language, if the ear accustomed to Russian speech was not to be offended. But more importantly perhaps, Tredyakovski's verse reform was to show that Russian poetry could compare with the poetic achievements of antiquity and modern France. In this sense, the reform was a national act, the more so since its author had introduced it under the influence of Russian folk poetry, which had impressed him with the appropriateness and the value of stress in Russian verse.[19] In all literature Tredyakovski called on Russians to display the "richness, strength, beauty, and pleasantness" with which the native tongue was so abundantly endowed. No matter how important it might be to learn a foreign language, even for the better mastery of one's own, one ought to be solicitous above all for the perfection of Russian. The wide sway which Latin held as the language of science, must also give way, Tredyakovski maintained, to the rise of national language. It was wrong to place any language permanently above one's own, and Russian, he did not doubt, would follow the example of the other European languages in proving itself adequate for science and learning as well as in verse, prose, or oratory. The replacement of Latin by Russian would assure an accuracy of usage which even the best Latinist could not approach and a universality which would further advance scholarship. He himself set an example in a philosophical article, employing newly created Russian words for rendering such terms as "substance," "existence," and "preestablished harmony." [20]

Tredyakovski reached a high point of linguistic nationalism in his dissertation "On the Primacy of the Slovenian Language over the Teutonic." [21] It was a curious mixture of etymological and historical speculation, whose purpose was to prove that Russian (and its linguistic ancestors) was the oldest European language. To make and to prove such a discovery would clearly be of more than purely academic significance, and Tredyakovski, disclaiming in advance an excess of love for the Slav-Russian language, showed himself aware of the interpretations that could be put upon his researches. If primacy could be proved for the language and the culture of the Slavs, national pride would be bolstered in the face of assertions by Western scholars that the ancestors of the Russians were a quite recent phenomenon in history and had become enlightened only as a result of contact with the more advanced Germanic peoples. Tredyakovski, in any case, claimed scholarly objectivity for his findings.

The "objective reasons" which led him to his rather startling conclusions may be summarized as follows: In antiquity, the proto-Slavic language was known by two designations, Slovenian and Slavenian. The first, derived from *slovo* (the Slavic for "word"), seemed to Tredyakovski the older, while the second derived from *slava* (glory) was of more recent origin. Tredyakovski accepted the older of the two designations as applying to the language spoken by the Scythians, the ancestors of the Slavs, as well as by the Celts. These latter he took to be the ancestors of the Germans, Danes, Swedes, Norwegians, and English. Since Slovenian was the oldest European language, it followed that the Teutonic languages had branched off from it and did not constitute an earlier, independent development. It was a matter of relative indifference to Tredyakovski whether Scythians or Celts had first appeared in Europe after the destruction of the Tower of Babel, for they had both shared the same language, namely; Scythian, "which must have been Slovenian, from the word *slovo*." In later centuries Slovenian put forth as many branches "as there are now languages in the countries of the West, the North, and the East." The primacy of the Slovenian language, according to Tredyakovski, was further supported by Chaldean sources. These, in referring to the darkness which reigned at the creation of the world as *omoroko,* revealed the extent of Slavic influence. Since *morok* or *mrak* mean dark in Slovenian, *omoroko* must be a Slovenian word. He even enlisted Persian, which called the first man not Adam but Mizh (clearly only a variant of the Russian *muzh,* man), in support of his thesis. The dissertation closed on the hopeful note that both the language (*slovo*) and the glory (*slava*) of the Slavs would grow for all eternity.[22]

Philologists place little credence in Tredyakovski's method or his conclusions.[23] But neither his rather naive etymologies nor his defective logic detract from the importance of his work as an indication of the growing national consciousness. The dissertation was written at a time (1757) when, in reaction against the headlong Europeanization of the forms of the language, a countertrend set in which aimed at restoring the rights of Church-Slavonic and resisted, more strongly than before, the neglect of Russian for French. Tredyakovski himself gave the impetus for a new appraisal of the stylistic properties of Church-Slavonic, and for certain festive and official purposes preferred its solemnity and richness to the "meanness" of everyday Russian. In line with his return to antiquity, Tredyakovski in 1752 revised his opening address to the Russian Conference of 1735, and eliminated from it elements of contemporary speech, replacing them with more archaic, Slavonic words and formulations. He reasserted the distinction between the different styles and demanded the return of the literary language to Slavonic roots. "Why should we willingly suffer the barrenness and narrowness of French, having the varied richness and expanse of Slavyanorussian," Tredyakovski asked in the introduction to his translation of Fénelon's *Télémacque* and added that, having become used to French and German, Russians were now wont to dismiss every Slavonic expression to which they were not accustomed, as foreign. The advantages which Russian enjoyed over French and

German, which had only "civic" uses, was precisely the existence of a language which was not of the market place and the government bureau. Why then take as models languages poorer than our own which can draw on all the riches of the past? Thus, to Tredyakovski, the uniformity of French and German, the very fact of their being "national" languages, generally employed and understood, seemed in his mood of linguistic historicism signs of a poverty of which Russian had to beware. From the early demand for a language "such as we speak among ourselves," Tredyakovski turned to a Slavophilism in matters of language, recommending the reading of Church books as the primary source for the enrichment and beautification of literary Russian.[24]

The problem of the relationship between Church-Slavonic and colloquial speech continued to preoccupy writers and scholars. Mikhail Lomonosov (1711-1765), saw in the retention of a body of Slavonic words and expressions the best protection against foreign elements which were in conflict with the character of the language, and the best assurance for its development in accordance with its native properties.[25] Unlike Tredyakovski, Lomonosov did not envision an archaization of the language, but the retention only of those living Church-Slavonic elements which were commonly understood and known. The proportion in which these were to appear as against contemporary speech was to be governed by the literary medium in which they were employed—high, intermediate, and low style.

To regulate linguistic and stylistic usage, Lomonosov divided the Russian vocabulary into three groups: the first included those Church-Slavonic words which were little used but understood by all literate people; the second, words employed in Russian as well as in Church-Slavonic; and the third, those purely Russian words which were not found in the Church-Slavonic literature. The high style, containing words

which were common both to Old-Slavic and Russian, was
to be preferred in the composition of odes, poems, and epics.
The intermediate style, most appropriate for dramatic literature, satires and elegies, would employ mainly Russian (but
not colloquial) expressions, while the low style, particularly
apt for comic genres, might contain colloquial Russian speech,
and on occasion even words used by the common folk
(*prostorechie*).[26]

To Lomonosov, the question of the relationship between
the major elements of Russian speech was not exclusively one
of defining aesthetic norms, but also of finding in a national
literary tradition, rather than in foreign example, the foundation for an organic development of the native language.
Church-Slavonic, therefore, was the fund which Russians must
draw on for the creation of new words and the basis for the
grammatical rules which their language still lacked. In a synthesis between Russian and the living elements of Church-
Slavonic, which he had outlined in his teaching of the three
styles, Lomonosov saw the best guarantee for the future development of the language, its integrity, and unity. The Slavonic language, Lomonosov felt, had a living tradition preserved
by the books of the Church which were in common use. There
existed, then, a common linguistic fund and standard for all
Russians, which made it unnecessary to turn elsewhere for
guidance.

Through this heritage which Russians had enjoyed for more
than 700 years they had become the direct heirs of antiquity
and of Christianity, without the intermediary role of a language, like Latin, which would have put them at one remove
from the source. The unbroken employment of Church-
Slavonic bespoke its vitality and distinguished it from the
languages of the West, where the formation of national idioms
had meant a break with the whole tradition of Latin and
medieval culture, a break in the cultural matrix in which a

language normally grew. How much richer was Russian than
German, for example, which could boast a literature of its
own only since that time when German had replaced Latin
in the books and services of the Church. How much more
fortunate Russians were always to have prayed in their native
tongue. Not only historical continuity and organic development, but uniformity had been made possible by the Slavonic
tradition. The fact that Russians, in spite of their dispersion
over a vast territory, spoke a language which was generally
understood, was due to the role played by Church-Slavonic
in the preservation of linguistic unity. In this respect too,
Russians were more fortunate than other people. "In Germany,
for example, the Bavarian peasant understands a peasant from
Mecklenburg, Brandenburg, or Swabia poorly, although they
are all of the same nation." [27]

All of this—the continuity of Church-Slavonic, its vitality,
its proximity to living speech—was to Lomonosov sufficient
ground for building the system of the national literary language
on foundations which had shown themselves so responsive in
the past and receptive to popular influences. But to keep
Church-Slavonic from turning, like Latin, into a language of
cult or theology, the intrusion or revival of pure archaisms in
vocabulary or morphology had to be prevented. As early as
1736, Lomonosov had objected to Tredyakovski's obsolete
Slavisms. The language of the Church which he wanted to
preserve was not the language of theology, of dogmatic· or
learned polemic, but the language of books in wide popular
use—Bible, psalter, the prologues and lives of the saints.

With the cultural and linguistic heritage of Church-Slavonic
to build on, Lomonosov did not doubt that the future of the
Russian language would be as great as its past, that it would
prove itself the equal, in every way, of other European languages. Lomonosov's many panegyrics to the native language,
to its abundance, beauty, and force bespeaking the power of

Russia, reached their high point with the dedication to the Russian grammar, the first scientific description and systematic study of the living Russian language:

> Charles V, the Roman Emperor, was wont to say that one ought to speak Spanish to one's God, French to one's friends, German to one's enemies, and Italian with the feminine sex. Had he been versed in the Russian tongue, he would certainly have added that it is appropriate for converse with all of these. For he would have found in it the majesty of Spanish, the vivacity of French, the firmness of German, the delicacy of Italian, and the richness and concise imagery of Greek and Latin. . . . The powerful eloquence of Cicero, the majestic stateliness of Virgil, the pleasant rhetoric of Ovid lose nothing of their qualities in Russian. The most subtle philosophical speculations and concepts, the various phenomena and essences which express the visible structure of the world of nature and the world of human intercourse, all these find in Russian appropriate and expressive terms. And if something should be found incapable of expression, the fault is not that of the language, but of our own incapacity.[28]

The fierce patriotism of Lomonosov quite naturally extended to his linguistic concerns. It is not surprising that after demonstrating the superiority of the Slavonic language in the past, he should find in Russian a unique combination of all the best qualities of the foremost modern and ancient languages. Russians were not alone in seeking in their language confirmation and support for claims of national greatness, and the apotheosis of the Russian language which introduced Lomonosov's Grammar can be found almost word for word and theme for theme in Richard Carew's *Epistle on the Excellencies of the English Tongue*. The natural beauty, power, and magnificence of Russian, Lomonosov predicted, would assure that in the future it would surpass all the other languages. It was inevitable that so great a nation with so great a language should bring forth its own Virgils and Horaces. Lomonosov was proud to have inspired others to the glorification of their fatherland in the native tongue and proud to have demonstrated its adaptability by being the first to use it in a lecture on physics.[29]

Lomonosov's attempts to base the future of his language on its past history and continuous evolution were doomed to failure in the face of a constantly growing intimacy on the part of literate Russians with the languages and literatures of the West. However vigorous the Slavic tradition may have been and however fruitful for the enrichment of Russian, the literate public, brought up on the more mundane works of European writers, found the high-sounding cadences of Slavonic pompous and unnecessarily complex; whereas the Russian components of the low style were still considered too vulgar, too base to be admitted into good, literary society. This placed on the middle style the burden of furnishing models for a simplified national language closer to the semantic system of French than the language of the Church. The problem was to bring the naturalness, simplicity, and facility of modern French to the modernization of Russian and yet to retain its character, to renovate it without making it merely a feeble copy of the French.

To these two tasks the poet and dramatist A. P. Sumarokov (1718–1777) devoted a considerable portion of his vast energies and talent. He declared for a literary language based on general usage (rather than Church-Slavonic) and preserving its uniquely Russian features without turning back to antiquity. This position was to bring him into conflict with Tredyakovski, whom he mercilessly satirized in his comedy "Tresotinius," and with Lomonosov, whose style he considered bombastic, graceless, and dated. Time and again he attacked Lomonosov, directly or indirectly, in critical articles or parodies, demanding naturalness of poetic diction as well as of everyday language. Neither the archaic Slavisms of Tredyakovski nor the bookish phrases of Lomonosov provided a standard which he would or could follow. "To feel truly, to think clearly, to sing simply and harmoniously," while avoiding excess "as nature's worst enemy," these are the rules which Russian writers should obey.[30]

If general usage was to govern the style, vocabulary, and morphology of the literary language, Sumarokov made clear that it was the general usage of polite, educated society that he had in mind, not the popular speech of the masses. To admit into the literary language the expressions and dialects of the common people would be to lower its standards. Sumarokov wanted to establish the speech of literate, educated society as a fixed, permanent, national standard to which all could look as guide and model.

Why do we not write as we speak? Such liberty would be immoderate, and finally no trace would remain of our ancient language. We change the old speech in conversation, having changed it in letters, then overload our language with foreign words; and finally we may forget Russian altogether, which would be a great pity, for no people has yet killed its native tongue, although ours is threatened with final extinction. Further, it is better to try and improve one's own, than to prefer to it what is foreign. . . .[31]

Sumarokov's fears that literary Russian might be buried under a flood of vulgarisms and foreign intrusions, more especially the latter, nearly amounted to an obsession. No writer or scholar during the entire century returned more frequently or more heatedly to the defense of the language against foreign influences, of whatever kind. And he saw threats to the purity of Russian from many sources. In an article addressed "To Thoughtless Rhymesters" (1759), he listed a number of quarters from which corruption and infection threatened. "The Germans filled it with German, the petimetry with French words, our ancestors with Tatar, the pedants with Latin, the translators of sacred texts with Greek." [32] At the time, French posed the main threat and it was the barbaric

French-Russian jargon of the petimetry that Sumarokov attacked most sharply. His defense of Russian was not a matter of blind conservatism. He himself introduced new words, admitted foreign terms for the designation of objects unknown to Russian, created literal equivalents of French expressions, and made the meaning of certain Russian words conform to the French meaning. The enemy in matters of language as well as in other spheres of life was Gallomania, undiscriminating preference for the French word or phrase where a perfectly adequate Russian one would do as well. The satire "On the French Language," while it paid generous tribute to the writers of France and the beauty of their language, warned Russians against believing that all French writers were Molières or Racines, against accepting the fashion of foreign lands as law.[33]

At one point, Sumarokov was carried so far by his patriotism in matters of language that he suggested the exclusion of terms which had by this time become accepted by precisely that social group whose speech habits he wanted to be considered the norm. *Frukty, serviz, mantilya, sup, tom, delikatno, antishambera* and others could, and should, he believed, be replaced by Russian equivalents. "The acceptance of foreign words is not an enrichment but a corruption of the language," [34] and he feared that if this process continued a few more years, it would be forever impossible to restore its original character. While Greek words had been taken over into Russian as a matter of necessity and logic and did not detract from its beauty, Sumarokov saw no need, except in some few cases, for the adoption of French and German words. Russian was as ancient and venerable a language as any other, closer, in fact, to its sources. He had concluded that the root-words of a language are all of one syllable and he found the root-words of Russian to be shorter than those of either Latin or German. For example, the word for "eye" in Russian is *oko*; in Latin—*oculus*; and in

German—*Auge*. Russian, therefore, was of one stem with Latin and German, but older than either. This fact made the Slavs one of the earliest European peoples and since Sumarokov thought the Celts were the original inhabitants of the Continent, Celts and Slavs became in his eyes part of the same ethnic group, as they had already been for Tredyakovski. Celto-Russian, or Slavyanorussian is thus the oldest European language. Nor was Sumarokov less inventive with regard to etymologies than Tredyakovski had been, and when he demonstrated that the word *tsar* bore no relation to the Latin Caesar, but came instead from the Slavic *otsar*, i.e., father of his subjects (*otets svoikh poddannykh*),[35] he was upholding not only the primacy of the Slavic language, but possibly also an idealized version of Slavic kingship.

The reigns of Elizabeth and Catherine marked a new high in the Westernization of the upper strata of Russian society which brought in its train an ever wider use of French to the neglect and, at times, total ignorance of Russian. The Princess Dashkova, who later became President of the Russian Academy and was one of the most vocal advocates of Russian culture, related in her memoirs what must have been a fairly frequent experience among the upper-class youth of her time. "According to the opinions of the time, we had the best of educations. We were instructed in four different languages, and spoke French fluently; a councillor of state taught us Italian, and M. Bechtieff gave us lessons in Russ [sic] whenever we would condescend to receive them." The result, "I spoke Russian very imperfectly," [36] was hardly surprising. It was only after diligent application, made necessary by her mother-in-law's ignorance of French, that the Princess finally mastered her native tongue. As late as 1790, Karamzin, then traveling in Europe, was deeply impressed by the fact that educated Englishmen, though all knew French, preferred their own language, quite unlike his countrymen who would rather speak French badly than talk to each other in Russian. "Is that not disgraceful for us? Why should we be ashamed of our mother tongue and turn ourselves into monkeys and parrots?" [37] The "disgrace" continued to call forth satire, to intensify theoretical interest in the language (and in the institutions dedicated to its perfection), and extensive demonstrations of the antiquity and adequacy, equality or superiority of the Russian tongue. In terms of content, none of these defenses of Russian differed markedly from those already noted. But the second half of the century, particularly the reign of Catherine, brought a new energy to the task spurred in part by the interest of the Empress herself, by the importance attached to language as an index of culture, and the growing self-consciousness of the gentry as a class.

To satirize was not, of course, enough. If Russian was to be brought to perfection, if its use was to be sanctioned by polite society, it had to be shown that it could be as responsive and elegant a means of communication for all purposes as the other European languages were. Tatishchev had seen in the work of his contemporaries Tredyakovski, Lomonosov, and Sumarokov practical proof of the high quality of Russian letters, but in the absence of a literary production which was universally acclaimed as equal to that of France or Germany, there could be no certainty that the native genius would reveal itself through literature. Attempts were made to demonstrate that there were native Homers, Pindars, and Racines, but for the most part the burden of proof had still to be borne by repeated insistence on the historical greatness of the language and its intrinsic wealth, both of which foretold a great future.

One way of realizing this future was the very practical one of making Russian the language of instruction in the institutions of higher learning and breaking the hold which foreigners had in the transmission of knowledge. Nikolai Popovski,

Rector of the Gymnasium at the newly founded University of Moscow, contested the monopoly of Latin as the language of learning by conducting his lectures entirely in Russian. He saw no need to discuss or teach his subject in Latin alone, for philosophy itself, after first speaking Greek, had subsequently had to learn Latin. Why then have Russians not the right to expect similar successes as the Romans? The means were given in the university itself, in the zeal and ardor of its students, and in the qualities of the native language. "As far as the abundance of the native language is concerned, the Romans have no advantage over us. There is no thought which it would be impossible to expound in Russian." Popovski believed that if philosophy were made accessible to all who spoke Russian, it would soon be shown that it was not lack of talent which accounted for the absence of Russian contributions to higher learning. "If it be your will and effort," he told his audience, "you can soon show that nature has endowed you with minds no worse than those on which other nations pride themselves; assure the world that it is a late beginning in the sciences, rather than the lack of ability, which has kept Russia from joining the ranks of the enlightened nations." [38] Popovski was not alone in stating the case for instruction in Russian, but the utilitarian side of the problem was most strongly stressed by a member of the Russian Academy who proposed that all sciences be taught in Russian: "The national language is the first means for the spread of enlightenment. Where the sciences are taught in a foreign language the nation finds itself under the yoke of that language, and this subjection goes together with ignorance. No matter how great the number of learned men in the state, if they will not teach the sciences in the language of the people, knowledge will be confined to only a small number of citizens." [39]

The poet M. M. Kheraskov realized Popovski's program while he was rector of Moscow University and in 1767 made

Russian the language of instruction in all subjects. In addition he wrote a "Discourse on Russian Poetry" in French which was designed to acquaint foreigners with the history and present condition of Russian letters.[40] Kheraskov began by asserting that the origins of Russian poetry were in every way comparable with those of other literatures, and he ascribed the subsequent delay in the development of Russian letters to the interruptions caused by the Tatar invasions. He then turned from the history of Russian poetry to its language. For him, as for Tredyakovski and Lomonosov, it was a matter of considerable pride that while most of Europe still prayed in Latin, the Russians were singing God's praises, reading the Church fathers and Holy Writ in the Old-Slavic language. His purposes, he told his readers, was to show how well his language lent itself to the translation of profound and important works, and that centuries-old translations of great authors could still astonish readers by the precision, power, and beauty of their style. All the conditions were given for a great flowering of native letters when the Tatar invasions cut short the bright promise until the time of Peter. Then, with Lomonosov, the promise was fulfilled and the potentialities of the language realized in every poetic style.

The persistence with which Russian writers pointed to the early use of Church-Slavonic as the language of Christian ritual while the West was still praying in a foreign tongue is an almost touching instance of the wish to show how venerable the history of the language was. Theirs was not a rude, barbaric dialect of some northern tribe, but a language which could compare favorably with the languages of the enlightened peoples of Europe. Quite clearly, the Russians did not feel part of that charmed circle of nations in the vanguard of European civilization, and they felt constantly constrained to explain why this was so. Not, certainly, because of any lack of native talent or endowment but because of special historical circum-

stances which had interrupted and so delayed the full flowering
of the national genius.

Fonvizin was so shocked to find that even educated Frenchmen did not know that Russians spoke and wrote a language
of their own, that he tried to overcome their ignorance on this
score in a speech to the members of the French Academy
which introduced his listeners to the history, the language,
and literature of his country. He, too, wanted it known that
it was not some inadequacy of the national character that had
kept Russians from matching the achievements of other states.
The national genius was capable of all things, and the national
language in its wealth and beauty was adaptable to any purpose. If there was some shortcoming, the blame had to be
placed elsewhere. If Russia was lacking in great orators, for
example, the reason was the absence of institutions which could
have given scope to their talents. In the Metropolitans Gavriil,
Samuil, and Platon, Russia had her Tillotsons and Bourdaloues,
proving to a sufficiency what Russian oratory could be like
"if we had some place to deliberate about laws and taxes, a
place to judge the conduct of ministers who guide the ship
of state." [41] Fonvizin expressed in an autobiographical sketch
how much he felt the Church-Slavonic tradition to be a living
part of Russian speech, and he credited his early reading of
religious texts for whatever knowledge of Russian he might
possess. "For in reading the Church books I became acquainted
with the Slavonic language, without which it is impossible to
know Russian." [42]

While Fonvizin instructed Frenchmen in the history of his
language and culture, a number of journals in Russia itself
repeated the thesis which he and Kheraskov had placed before
Europe. In their contentiousness and in the exaggeration of
their claims, they made very explicit the slight Russians must
have felt at having been presumed to be without a language of
their own. Such mistakes, one of the articles pointed out, were

a slander not only on the literary culture of the nation, but on its conditions of life, its character, feelings, and thoughts. The fact that Russians had been conducting their church services in their own language, while the rest of Europe still worshiped in Latin, was once again brought forth. Another writer claimed that the long history of Russian not only gave it preeminence over the modern languages, but also demonstrated its equality with Latin and Greek. In one instance, the ancestor-language of modern Russian was described as one of the first and basic languages of humanity, older than Hebrew or at least its contemporary.[43]

Although he made no such extreme claims, the historian Boltin, in denying a Frenchman's assertion that Russian lacked the means for an expression of abstract concepts, also used the evidence furnished by Old-Slavic literature. If the Frenchman were right, it would have been impossible to render into Slavic the works of the most renowned fathers of the Eastern Church and the beauty and elegance, clarity and grandeur of Greek rhetoric. Admitting that the language of modern Russia was perhaps not as rich as Church-Slavonic, Boltin was a degree more sophisticated than most of his contemporaries who wanted mainly to prove that Russian was as good as any other language. Boltin was ready to grant, without fear of admitting the inferiority of his language or his nation, that Russian did lack certain terms, expressions, or concepts. If Russia, or her language, could not point for point compare with the West, this was not necessarily deplorable. It might, on the contrary, be cause for rejoicing and evidence of originality. This point, which Boltin developed fully in the works which he devoted to the history and institutions of his country, he also applied to its language. "I do not say," he replied to the Frenchman's taunts, "that the words of all languages are to be found in Russian with equal meaning and strength. Each language has something which is special and unique unto itself, and in this sense one may say that even in the most inadequate are found such words as cannot be translated into the richest language by one word." [44] Boltin did retain a belief in a hierarchy of languages—some were apparently inadequate, though he does not say why or for what—yet he came closer than any of his contemporaries to demanding respect for Russian not because it was like other languages, but because it was different, possessing wealth and beauty of its own.

The reign of Catherine saw the resumption of organized approaches to the study and normalization of literary Russian. The Empress shared with the other monarchs of enlightened despotism a firm belief in the efficacy of governmental measures in all fields of human endeavor. Language, to Catherine, was a human artifact; its growth and development could not be left to take place naturally but had to be stimulated and guided by the conscious intervention of the ruler. In her "Notes Concerning Russian History," Catherine expressed the view that the efforts of the Princess Olga had brought the Slavic language into common usage, and she proclaimed with axiomatic certainty her belief "that nations and their languages grow and spread through the wisdom and care of rulers. As the monarch is prudent, and labors diligently for the honor of his nation and his language, so also will the language of that nation flourish." [45] The languages of many nations have disappeared as a result of the monarch's negligence. Catherine was certain, and tried to make certain, that this would not happen to Russian. Her certainty went so far that she was moved to tell the Princess Dashkova that "our Russian language, uniting as it does both the strength, the richness, and the energy of the German with the sweetness of the Italian, would one day become the standard language of the world." [46] She did not even feel constrained to abandon this chauvinistic pose before foreigners and managed to combine it with a nicely turned compliment for the sage of Ferney, when she told him that it took a Voltaire to make something of a language (French) so poor in comparison with Russian.

Catherine's nationalism in matters of language often went to extreme lengths, as when she chided the Princess Dashkova for speaking French to an officer before his soldiers, or when, according to an anecdote related by Karamzin, she punished members of her entourage for use of a foreign word by making them recite one hundred lines of Tredyakovski's *Telemakhida*.[47] For what Catherine's Russian lacked in accuracy or purity she tried to compensate by a liberal use of simple, proto-Slavic words (*korennye slova*), popular expressions, and proverbs. Catherine carried her devotion to simplicity and directness of language and her opposition to barbarisms and foreign borrowing into her prescription for Russian authors. Echoing Sumarokov's opposition to bombast and bookish Slavisms, she asked that short expressions be preferred to long ones, that he who write Russian think in Russian, that foreign words be avoided and no new borrowing take place, "for our language is sufficiently rich without them." [48] Catherine's abhorrence of pompousness and bookishness was natural in one to whom the simplicity of French denoted elegance and who was not from birth steeped in the culture of the Church texts. Happily, her tastes coincided with the more general trend, represented above all by Sumarokov, which wanted to raise the speech usage of the upper classes (formed by French tastes), to the level of a national literary standard.

In keeping with the broad interpretation of the duties of her office, the Empress did not limit her efforts for the purification and standardization of Russian to casual remarks and articles. It was with her support that the tasks outlined by Tredyakovski for the "Russian Conference" were again taken in hand. The first institution to devote itself to problems of language after the closing of the "Conference" in 1743 was the Commission for Translations founded in 1768. Catherine donated 5,000 rubles to facilitate its work. Its purpose was to bring some uniformity into the vocabulary and style of translators who had been working in isolation from one another. The Commission (its Russian title was *Perevodcheski Departament*) was headed by the Empress' secretary Kozitski, Counts G. V. Orlov and A. P. Shuvalov and functioned for a period of fifteen years when, with the founding of the Russian Academy, its operations were transferred to the new body.[49]

Another institution concerned with linguistic tasks was the Free Russian Assembly (*Volnoe Rosiiskoe Sobranie*). Established in 1771 at Moscow University, it remained active until the founding of the Academy in 1783. Its aim, like that of its predecessors, was the "improvement and enrichment of the Russian language . . . , the compilation of a correct Russian dictionary alphabetically arranged," and the publication of historical documents. The most tangible result of the Assembly's labors was the publication, in 1773, of Petr Alekseev's "Ecclesiastical Dictionary" (*Tserkovni Slovar*). Not a dictionary in the strict sense of the word, but a guide to the reading of Church books, it contained, in addition, explanations of archaic Slavisms and excursions into history, old Russian literature, ceremonial and customs. That Alekseev's dictionary could later serve as one of the more important sources of the Dictionary of the Academy, shows how useful a work of even so limited a character was at the time.[50] How broad a view contemporaries took of its usefulness is indicated by the publisher's preface.

And thus, besides the great personal benefits which the true Christian will receive from the zealous reading and imitation of the books of the Church, there will accrue an additional benefit to society, which is that our beloved fatherland will in a short time have worthy orators, poets, and historians in its native tongue; men, who leaving behind foreign expressions which we do not understand, will seek the inherent beauty of the Russian word . . . and with it praise the glorious deeds of our century.[51]

All the brave words about the future could not, however,

conceal from the impartial observer that the condition of Russian letters suffered immeasurably from the absence of firm and generally accepted linguistic norms. The proposed reforms of Lomonosov, the example of Sumarokov, and the work of Tredyakovski had served only to confuse further an already complex situation. No matter how loudly patriots might inveigh against the corruption of the language, the fact that the reading public continued to remain unusually receptive to foreign influences in its total culture was clearly reflected in its speech habits and in its literary preferences. To hold up as a model to this public and to those who had literary ambitions, the language of the Church books (however much modified), or the style of the chancellery, or to insist that it cleanse its speech of foreign elements, was entirely unrealistic in the second half of the eighteenth century. The difficulties which the clash between varying literary norms presented to the writer were widely recognized, and the misunderstandings to which the coexistence of differing sociolinguistic spheres could give rise, was amusingly portrayed by Fonvizin in "The Brigadier." The speech of the Councillor is a mixture of Church-Slavonic and government jargon; Ivanushka and the Councillor's wife have adopted the fashionable prattle of French and Russian which denoted the young fop; the Brigadier bellows in good army style, with an occasional admixture of low vulgarisms, while his wife typifies the uncultured speech of the provincial gentry, and sounds not too different from the common people she holds in such strong contempt. Only Sofia and Dobrolyubov speak in a way which Fonvizin considered literate and acceptable. The Brigadier's wife does not understand the Councillor, the Brigadier is at odds with his son, and like them the gentry had no common literary standard. The Russian language, wrote one contemporary in the organ of the Free Russian Assembly in 1776, though rich, needs to be developed further.

It stands in need of many improvements . . . lacks many words, but above all it needs to be firmly fixed. We still flounder about in different grammatical rules, and there are a great many words in our language which have no clearly defined meaning. We have no metaphysical language, without which it is impossible to write about many matters. . . . To bring order into our language, it is necessary to affirm grammatical rules . . . and to exclude from it all that does not belong. In order to expand the language it is necessary to invent many words, or to borrow them from foreign languages. In order to regulate it, we need dictionaries, determining the sense of words, and other works where their value will be indicated with accuracy.[52]

The demand for uniformity and for the means of its enforcement was not new. Rather more unusual, however, was the admission that for the expression of new concepts Russian might not only have to invent new words but also to borrow them from other languages. One member of the Free Russian Assembly thought harmful the practice of eliminating all foreign words from Russian, especially those which had already become naturalized, and of replacing them with Russian words which no one understood. Sooner or later, in the process of the formation of a common literary language, it had to be recognized that in their contacts with Western thought and literature, the educated classes of Russian society, and with them their language, had become Europeanized to an extent which could no longer be undone. This was the direction which future reforms were to take, and the one which Karamzin in his creation and advocacy of the "new style" prescribed. It led Russian away from its Church-Slavonic heritage and set up as model and standard the speech practice of the salons of the capitals. Fluency, elegance, and the elimination of all that was merely local, dialectal, cumbersome, and archaic, were to become for Russian, as they already were for French, the most highly valued qualities.

When the Russian Academy (*Rossiiskaya Akademiya*) at

last became reality in 1783, the example of foreign institutions, the wish to free Russian of foreign encumbrances, and the need for lexical and grammatical systematization were uppermost in the minds of those most directly concerned with its foundation. The Princess Dashkova, Catherine's friend and fellow-conspirator at the time of her accession, was appointed President, and she was convinced that nothing was wanting but "rules and a good dictionary to render our language wholly independent of those foreign terms and phrases, so very inferior to our own in expression and energy. . . ."[53]

The tasks set for the Russian Academy were much like those that Tradyakovski had defined in 1735 and centered about the publication of a grammar and a dictionary. If, in spite of its native riches and limitless resources, the Russian language had not attained perfection, it was, as the President of the Academy said in her inaugural address, due only to the lack of determinate rules—rules for the inflection of words, as well as an authorized definition and limitation of their meaning. In this lack of determinate rules she saw the cause of those varieties of construction, those improprieties of imitation and foreign idiom which had hitherto disfigured the native tongue.[54] Whatever the flights of patriotic fancy to which the Princess or others connected with the new Academy might be led—whether they saw (as she did) Russian uniting the excellence of Greek and Latin, or talked of the brevity and pungency of its expression (as did the Academy's permanent secretary, Lepekhin)—they all returned eventually to the foremost and most basic need: "a grammar of our language exact and methodical, and a rich and copious dictionary" (Dashkova); or, as Lepekhin expressed it, "to formulate for it unchangeable rules."

The Academy immediately began work on a dictionary, and enlisted for this task the cooperation of almost every writer of note: Derzhavin, Boltin, Fonvizin, Knyazhnin and some forty-two others. Their joint efforts were crowned with success and the first volume of the Dictionary of the Russian Academy was published in St. Petersburg in 1789; the last, and sixth, appeared in 1794. Now Russia too had a dictionary of her language, and the concrete evidence of having reached a level of cultural development where she need no longer feel inferior to the nations of Europe. In the view of one writer, who congratulated the Russian reading public on the appearance of the fourth volume of the dictionary, the work was superior even to the dictionary of the French Academy. His opinion that language is a mirror of civilization left little doubt where he placed Russia's achievements.[55]

The Grammar which together with the Dictionary was to have been the Academy's foremost task did not appear until 1802. In the meantime, the number and popularity of various independently produced grammars showed that the search for order and system in the Russian language continued. As the blessing of literacy spread, as Russian was becoming increasingly respectable and young gentlemen felt encouraged by famous and successful example to give elegant expression to their feelings in their native tongue, the need for rules became more pressing. If patriotism demanded that one speak Russian in preference to French, good taste and good breeding demanded that one speak and write Russian well.

The first and most popular of the many grammars which appeared in the last third of the century was Nikolai Kurganov's "Universal Russian Grammar" which in the years 1769–1837 ran through a total of ten editions. Fearing that the "science of the Russian language" might not of itself assure a wide sale of his book, Kurganov astutely added to it a number of sections which had little to do with grammar. There were helpful hints on how to write a letter, collections of proverbs, riddles, songs, and poems. Whether these special features accounted for the success of the volume is difficult to say. The demand for grammatical knowledge was in any case great enough to cause another such work, not similarly equipped, to go through eight printings: "The Short Rules of Russian Grammar," compiled by A. A. Barsov in 1771 for the "use of the youth studying in the gymnasia of Moscow University." Another of Barsov's works, "Extensive Russian Grammar," which he prepared on orders of the Commission for the Lower Schools in 1784–85, remained unpublished. The School Commission did publish "A Short Russian Grammar" in 1787, and this, in turn, was followed by a number of works designed for general use, such as Peter Sokolov's "Basic Principles of Russian Grammar" (1788), and Vasili Svetov's "Brief Rules for the Study of Russian" (1790).[56]

The completion of the Academy's labors on the Dictionary was an event of major importance in the history of Russian letters, and it was so regarded by the men to whom language was an artistic medium. Among the writers it was Karamzin, with his concern for the flourishing of native literary talent, who greeted the Dictionary as a phenomenon of Russian intellectual life which would evoke the astonishment of foreigners. It bore testimony to the speed with which Russians had reached a high level of literary culture; it was a sign that Russian culture had come of age: "We do not mature in a matter of centuries, but in decades. Italy, France, England, and Germany were already famous for great writers before we even possessed a dictionary . . . and we developed a language system which can measure itself with the famous creations of the academies of Florence and Paris." [57]

In a somewhat less sanguine frame of mind, however, Karamzin was the first to note with critical impartiality that Russia had not yet given sufficient proof of her right to citizenship in the republic of letters. It was not alone the lack, now partially remedied, of a dictionary and a grammar which had

held Russian talent back from that outburst of creative energy
of which Karamzin knew it capable; it was much more the
absence, he felt, of a literary language which would meet the
demands and the tastes of educated society and which would
correspond to the spirit and the style of the European civilization which he, and the class from which he expected readers
and writers to come, took as their model. From his discussion
of the problem, entitled "Why is There so Little Literary
Talent in Russia?" (1803), there emerged quite clearly his
belief that in order to develop a living literary culture of their
own, and one which could compare favorably with that of the
West, Russians had first to abandon the incubus of the old
Russian tradition. Though he admired that tradition in the
ethics and the conduct of public and private life, he felt that
in matters of speech and literature it was a dead weight which
prevented further development in the direction of vitality and
innovation. He was as unwilling to make himself the proponent
of an archaic nationalism in matters of language, as he was
reluctant to undo the work of Peter in politics and social
life. True Russian patriots, in the one as in the other sphere,
would take the Western format which had been prescribed,
and make its externals so completely their own, that they
could then proceed to give it a truly national, truly Russian
content.

Peter the Great, with his powerful hand transforming the
fatherland, made us like other Europeans. To complain of that is
useless. The link between the mind of the old and the new Russia
is broken for all time. We do not want to imitate the foreigners,
but to write as they write, for we live as they live. . . .[58]

"To write as they write" required for Karamzin that the
Russian author stop patterning his language after that of the
old books, even those of Lomonosov, and listen to the living
speech around him. On that basis, and on that basis alone,
could a language which had life and vigor be constructed, a

language which was Russian not only in name, but in the fact of wide usage and comprehensibility. This was the program for the new style of which he was the chief advocate and architect, and which was to put Russian into the first rank of modern European languages. The fact that the new style bore the imprint of French in syntax, in grammar, and in vocabulary disturbed Karamzin not at all, for the available alternatives— a bookish and outmoded Russian or a second-hand French— were even less desirable. If the upper classes spoke French so widely, it was because Russian literature had not yet succeeded in enriching the colloquial idiom with the terms which it needed for the expression of tastes and sentiments which had been formed by a reading of Western books. Even the Dictionary was of little help here. "What is there left to do for the author," Karamzin asked, "but to think up, to compose new expressions, to guess at the best selection of words." [59]

The transformation and normalization of the literary language which Karamzin brought about with his new style was the culmination of more than a half century of dispute, confusion, and irritation to anyone wanting to write Russian. Its result was the exclusion of Church-Slavonic—which by Lomonosov's definition had served as the primary example of high style—from all but the most specialized literary genres, and the Europeanization of Russian on the basis of the usage of high society. Sumarokov had carried the victory over Lomonosov, and the common speech (i.e., the speech of the salon) became the national literary language. It was not a development which saw its completion in the eighteenth century, nor even full acceptance. But in this, as in so many other areas, the eighteenth century had prepared the necessary ground. The final victory of the colloquial speech of a Westernized upper class had been signalized in a variety of ways. Sumarokov had helped to win importance and acceptance for the "middle styles"; the curricula of the Corps of Cadets, and of Count

Betski's boarding school, began to give precedence to Russian, rather than "Slavonic," as the "language of the fatherland."

Karamzin's recasting of Russian in a European mold was not received without opposition. The new style, although it was the only one which could hope successfully to contest the predominance of French and gave every prospect of furthering the evolution of a national literature, had borrowed too many non-Russian literary and linguistic concepts to please entirely the religious, conservative, and parochial outlook of a man like Admiral Shishkov. The story of his opposition to the reforms of Karamzin does not strictly speaking constitute part of this survey, but since it appears to hark back to the work of Lomonosov and to derive inspiration from it, it may serve as an illustration of the historical continuity which links the two generations.

Shishkov's fears for the survival of a Russian which was closer to the Church-Slavonic tradition than the new style of Karamzin, was grounded in a justified apprehension about the survival of a way of life. The fact that the young children of the aristocracy and the gentry, from their earliest years, not only were taught French, but that their entire education should be entrusted to Frenchmen, made the eclipse of religiosity, morality, and modesty inevitable. For with the language they imbibed from their tutors, the young Russians learned also to accept standards of behavior which Shishkov thought un-Russian. "They never look into the Church books or the old Slavonic-Russian books," he complained, "but read French novels, comedies, tales, and similar works." [60] To Shishkov this spelled moral laxity as well as ignorance of the true mother tongue. He was not alone in his skepticism towards the new language which the *haut monde* of the capitals was quick to accept. His view that it was not sufficiently national, that it was, like the language of the petimetry of an earlier generation, *un petit jargon de coterie*, lasted well into the twenties and thirties of the new century.

What Shishkov demanded, and what he failed to find in the Europeanized style of Karamzin, was the expression of Russian thought patterns on the basis of long-accepted rules and concepts. Karamzin's language, since its structure was not Russian, could not, by definition, be Russian in content. Russian thoughts asked to be clothed in Russian form, and only the language which was Slavonic and derived from the literature of the Church, could answer that requirement. Thus the first Slavophiles, as the defenders of the Slavonic language tradition were then called, were born. Shishkov wanted his countrymen not only to stop speaking French, but what was more important, he wanted them to stop thinking in French. "If, in writing Russian, we don't stop thinking in French, then we shall always lie, and lie and lie in our own language." [61] It was Karamzin's fault that Russians had stopped speaking French without realizing that they had never fully escaped its style and thought patterns. Shishkov gave numerous examples of the way in which idiomatic expressions had been taken over quite mechanically and had lost their resonance. Some of his criticisms on this score, and of the continued wide-spread use of untranslated foreign words, were not without justice, as Karamzin was one of the first to see; and in the later editions of his "Letters of a Russian Traveler," he substituted Russian, or even Slavonic words, for the foreign ones he had first employed.

It was, however, too late for a reversal of the trend. As Shishkov correctly complained, the Slavonic language was looked upon with disdain. Even the priesthood could no longer be relied upon to cultivate it, except in the most perfunctory manner. The high, half-Slavonic style had definitely lost out to the forces of modernism, of secularism, of Europeanism.

Unlike Shishkov, Pushkin valued the work of Karamzin as a national act, a liberation and a return to the living sources of the Russian word. By Pushkin's time, the process of the formation of a national literary language had gone a long way toward its completion. In the area of language, at least, Russia's answer to the challenge of the West was a language European in form, national in content.

## CHAPTER IV

# The Discovery of the Folk

A variety of motivations had led Russians of the eighteenth century to view the contrast between town and country in national terms. The artificial city created by Peter, the seat and source of a bureaucratic absolutism and its foreign servitors, had come to be regarded as alien to the true interests and traditions of the Russian land and its natural representatives. Eventually, the rejection of "foreign" influences was extended to a wider sphere: the society of both capitals came to be looked upon as having abandoned the Russian way of life for an immoral and ill-considered imitation of foreign ways. Implicitly, and often explicitly, the reader was invited to turn away from urban corruption, insincerity, and fickleness to rediscover in the village, in its isolation and constancy, in the figures of its plain but noble masters and serfs, the true, historic image of the nation. As Russia's very backwardness seemed in the eyes of her defenders to assure a brilliant future, so the very remoteness and backwardness of the village insured there the survival of virtues and traits coming to be considered truly Russian: spontaneity of feeling and expression, an artless honesty, generosity, and humanity.

The picture of this contrast was painted almost exclusively in primary colors. It was devoid of subtler shadings, devoid certainly of realism as far as the situation in the serf village was concerned. But this did not keep it from being employed effectively and frequently to teach a lesson. The lesson began with the discovery of the village and its inhabitants; progressed to a tentative assertion of their equality and eventually to a belief in their superiority and uniqueness. No matter how remote pastorals and pastoral idylls, shepherds and shepherdesses in Arcadian dress might be from Russian reality, they served to direct the reader's attention to the countryside and to the village, and subsequently to the discovery that true Russian hearts were hidden beneath the pastoral disguise. This process was not, of course, completed until the glorification of the folk by Slavophiles and Populists, but most of its ingredients and materials had been discovered and made ready by the idealization of the village and its ways. This preparation also embraced the decline of classicism and the admission of new aspects of Russian reality to literature, an interest in folklore, and finally, the revelation, so striking in view of the time and the place, that peasants too are human beings, more human quite often than their thoughtless and cosmopolitan masters.

The view of the countryside and of the village as the repositories of true human worth, was not unique to Russian literature. In England, William Cowper (1731–1800) expressed the view that the urban classes knew "no fatigue but that of idleness and taste no scenes but such as art contrives"; man was closer to nature and to nature's God in the country than in the town:

> God made the country, and man made the town:
> What wonder then that health and virtue, gifts
> That can alone make sweet the bitter draught
> That life holds out to all, should most abound
> And least be threatened in the fields and groves.[1]

In France, Rousseau was the most famous and outspoken representative of a school of thought which held that the natural man was essentially superior to the product of civilized societies. Since natural was taken to mean primitive, and the fiction of the noble savage still enjoyed wide currency, Russia, too, could benefit by the prevailing definitions of primitivism. If proximity to nature were the test of virtue, then Russians could consider themselves closer to the ideal of the age than did citizens of the more highly civilized (i.e., urbanized) countries of Europe. Russians did not as yet employ this argument to proclaim their superiority over the West, but to Rousseau it was self-evident, and he revealed an almost Slavophile streak when he deplored in the *Social Contract* Peter's attempts to make his subjects into Germans or Englishmen. Had they remained Russian and rejected the false civilization of the West, they would have found themselves much closer to the virtuous primitive man.[2]

In Germany, Herder was the most characteristic and original representative of a trend which discovered the charm of primitivism, of closeness to nature and creativity. Among the *Kultur-voelker* he found the folk, the wide rural masses, to be closer to the sources of national feeling than the learned upper strata of society. The savage, he wrote in 1784, "who loves himself, his wife, and his child with quiet joy and glows with limited activity for his tribe as for his own life is, it seems to me, a more genuine being than that cultured shade who is enchanted by the shadow of the whole species. . . . The inundated heart of the idle cosmopolitan is a home for no one. . . ."[3]

To a very considerable degree the idealization of the village and its inhabitants was a reflection of European literary trends, of the prevailing mood of literary "naturalism," but at the same time there existed in Russia an indigenous ruralism which stemmed from purely local concerns and preceded the Western influence in point of time. It could thus create a more receptive soil for the foreign model and merge with it.

This Russian ruralism had as its native sources the wish of significant portions of the gentry to be spared the supervision and demands of autocracy and the desire to escape the luxury, the expense, the loss in status brought about by life at court. The patriarchal village in which he was still unquestioned master, where he was not at every step reminded of his relative impotence *vis à vis* a powerful state, where young fops could not outshine him—this was the place to which many a Russian nobleman began to look with longing and nostalgia. If, formerly, his enjoyment of Latin pastorals in Russian translation had been primarily an aesthetic one, if Tredyakovski's "Verses in Praise of Country Life" had seemed a pretty but not very realistic picture of the village as he knew it, towards the end of the fifties literature began to sound notes which evoked from him a more direct, more interested response. The idyll which was devoid of social implications continued to be popular, but Sumarokov's "Epistle on the Beauties of Nature," though it was still dominated by traditional motifs, introduced a sharpened statement of the urban-rural contrast. It not only celebrated the natural beauties, the simplicity and solitude of the rural retreat but also its freedom: "My sleep is not disturbed by somber thoughts; with joy I go to sleep, with joy awake again. No falseness see I here, and meanness is unknown. I dress as I please, do what I will, and owe accounts of my deeds to no one." [4]

Superficially, Sumarokov appeared to view the contrast between rural solitude and the venal city in classically stylized fashion; but his sponsorship of a privileged gentry with its roots in the village versus an upstart bureaucracy drawing its strength from the court lent added meaning to his lines. His themes were echoed frequently in the journal "Useful Enjoyment" (*Poleznoe Uveselenie*, 1762). Beginning with an ode attributed to M. M. Kheraskov (1733–1807), the rural virtues of simplicity, independence, and freedom from vanity were opposed to the city's empty riches and pride of station. In the poem "A Pleasant Night," Kheraskov sounded what must be among the earliest notes of romantic nature poetry in Russia, the cult of nature set in a nocturnal landscape charged with feeling. There alone nature could reveal herself to the feeling heart, enrapture and instruct—not amidst the bustle of town life, where beauty had been driven from the hearts of men. But it was not beauty alone that nature gave to those who lived in conformity with her law: "The innocence of the country-dweller goes hand in hand with freedom; in a word, all of life is beautiful here." Kheraskov's friend, A. A. Rzhevski, made equally clear his preference for the country, its peace and freedom, equality and simplicity. In the city, hatred, envy, hypocrisy, and oppression "by the common enemy" prevailed.[5]

This evocation of the "sweet liberty," the "golden days" of the village was to be in its effects something more than the acceptance of a literary convention. To locate all the evils of Russian life in the town, to view the village alone as undefiled was patently absurd, but this distortion had a didactic purpose. Close to Sumarokov in their conception of the gentry's role and its obligations to the state, Kheraskov and his group saw in the village the true sphere of activity of their class, at least as long as they were condemned to be without real influence in the state. Unwilling or not sufficiently strong in their opposition to the government to shun participation in its activities altogether—Kheraskov, for example, served for almost thirty years as rector of Moscow University—they helped their countrymen to discover a Russia which was not to be seen in the pomp and circumstance of Moscow and St. Petersburg. They had set out, as Kheraskov said, to sing of little things as well as heroes.[6] It was an important step in the history of Russian letters and of Russian thought.

The idealized, poeticized village remained throughout the

rest of the century the model held up to the town to demonstrate its corruption. The journals, even the satirical ones,
were filled with these rustic idylls, and it was rare that a
realistic note was heard in them. Even the sternest critics of
the serf village occasionally softened the outlines of reality
so that the village might serve them as a social and moral
yardstick by which to measure the town and find it wanting.
Both Novikov and I. A. Krylov ridiculed the prettified picture of rural bliss painted by the pastoral poetry of their time,
but they were themselves guilty of such distortion. Novikov
pointed to the village as the place in which the Russian virtues
could best be preserved—that very same village which he also
knew and described as the scene of misery and brutality.
Nothing can compare with the pleasantness of village life,
he wrote in "The Drone." There life is active and simple, close
to nature, foreign to flattery and lying; in the village there is
no artificial beauty, but singing birds, budding groves and
meadows filled with flowers. And there the moral precepts of
old Russian family life are still being practiced.[7]

The case against the town was put most succinctly by
Krylov, when a French storekeeper in St. Petersburg is made
to say: "One of our stores can ruin 100,000 peasants a year." [8]
A. I. Klushin, his associate on the "Spectator" (Zritel), advised the noble who squandered his estate in order to gratify
his whims not to forget the fate of his serfs: "If you would
only consider the condition of your peasants with greater
care! You would realize what your pretensions cost them;
not only their sweat . . . but tears and blood as well." [9]
Whether the village was depicted with realism or nostalgia,
the purpose was almost always didactic, and its inhabitants,
either as objects of pity or subjects of a rural romance, were
brought forth to demonstrate to the town the evil of its ways.
Two very popular literary genres, the comic opera and the
comedy, which more often amused than instructed their

audiences, were also caught up in the trend. In town, they repeated, people are without principles or sincerity; everywhere there is craft and deceit, but the true countryman knows where happiness lies. Knyazhnin's Lukyan, singing that he is a hundred times happier than the elegant townsman, tells his bride that "noise, luxury, and rivers of gold" were all he saw in the city, "but of happiness not a drop." The special attraction which the village held for its advocates lay in the absence of sharp distinctions of rank and wealth. This fiction helped to make more palatable the rosy and inaccurate versions of Russian rural life which were shown on the stage. If one wanted to believe in the choruses of happy peasants singing of their love for work, for master, and for country, belief was made easier by the presentation of a pseudological argument which held that there were, after all, real compensations to be found in the countryside, even for the serf. All are alike, there are no rich and no poor, and the country nobleman, living close to his peasant, sharing his joys and sorrows, treats him like a comrade, not as if he were the lowliest creature on earth.[10]

The closer we come to the end of the century, the clearer is the rural-urban distinction expressed in social terms. Town and court are corrupting influences not merely by the accident of environment or geography, but by the fact that the social groups that consider them *their* territory have become estranged from the real Russia. Having become less Russian in their pursuit of worldly goods and values (mostly of foreign origin), the urban classes of Russian society had also become less human. This is the view of Alexander Radishchev (1749–1802) in his *Journey from Petersburg to Moscow*. It is a realistic portrayal of rural conditions which goes hand in hand with a sentimental view of the natural goodness and beauty which these can produce.

Having reached a settlement, I left my carriage. Not far from the road ... stood a crowd of women and girls. The passion which has governed me all my life, though now extinct, by force of habit directed my steps to this crowd of village beauties. It consisted of more than thirty women. They were all in holiday attire, with neck and feet uncovered, arms akimbo ... shirts white, eyes full of joy, and cheeks glowing with health. Charms, which were somewhat coarsened by heat and cold, but delightful since they were without the cover of slyness; the beauty of youth in its fullest brilliance, on their lips a smile or hearty laugh, revealing rows of teeth whiter than the purest ivory. Teeth which would drive our ladies of fashion out of their minds. Come here, dear ladies of Moscow and Petersburg, look at their teeth, and learn from them how to keep them white. They do not have the services of a dentist here, they do not scrape their teeth with brushes and powders every day. Stand close to any one of them, mouth to mouth; her breath will not infect your lungs. But yours, yours may, perhaps, infect them with the germ of a disease ... a disease ... I fear to name it; though you will not blush, you will be angry.[11]

The infections to which the ladies of St. Petersburg and Moscow are exposed are only in part physical. They are equally the result of the corruption and debasement of all moral standards in the town. Fidelity is no longer in fashion; it is, in fact, considered backward, reminiscent of the times in which Russian women spent their lives in the semi-oriental seclusion of the *terem*. All that reminds them of their past and their provincial remoteness from the main stream of European fashion, the ladies of Russian society are eager to conceal. Unlike their country cousins, they hide their true appearance behind paints and powders. If whatever is left of health and virtue in the village is to be preserved from infection, it is best to isolate the villagers. This is Radishchev's advice to the peasant-maid Anyuta whom he meets in Edrovo. She is a girl whose purity and beauty are so overwhelming that they are scarcely credible. She tells the traveler that her lover wants to take service in St. Petersburg, there to earn the 100 rubles which are necessary to buy his freedom and

make their marriage possible. This project so alarms Radishchev that he cries out to her: "Don't let him go, dear Anyu-
tushka, don't let him go; he will go to his ruin," and he tells
her of the dissipated ways her lover will be taught, how he
will learn contempt for her and for his work in the fields.
"And all the more so, Anyuta, if he should happen to serve
in a noble household." Moved by Anyuta's innocence and
the recital of her woes, the traveler offers to pay the sum
which will enable her to marry; but Anyuta and her mother
are immediately suspicious of such unwonted generosity. The
girl's mother even turns down the gift, thinking that the barin
is offering it in expiation of some injustice done her daughter.
This only confirms for Radishchev the innate nobility of the
peasant character. "I could not help but wonder at so much
nobility of thought among these village people." [12]

The village alone is the reservoir of purity and health from
which Russian society can recover its lost virtues, just as from
the chaste kiss implanted on Anyuta's cheek the aging *bon
vivant* hopes to recover some measure of moral health. It is
altogether too saccharine a scene which Radishchev draws and
a great deal less effective than his more realistic descriptions
of the impact of serfdom on the peasantry. Yet the more
sympathetic among his readers were probably ready to accept
the idyllic picture of Edrovo, and in their turn contributed to
its perpetuation as model, example, and wish-fulfillment.

The whole complex of feelings in which Russia seemed to
take on the features of the unspoiled village, and the West
those of the town, was rather crudely expressed in Ippolit
Bogdanovich's drama "The Slavs" (1781) which found special
favor in the eyes of the Empress Catherine. It tells of Alexander the Great crossing the lands of the Russian Slavs with
whom he is at war, of his meeting and falling in love with a
daughter of the town of Slovensk, the Princess Dobroslava;
of his generosity in leaving her to her beloved Ruslan; and of

the peace which he concludes with this noble people. Alexander is a figure of heroic dimensions, generous and wise enough to recognize that the simple good manners of the "backward" Slavs, their home-spun wisdom and decency are superior to the supposedly advanced ways of his Athenians, who are scored off in the person of Alexander's adviser, the philosopher Pansofi. There is not a character on the Russian side of the debate, beginning with Dobroslava's nurse, who in argument does not best the Athenians, especially Pansofi, whose formal learning is of no avail against the sound good sense of his untutored opponents. When Pansofi remarks to his master that Dobroslava doesn't know the ways of the world as taught at Athens, Alexander replies that she has a special education, a virtue unknown to Athens:

> To the Athenian sage, the simple ways of the Slavs seem comical; but more comical is the sage who finds nothing of worth outside of Athens. Such is the vanity of the learned Athenians! Depraved themselves in every possible way, they cannot conceive that somewhere there should exist a dignity unattainable to them. Their minds and hearts are infected with such a deep mistrust of all humanity, that they find justification for their cheerless and doleful outlook. O, Aristotle, your teachings would be more useful among the Slavs, under the scepter of righteousness.[13]

Alexander is so impressed with the way of life of the Slavs that he asks Ruslan for the books in which their moral precepts are set down, so that he may collect and employ them for the edification of his Athenian subjects. There are no books, Ruslan replies, for among us the virtues are taught and preserved by life and by example. Whatever it is that the Slavs lack, refinement of customs, of entertainments, of thought or political life, appears to Alexander an advantage and a token of the greater constancy of their polity. Here there is no chasing after phantoms inspired by conflicting political philosophies; no factional strife, but quiet and orderly obedience to the rules and institutions of a benevolent authority.[14]

The case for official nationalism could hardly have been stated more directly if Paris had been substituted for Athens, the Enlightenment for Athenian philosophy and Catherine for the Slav ruler who had established sound morals and institutions in his country. The giddy inconstancy of an urban people, led by its life to expect ever new thrills, became even more of a commonplace in Russia (as elsewhere in Europe) when the course of the French Revolution justified deep-seated prejudices. The "impartial citizen" who signed as the author of a pamphlet entitled "Thoughts . . . on the Turbulent Events in France" [15] was only reiterating a commonplace when he denounced as the most basic evil of the times the multiplication of towns, the breeding grounds of revolution. The unstable conscience of the townsman was the source of baseness and selfish materialism, and these alone made revolution possible. The trading spirit, which is the town spirit *par excellence*, destroys all natural feelings of loyalty and faith. It causes man to look on man as a commodity, to rebel against custom, tradition, and authority, whose survival was much more likely in the village, and by extension of the argument, in the country of villages.

Karamzin, too, under the impact of events in Western Europe, turned to Russia's rural past, to the Russian countryside and the Russian village to discover the traits which would inspire resistance to the blandishments of foreign philosophy and stir feelings of loyalty to monarch and to country. The village was the source of personal and social harmony, the place where he could refresh his spirit away from the turbulence of the town.[16] The Russia of Karamzin's historical imagination was a country of "flourishing fields and prosperous villages from which the industrious villagers march out to their work to the accompaniment of joyous song—peasants who to this day have remained unchanged, who dress, live, and work as they always used to . . . and still present to us the true face of Russia." Those were the times when Russians were still Russians, when they dressed in their own fashion, walked in their own way, lived according to their own customs, and spoke in their own language what their hearts dictated. Karamzin's heroine, like Bogdanovich's Dobroslava, is lovely, innocent, and well-brought up, without benefit of foreign philosophy, of Locke or Rousseau. She is the product solely of native endowment and a traditional Russian education.[17]

By the end of the eighteenth and the beginning of the nineteenth century, all the elements were at hand for the elaboration of a nationalist theory whose basic ingredients were the peasant village and its inhabitants as the microcosm of Russia. In the confrontation of good and bad, of town and country, Russia and the West, the heart was ranged against the head, true feeling against convention, nature against art. But before the emergence of the peasant as the embodiment of wisdom and of virtue, before the Arcadian shepherd became the Russian *muzhik* and a literary commonplace turned into the village commune of Slavophile cast, certain changes had first to take place in Russian literature itself.

The records of the Third Section of His Imperial Russian Majesty's Private Chancellery (the secret police) contain a number of reports on Alexander Pushkin. Exiled to his estate, the poet, in the year 1826, was said to have behaved in a most suspicious manner. Dressed in a peasant shirt, he walked or rode about the countryside, attending village fairs and peasant festivals, seeking every opportunity for contact and conversation with the peasants. This was strange behavior for a gentleman, especially for one who had incurred the displeasure of His Majesty for a lack of political discretion. The Third Section, on investigating, found that all Pushkin had been doing was to collect folk material—the songs, proverbs, and tales of the region. By the second decade of the nineteenth century, such behavior seemed reasonable even to the police, though it was by no means common. The activities of Pushkin were only the beginning of a trend which set in with real force after the middle part of the century, but its roots go back to the second half of the eighteenth century. These roots have often been ignored, so that the folkloristic interests and researches of Russian writers and ethnographers came into sudden view only with Pushkin, or even later.

In Russia, as elsewhere in Europe, this interest in the people and its artistic product, in *Volkstum* or *narodnost*, occurred together with those elusive phenomena, nationalism and romanticism. They played an important role in returning art to its national sources, prodding it to search for the most faithful expression of the national character. In the process, such aspects of the nation's life as its history, its common folk, their speech and song were admitted into literature.

Though the appearance of the folk, its life and art, in nineteenth century literature was not an absolute innovation, it was an event of momentous importance in the history of Europe. It was as if the servants, heretofore restricted to a remote part of the house, and only rarely heard or seen, except in the performance of their duties, had suddenly burst into the salon, demanding to be treated as equals, as real human beings rather than as abstractions. Eighteenth-century canons of literary taste had prescribed that the people be excluded from all serious forms of literature, just as social convention demanded that they be denied participation in political or social life. Nor was it easy for any part of living or historical reality to fit anywhere into the closely ruled scheme of neoclassicism.

This classicism of the eighteenth century which everywhere found ready imitators, derived in great measure from the example of Racine and the teachings of Boileau. When Pushkin complained that Lomonosov's main failing had been the absence of every trace of the folk element (*narodnost*) and originality from his work, he was accusing him of blindly applying to his native language the aesthetic lessons which Lomonosov had imbibed in Western Europe. Similarly, when Nikolai Chernyshevski denied to the tragedies of Sumarokov or Knyazhnin any truly Russian elements, he deplored what he considered slavish imitation of the neoclassical doctrine of the three styles and the dramatic unities. There was nothing truly Russian about the Roslavs and Dmitris of these works, Chernyshevski felt, and it would have been more honest to have called them Oedipus or Hector.[18] Pushkin and Chernyshevski were too severe, for no amount of neoclassical doctrine could keep all aspects of Russian reality—its speech, its settings, and its characters—from penetrating into literature. The teaching, however, was clear, and Boileau expressed his astonishment over the ignorant novice who would prefer Hildebrandt to Hector, the national to the classical hero.[19] This gave to much of eighteenth-century literature a character which made it at one and the same time remote and cosmopolitan, artificial and universal. Whenever and wherever a national literature wanted to come into its own, it had first to shed the confinement of European classicism as defined in France, to rediscover and to reassert its own literary and historical tradition. The decline and final unseating of classicism was a necessary prerequisite for the full emergence of the folk and the nation in the history of Russian literature and national consciousness.

The stylistic theories of neoclassicism, as they were received and applied in Russia, did not make impossible the expression of patriotic sentiment or of devotion to monarch and to country. Patriotism and civic duty for the classical hero had little to do, however, with his place of birth. They derived instead from his high station in life or his personal morality, and were the same for the Roman citizen and the Russian aristocrat. The national consciousness demanded a hero whose motivations were less schematic and more uniquely Russian, no matter from which stratum of Russian society he came. Once the rigid observance of the classical rules weakened and "the people" began to enter into literature and the awareness of the literate public, the way was cleared for a theory which extolled the folk, its wisdom, and its greatness. What were felt to be the homeless generalities of classicism were superseded by the local color of an early romanticism. It was the populist "going to the people" *avant le mot*. Even sentimentalism, which stressed the individual and his feelings, served to strengthen interest in the peculiarly national, Russian qualities which distinguished the peasant and his ways: his dignity in the face of adversity; the tenacity of his belief in a Russian God; his devotion to the Russian soil. All these were in sharp contrast to the cosmopolitanism of his betters. It was not unlike the emergence of the "sturdy yeoman" in the literature of English romanticism.

The openness of Russia to Western influences in the eighteenth century brought about the rule of classicism in Russian letters. This very receptivity was also one of the factors which helped to remove it from its position of eminence. The literary currents of Western Europe which counteracted classicism were quickly transmitted to Russia. Western sentimentalism and the bourgeois drama, early romantic poetry, and the novel of sensibility found an echo in Russia so shortly after the reception of classicism that the latter never had a chance to become firmly rooted. Only thirty or forty years elapsed between the appearance of the first Russian products of classicism and its countercurrents. Prince Kantemir's first satire, an imitation of Boileau's ninth, was written about 1739; Lomonosov's first ode, a translation of Fénelon, in 1738, when he was still abroad; Tredyakovski, the translator of Boileau's *Art Poetique*, wrote his "Ode on the Surrender of Danzig" in 1734 and modeled it after the French master's *Ode pindarique sur la prise de Namur*. Sumarokov's first odes, epistles, and satires were written in the forties, and his first tragedy, "Khorev," closely patterned after Racine, appeared in 1747. With the "Rossiyada" of Kheraskov (1779)—a work which the author himself likened to the *Henriade* of Voltaire—the classical wave in Russia began to recede.

In the sixties, the novel of sensibility, in the form of translations from Fielding, Richardson, and Marmontel, began to be widely read in Russia, and by the end of the century the tears which it released were, on the testimony of Karamzin, flowing freely.[20] Every literary trend which called for a return to the primacy of feeling and simplicity, as against reason and stateliness, and which demanded that literature turn to nature and to one's native land for inspiration, found a speedy echo. The *Nouvelle Héloise* of Rousseau became known through the reports of travelers, was imitated in 1766, and translated as early as 1769. The satirical journals, which followed their European models in demanding simplicity and naturalness, began to appear in that same year. Translations (and soon imitations) of Thomson, Young, Ossian, and Sterne, followed. Young's *Night Thoughts* were partially translated in 1772, and four more times before the end of the century. Portions of Sterne's *Sentimental Journey* were known in Russian translations from 1779, while Radishchev, whom it influenced so profoundly, had read it even earlier in a German version. Only two years after a translation of Richardson's

*Pamela* (1787), a "Russian Pamela" appeared, and when the poems of Ossian were translated in 1792 many Russians had already felt the influence of Ossianism through French and German translations, or during their travels abroad.[21]

An additional reason for the relatively speedy decline of classicism in Russia was the continued survival of old-established literary forms and traditions which it had never succeeded in displacing. Like so many other importations from the West, French literature, although it was readily embraced by the professional litterateurs and their audiences in the capitals, remained foreign to the majority of the reading public, including the provincial gentry, and left them unmoved. The elegant satires, ponderous odes, and thundering declamations of the classical lyre were too strained or courtly to replace in the affections of all the stories of knights and sorcerers, of pranksters and Eastern princes, the folk-songs, tales, and epics to which they were accustomed. The literature of Muscovite Russia and the oral tradition of even more remote origin continued to flourish. Many of the gentry never lost their taste for their native art, and there are numerous examples of members of this class gathering singers and story-tellers about them at their estates, even before the fashionable interest in folklore set in. Their peasants and servants, at the same time, would read, or would have read to them, the tales of "Prince Bova," of "Peter Goldenkeys," or of "Vasili Koriotski, the Russian sailor." The survival of these older traditions guaranteed their renewed popularity when interest in folklore and the native literature was spurred by nationalist or scientific concerns. It led also to the penetration of folk and local elements into the literature which was fashioned after Western models. It is this which explains the presence of folk motifs, or elements of popular speech and poetry, of local and historical color in the work of the most confirmed among Russian classicists.[22] Even Sumarokov, who in his manifestoes of Russian classicism, the "Epistle of Poetry" and the "Epistle on the Russian Language" laid down the theoretical positions which he defended to the last, in practice admitted into his work materials of which his French masters would not have approved. Of his eight tragedies—and tragedy was the highest achievement of the classicist's aesthetic and its most sacrosanct form—only two do not take place in Russia. His heroes may not, in their motivation and behavior, differ much from their French counterparts, but the names they bear are Russian names, and the events in which they participate are events of Russian history. The Russian history of Sumarokov's tragedies was quite often the product of his own imagination, but in his drama, "Dmitri the Pretender" (1771), he drew on his knowledge of historical events which were a familiar part of the Russian past. In spite of Sumarokov's strict observance of the classical rules, Dmitri is more than an abstract personification of evil. His evildoing has specific historical and national connotations. He is not merely an enemy of society in general, but of Russian society specifically, the candidate of Poles and Papists to the Russian throne. A Russian audience could not help but react with emotional immediacy to scenes from its own history, and a contemporary recalled how when he saw "Dmitri" on the stage his heart beat in a way it did not when he was watching the heroes and villains of Corneille and Racine: "My imagination was afire with love for Church and fatherland; it carried me off to Red Square, compassionate for the suffering of Moscow . . . and I rejoiced as holy Russia acclaimed the manly appeal of Shuiski." [23]

While tragedy, in Sumarokov's definition, limited itself to depicting the passions and virtues of "nobles, marquises, counts, princes, and rulers," [24] comedy, occupying a less exalted position in the classical hierarchy of values, could portray the lesser acts of clerks and judges, fops and pedants. It was inevitable that in pillorying the minor vices of vanity, pettifoggery, and bribery, Sumarokov should draw more freely on the material furnished by Russian reality than he was prepared to do in the case of tragedy. As the artificiality of his tragic heroes could not be concealed by clothing them superficially in Russian dress, so the fact that some of his comic protagonists bore such un-Russian names as Dyulizh, Minodor, Tresotinius, or Bombembius did not keep his audiences from recognizing them. The comic genres of classical literature were altogether more receptive to reality than the epic and tragic forms and in the later comedies of Sumarokov there is an increasing number of realistic elements: proverbs, folk-sayings, popular humor, and naturalistic renditions of the speech of the country squire. A similar process of admixture, a kind of domestication of Western classicism, also took place in the writings of Kheraskov, after Sumarokov its outstanding representative in Russia. Side by side with typically classical elements in his "Rossiyada," there are bits of folk-tales, old Russian legends, historical songs, and materials drawn from his study of the chronicles. As the author of two sentimental dramas, the first written in Russia, Kheraskov came into direct conflict with the position held and defined by Sumarokov.

The most spirited attack on Sumarokov came from V. I. Lukin (1737–1794), a writer and translator of comedies, who found inadequate whatever elements of Russian reality had already made their way onto the stage. He bitterly mocked what seemed to him the totally un-Russian character of the contemporary theater and its stilted speech. Comedy, if it was to point to specific social ills, had to do so in a specific and concrete way, not, Lukin believed, by drawing human failings which were common to all climes and periods.

It has always seemed unusual to me to hear foreign dialogue in works which ought, by their representation of our morals, not only to correct defects of mankind in general, but the more specific vices of our nation. More than once I have heard visitors to the theatre say that not their good sense alone, but their ear as well, had been offended by stage characters who (though they have been made to conform somewhat to our manners) are called Klitander, Dorant, Tsitadinaya and whose speeches indicate conduct which is not characteristic of us.[25]

Lukin set forth his theoretical position in a series of polemical prefaces which, with unmistakable thrusts in Sumarokov's direction, questioned the classical rules of dramatic composition. Wasn't it strange, Lukin asked, to introduce into a supposedly Russian comedy a clerk who wants "to draw up a marriage contract" at the house of a gentleman called Oront, to parade across a Russian stage characters bearing such names as Geront, Fontitsidius, Fineta, Krispin, and Notarius? "This is indeed a strange business, but what is stranger still is that it should be considered correct." [26] Correctness, as it was understood by Sumarokov and his followers, was not a criterion which Lukin was willing to employ. To him correctness meant above all verisimilitude, some correspondence between what took place on the stage and in the life around him. It mattered little whether his comedy was of five or of six acts, as long as it was a "Russian comedy." His protest was not informed by aesthetic beliefs, but derived from a practical insistence that what a Russian audience was given to see should bear some relation to its experience. He demanded that the characters and situations of dramatic literature, especially of the comedy, be Russian. Whether their originals were French or English was of little importance, as long as they were truly transposed into a Russian key. "The French, the Germans, the English, and other peoples who have a theatre portray their own image in it . . . and why should not we do the same?" [27]

As long as there was not yet a Russian dramatic literature on a level with that of Europe—and Lukin felt that in time this would be the case—it was best to borrow and to adapt the foreign work to Russian conditions. Borrowing was no disgrace, as long as it was not slavish imitation but a creative reworking. "We are born to borrow, and it is necessary that we do so; but one must acknowledge the fact; to appropriate someone else's work is shameful." [28] Lukin adhered to his own prescription and tried to force his foreign models into a Russian mold. He was himself conscious of the strain to which he put some of his material, and notably in the *Shchepetilnik* felt it necessary to explain why he preferred this little-known Russian word to the widely employed and understood *bijoutier*: "publishing this comedy in Russian . . . I did not want to write this French word with Russian letters." [29] His servants bear names like Vasiliev, Ivanov, Mironov, Stepanida, Andreev, and some of them even speak dialect on the stage. Their masters bear such contrived but Russian-sounding names as Dobroserdov (Goodheart), Pryamikov (Upright), Chistoserdov (Pureheart), and Legkomyslov (Flighty).

While there was much of a personal nature that embittered the literary quarrels of Sumarokov, Lukin, and their respective camps, the disagreement which divided them went deeper. It went beyond the fact that Lukin, a relative newcomer of insignificant social position, had dared challenge the authority of Russia's greatest living poet, or that he had had the temerity to issue a collection of his works at the age of twenty-eight— something which only Lomonosov and Tredyakovski had done before him. Their conflict extended to differing views on the nature of comedy, with each participant to the dispute trying to enlist European authority on his behalf. Sumarokov felt threatened not only in his personal authority, but also in his role as chief exponent of the classical position, while Lukin looked upon him as a man who had unjustly arrogated to himself the role of Russia's only literary arbiter "who has condemned me to be driven out of the city, because I dared write a drama of five acts, and thus started an epidemic among the young people." The "epidemic" was the growing taste of

Russian audiences for the reflection of sentimentalism and middle class life in dramatic literature. In response to this taste, Lukin had announced that he would introduce into his "Wastrel" elevating and sentimental ideas.[30] These developments, reflecting a wider European trend, were viewed with growing alarm by Sumarokov. At the beginning of 1769 he dispatched a letter to Voltaire at Ferney, trying to enlist the great man's help and prestige in restating once and for all the unshakable tenets of dramatic composition. Voltaire obliged, and his letter, together with Sumarokov's "Reflections on the Comédie Larmoyante," which had been provoked by the unusual success of Beaumarchais' *Eugénie* in Moscow, formed the preface of Sumarokov's "Dmitri" which appeared in 1771.

Voltaire declared himself proud to share Sumarokov's horror at the way in which literary standards were being debased. His assertion that after Molière and Regnard only monstrosities had appeared in French comedy showed how much he, like his Russian correspondent, had closed himself off from some of the most vital currents of contemporary literature. Agreement between the two men was complete. "I regard Racine as the best of our tragic poets. . . . I subscribe wholeheartedly to all you say about Molière and the *comédie larmoyante*; to the shame of the nation, it has taken the place of the only true comic genre, which was brought to perfection by the inimitable Molière." Further, Voltaire noted with horror that some dramas presented tragic events with bourgeois protagonists. Voltaire's enthusiastic support may have given some comfort to Sumarokov but it was small in view of the fact that his tragedies were now less popular than the "vile products" of Beaumarchais and his kind. At performances of Sumarokov's "Semira" and "Sinav and Truvor" the audiences had been disrespectful of his tragedies, and he felt it necessary to take up their defense in the "Reflections." The source of the infection is France where there are now neither Racines nor Molières, though comedies and tragedies are still being written. But whereas France, too, is being flooded with examples of the vile *comédie larmoyante*, she has standards of taste which cannot easily be uprooted. In Russia, the situation is different and therefore more dangerous. There, Sumarokov felt, lowly quill-drivers and lackeys had replaced him as arbiter of taste.[31]

The quill-driver was Nikolai Pushnikov, the court lackey was Mikhail Chulkov who had begun to publish a collection of songs in 1770. It was one of the first attempts to collect and record folkloristic materials. In the lackeys and copyists, the Lukins, Pushnikovs, and Chulkovs, Sumarokov saw, not without justification, the forces which would eventually assure the defeat of his position. The adapters of sentimental comedies, the translators of bourgeois dramas, and the collectors of folklore sensed more accurately the trends and tastes of their time than did their illustrious contemporaries Voltaire and Sumarokov.

Sumarokov died in 1777, a bitter and lonely man. His teachings and influence lingered on and were not finally displaced until well into the next century. Twenty years after his attack on Beaumarchais and his Russian admirers, the debate was once more resumed. Lukin's position was restated with greater theoretical sophistication by a man who felt that it had not yet found full acceptance.

P. A. Plavilshchikov (1760–1812), son of a merchant family, actor, journalist, and playwright, brought to all his activities a great amount of patriotic pathos. So much so, that patriotism (*otechestvennost*) seemed to him the primary subject of dramatic literature. In two articles, "Theater" and "Comedy" both of which appeared in the magazine "Spectator" in 1792, he stated the patriotic and aesthetic requirements which writers for the stage had to meet. The starting point of his thesis is that the subject matter of the play must correspond to the interests and experience of Russians. He goes beyond this, however, and beyond Lukin, in suggesting specific events from Russian history.

Of what interest is it to a Russian to know that some Tatar Dzinghis-Khan was the conqueror of China. . . . ? What need is there for us to see some Dido pining away for love of Aeneas and Iarbas driven mad with jealousy? What have we to do with the eternal feuds played among the tombstones of Verona? First of all we must know what happened in our own fatherland. The merchant Kuzma Minin is most worthy of being glorified on the stage: his constancy, his love for his fatherland for which he sacrificed all he possessed, the insurmountable bravery of Prince Pozharski . . . all this would serve as instruction in how to love the fatherland. . . . We cannot blindly imitate the French or the English; we have our own manners, our own character, and consequently must have our own taste. . . .[32]

The development of taste as well as of the arts would only be delayed, Plavilshchikov feared, by a continued dependence on foreign models. The prejudice that a Russian theater could exist only if it modeled itself after the French stage seemed to Plavilshchikov added proof of the infection which a fashionable education had spread among Russians. He would not deny that there was much that was exemplary in French dramatic literature, but there was also much in it that was incomparably remote from life. When a French author dressed his Asiatic heroes in the appropriate costumes, but left them the character, the mind, and the speech of Frenchmen, that was not worthy of imitation. Why cannot we, asked Plavilshchikov, create a theater in Russia which is in keeping with our character? "And why can it not be, in its way, perfect?"

The way to perfection demanded, first of all, the abandonment of classical constraint as far as the matter and the manner of the drama were concerned. Abandon the rule which considers criminal the writing of a six-act play, the rule which demands the unity of time and place, if it interferes with the representation of reality on the stage. If it is a question of sacrificing purity of style or the dramatic unities to true beauty, then the author sins both against himself and his audience if he bores them with a play written according to the rules. The strictest observance of the rules cannot guarantee the quality of a play, while a work which has broken every law may appeal in the most direct way to the hearts and souls of its hearers. The appeal to heart and soul, however, could only be made if the legacy of the "rule-makers" were ignored, and among these was Sumarokov, whose memory and services to Russian letters Plavilshchikov wanted to respect. He discharged his obligation by praising Sumarokov in general but disagreeing with him on the scope of dramatic literature. Sumarokov, "the father of our literature," and his model Voltaire, had held too narrow a conception of drama, which is a combination of tears and laughter. "It is as impossible for a man to spend a whole day sobbing and in tears . . . as it is to keep guffawing for twenty-four hours. . . . Dramas are not in vain called honorable children of the theater; they are closer to life than the tragedy, and the smiles they produce are nobler and more pleasing than comic laughter." [33]

The product of Plavilshchikov's union of tears and laughter, the tragicomedy, which he called *dramma*, was a hybrid to horrify every purist, but it met a need which more orthodox playwrights did not fill. Plavilshchikov observed with some satisfaction that Molière's *Misanthrope* constantly played to half-filled houses, while Ablesimov's comic opera "The Miller" for all its weaknesses, for all its neglect of the Aristotelian rules, played for more than 200 performances to capacity audiences. The reason was clear: "It is because the miller is one of ours; the misanthrope is a foreigner." [34]

The popularity of comic opera contributed materially to the acceptance of the trends which were destined to drive classical poetry from the scene. It brought native materials and native characters before the public in great profusion; it entered not only the milieu of the gentry, but also that of the merchant class, of workmen, sailors, and peasants. Even when its pictures of the life of the people were prettified and its folk-songs imitations, it developed among its listeners a sympathetic attitude for the people and for its artistic inheritance. Unlike the classical stage, which, with few exceptions, portrayed the lower orders of society only as comic and secondary figures, the comic opera drew them with understanding and sympathy, though not always without condescension.

M. I. Popov's "Anyuta," [35] performed at Tsarskoe Selo in 1772, was the first of a long series of successful comic operas. Although Soviet claims for its folk or popular character are exaggerated, its subject matter, the speech of its peasant characters, its songs and proverbs mark it as a significant innovation in Russian theatrical history. All of these were elements which the audiences of Moscow and St. Petersburg met as rarely in literature as they met them frequently in everyday life. There were things about it which did not ring quite true perhaps—the fact that the peasant heroine is discovered in the end to have been of the gentry all along—but even this helped to make more palatable a crossing of class lines which might otherwise have called for protests. It is characteristic of the position of Anyuta's author in the history of Russian literature, that along with Chulkov he was one of the most zealous and serious collectors of folklore.

The most successful comic opera was A. A. Ablesimov's "The Miller," first performed in 1779.[36] Not taken off the boards for the rest of the century, it played to enthusiastic audiences well into the beginning of the next. There is some dispute whether it is really a folk comedy, or whether some of the characters are not travesties of the Russian peasant,[37] but it brought into literature, onto the stage and before the public, aspects of Russian life which had heretofore been shunned or neglected: wedding-songs, some genuine turns of speech, and folk expressions. After 1779, comic operas with lowly themes appeared more frequently; Kheraskov ("The Good Soldiers"), Nikolev ("Rozana and Lyubim," "The Bailiff," "The Knife Grinder"), Knyazhnin ("Misfortune from a Carriage," "The Drink Seller") and V. I. Maikov ("A Village Feast"), N. A. Lvov ("The Coachmen") and Mikhail Matinski (whose "Merchants of St. Petersburg," was the first introduction of that class to the stage), continued the work begun by Popov and Ablesimov. Even the Empress Catherine, as open to the winds of fashion in literature as in political thought, composed a number of comic operas liberally sprinkled with local color and themes taken from Russian history and legend. The subject matter of her comic opera "Boeslavich," came from the cycle of folk epics known as the *byliny*, and in her treatment the Empress drew freely on "Russian tales, songs, and other compositions." The same is true of Catherine's three other operas which employed, as she informed her readers, the language of the original tales.

Catherine also discovered Shakespeare, whose loud and bustling vitality was in such sharp contrast with the well-mannered tones of contemporary dramatists. The eighteenth century's discovery of Shakespeare was one of the most important factors in the decline of the classical theatre and its rules, lending influence and encouragement to the tragedy which had events of national history as its subject matter. Shakespeare had refused to let himself be bound by the three unities and to imitate his disregard for them was a sign of literary progressivism. The very titles of Catherine's historical dramas about Rurik, Oleg, and Igor signified her intent: "An imitation of Shakespeare," or "a historical representation without observance of the usual theatrical rules." Almost the entire third act of "The Beginning of Oleg's Rule" was taken up with a description of ancient wedding rituals and included three folk-songs.[38]

The mock-epic, accepted by the classicists as a parody on the heroic poem which glorified noble deeds and noble men in the grand manner, also helped to subvert the ruling literary tradition and to widen the horizon of writer and reader alike. It took them away from Mt. Olympus, from courts and battle-fields, into the back streets and taverns, among sailors and clerks, peasants and bargemen, into a social milieu where behavior and speech were worlds apart from those of the true epic. The poems of Chulkov, Osipov's "Aeneid" and "Orpheus," Kotelnitski's "Aeneid" and "Proserpine," and especially V. I. Maikov's "Elisei, or Bacchus Enraged," in their choice of heroes and locale, their irreverence and vulgarity marked a shocking departure from the reigning canons of good taste. They were a fresh and vital influence which turned the Russian author to sources of his imagination and language which were close at hand.[39]

The last decade of the century brought ever more insistent and frequent calls for the abandonment of literary forms which were foreign to Russian tastes, and for giving Russian content to those which were to be retained. In language almost identical to that in which Lukin and Plavilshchikov had demanded the nationalization of dramatic literature, Andrei Bolotov, writing in 1791, called for the "Russification" of the newly popular novel. In an article primarily devoted to a review of P. N. Lvov's "Russian Pamela," Bolotov remarked that in spite of its title, it was still far from being a truly Russian novel; that neither its locale nor the names of its characters were really Russian, and that they had a theatrical quality about them which lessened the "romantic" quality of the novel as well as its naturalness. "It would be well, if someone were to write a Russian novel which would strictly observe both naturalness and plausibility, and in which everything were conceived with Russian features, manners, and customs. But so far, not a single such novel exists; all that remains for us is to hope for it." [40]

Russia did not escape the infection of Ossianism which was sweeping Europe and the efforts which it inspired to discover a remote and romantically obscure antiquity, national ballads, bards, and folk-heroes. The dryness, the order, the all-too-great familiarity of classic poetry readily gave way in Russia, as elsewhere, to nostalgic visions of a romantic past. And just as the vogue of Ossianism and Celtic balladry in the West called forth a host of "discoveries" and imitations of ancient lays, Russia too had her forgeries and impostors. Bayan, the mythical bard mentioned in the *Lay of Igor's Host*, was purported to have been the author of one such forgery, a hymn "discovered" in a parchment scroll of the first century together with some prophecies (*proizrecheniya*) of Novgorod priests of the fifth century.[41] Kheraskov, the last of the great eighteenth century classicists, invoked Bayan, whom he presumed to be the author of the Igor tale, in his *Bakhariyana*, itself an attempt to sing in the fashion of the "Russian troubadours."

> There is a worthy example for us,
> How to sing the deeds of heroes;
> Here the art of Homer and Ossian
> Combines with the greatness of Lomonosov;
> But Bayan was greater still,
> The falcon-like, glorious bard.[42]

M. N. Muraviev and I. I. Dmitriev, N. A. Lvov, G. R. Derzhavin, and Karamzin, were all caught up in the wave and paid their tribute to the period when, presumably, Russian knighthood was in flower. There was Muraviev's "Oskold," Lvov's epic poem (*bogatyrskaya poema*) about the knight "Dobrynya Nikitich" (both unfinished), Dmitriev's poetic treatment of the exploits of Ermak in Siberia, Derzhavin's "Dobrynya" (a play), and Karamzin's ambitious "Ilya of Murom" (1795). The latter was written, its author assures us, in Russian meter, the same as used in the old ballads. It opens with a ringing farewell to classical antiquity, and invites the reader to come away from Greece and Troy, to turn from the shores of Italy to his native land and the records of its past. "We are not Greeks, not Romans. We don't believe their legends. . . . We heard different tales from our mothers. And now I shall tell one of them in the old way." [43]

Many factors were at work in the long transition from classicism to romanticism, from an essentially cosmopolitan to a national literature. Aesthetic beliefs and national pride, a consciousness of history and of social duty, sense and sensibility, phantasy and fashion all contributed to the decline of the reigning literary theory. It was a process which had been a long time in the making, and in its course folklore and national history, the simple folk and the intensity of private feeling had gained rights of citizenship in the republic of letters. Measure, order, rule, and line gave way before creative confusion, universality before uniqueness, the symmetry of Versailles to the apparent disorder of the English garden.

Dmitriev's lines describing the reaction of an unsophisticated oldster to the reading of an ode, was a fitting epitaph for the poetry of classicism in eighteenth-century Russia.

> It is indeed a solemn ode!
> Though I can't say exactly of what kind,
> It's very long. . .
> And all there's in it, is correct:
> At the beginning, there's an introduction;
> The exposition follows it, and finally the conclusion!
> It's learned, like the talk in Church.
> For all of that, my wish to read it is but slight. . . .
> It's full of things which such a simple mind as mine
> Could never have thought up: there is the

'Rosy-fingered dawn,' 'the lily of Paradise,'
And 'Phoebus' and 'the open Heavens!'
How great and noble, but not merry in the least!
Our feeling hearts, it leaves entirely unmoved! [44]

As Radishchev put it in the introduction to his "Bova": The lyre is no longer in fashion, let the *gusly* ring out!

The decline of classicism as the reigning literary formula was one of the conditions, not the cause, of the widespread acceptance of a belief dear to romantic philosophers and historians: that the voice of the folk, as it expressed itself in myth and legend, tale and song, was the most faithful expression of the qualities of mind and soul of a people. Changes in social life and thought acted jointly with the revolution in taste to bring about that "national romanticism" of which the interest in the folk and its lore constituted an integral part. The romantic articles of faith soon spread from Greece to Norway, from England to Russia.

The folk tales, it was said, had "grown organically" from within the peculiarity of each people; they were the clearest revelation of the folk spirit. The folk-literature, having sprung from the people's "innermost uniqueness," belonged "to us and to no one else"; in it was enshrined the "soul of the nation." A Swedish writer referred to the traditions as the records not of individuals but of a distant folk past, and much later they were spoken of as "living portraits of the spirit which has coursed through the people from earliest times." [45]

In Russia, national romanticism took the form of Slavophilism, and found in Konstantin Aksakov one of the most spirited spokesmen for the point of view which equated folklore with folk-soul, and folk-soul with the national character. In the folk song he saw the expression of the life of the people, but of the people defined nationally, for to him the folk song was devoid both of universality and individuality and received its imprint solely from the collective life of the nation. For Aksakov the folk song (*narodnaya pesnya*) became the national song (*natsionalnaya pesnya*) and its study, "with which the literary history of the people must begin" would, he was convinced, reveal the national spirit (*dukh narodny*).[46] The premise that a people's character could be made manifest through its songs was not entirely novel to the nineteenth century or to Aksakov. Herder had declared in 1777 that a modest collection of a people's songs—the treasury of its science and religion, the repository of its memories, hopes, and fears—would be more enlightening and exact than all the gossip brought together by travelers.[47] Radishchev, in the *Journey From Petersburg to Moscow* (1790), had proposed that Russia fashion her government after the spirit expressed in the heart-rending songs of her people, and he found that the art of the blind village minstrel spoke more directly to his listeners than the warblings of the Italian singers in St. Petersburg or Moscow to the spoiled ears of their audiences.[48]

Even if one is inclined to dismiss Radishchev's proposal as the generous response of a sensitive nature to the suffering of fellow-beings, the fact remains that it is one of the milestones marking the distance which educated Russians had traveled in less than thirty years. It was a long way from Sumarokov's decisive denial that there were any noble feelings among the lower orders to Radishchev's generous sponsorship of their humanity and wisdom. The two positions marked the extremes between which attitudes towards the peasant and his life and art were likely to move. There was, however, no necessary relationship between a writer's conscious attitude towards the peasantry and the folk elements contained in his work. Sumarokov, the most typical adherent of classicism and one of the most insistent spokesmen for the rights and privileges of the gentry, was more receptive in his writing to the oral tradition of the peasantry and its speech habits than was Radishchev, whose attitude towards the folk was a great deal more sympathetic.

The ambivalence which often marked the attitude of the upper classes towards its inferiors was mirrored in the attitude towards folklore and the register of feeling ranged from contempt, amused tolerance, delight over the picturesque, to warm human sympathy and serious scientific interest. When in 1784, the Princess Dashkova wanted to entertain an English visitor *à la Russe*, she did so by arranging a village feast which combined features of Marie Antoinette's pastoral idylls and Russian comic opera. Perhaps unconsciously the Princess believed that for all the curiosity of the scene, her visitor was being shown the real Russia.

A village had been newly built on my estate . . . and here I assembled all the peasants who were about to occupy it, dressed in their holiday suits, embroidered as is the custom with us by the females. The weather was delicious, and I encouraged them to dance on the grass, singing in accompaniment, according to our country fashion. Mrs. Hamilton, to whom this sort of fete was quite new, was no less charmed with the nationality of the scene and beauty of the dresses than with the picturesque effect of the groups which sang and danced before her. To give it all the effect we could, refreshments, consisting of Russian dishes and drinks were not forgotten; and the whole formed a picture so striking and so interesting that she was infinitely more pleased with our little rural entertainment than she could have been with the most magnificent court festivity.[49]

The Princess Dashkova's attitude towards her peasants, as she dressed them up for her English visitor, had something patronizing about it. Condescension may not have been what a latter-day populist or liberal would have approved, but the Princess was creating for herself and for the foreigner an image of Russia in which she wanted to believe.

This portrait of the Russian folk, to which the writers of the eighteenth century contributed so many important features, was in a sense a self-portrait of the Russian intelligentsia. The fact that the portrait of the folk was not an accurate likeness did not detract from its importance as an element of growing national consciousness. It was accurate enough as a mirror of the intelligentsia's wished-for picture of Russia and of itself, and as such it survived with amazing tenacity. The patronizing was there, so were the artificiality and the falseness, but they were born of a real need: the need to see in Russia and the mass of her people more than a backward, benighted country on the outskirts of civilization, more than a beastly mass of ignorant serfs.

The ambivalence of writers and members of the upper classes in general towards folklore was only another aspect of a deeper split which divided Russians within themselves. On the one hand there was the attraction of Europe, the wish to see in the Russian landowner the equivalent of the European aristocrat. On the other hand there was the counterpull of native loyalties, habits, and tastes. This conflict caused many Russians to look down upon and shun the literature of the base rabble, while at the same time they continued to use and enjoy it. While folklore and local color were barred from the more serious literary genres, they found their way into comedies, comic operas, parodies, and fables. And while the gentry were trying to acquire Western polish and tastes, many of them continued to watch the peasants' choral dances, to listen to their singers and story-tellers. The notice inserted by a blind story-teller in the "St. Petersburg News" (1797) offering his services to some "lordly house" (*gospodski dom*), Tolstoy's recollection of such a *skazochnik* on his grandfather's estate, the famous collection of byliny prepared for the mill-owner Demidov in the middle of the century, the numerous manuscript collections of folksongs, all bespeak the continued and lively enjoyment by the upper classes of the popular art.[50]

The first Russian scholar and writer to concern himself consciously with folk poetry was Tredyakovski, the translator of Boileau and Fénelon. Seeking for Russian poetry a meter which would be more in keeping with the properties of the language than the syllabic verse taken over from Ukrainian and Polish, he turned his attention to folk poetry and song, and came to the conclusion that Russian authors would do well to use these as the basis for a new theory of Russian verse. His "Aid to the Composition of Russian Verse" (1735) actually introduced examples of peasant song and folk poetry. Composed in metrical feet, tonic and without rhyme, theirs was the verse form which Tredyakovski thought most appropriate for Russian poetry. Realizing that he was taking a revolutionary step which infringed the classical canon, he felt that he owed his readers an explanation, if not an apology. "I beg the reader not to be angry with me, and to forgive my quoting some fragments from our lowly but native verse: it is done only by way of example." [51] Twenty years later he still assured his readers that if he introduced folk material to print at all, it was done purely to illustrate the nature "of our primitive poetry" and for no other reason. Even Tredyakovski, who was willing to employ folk poetry as a model, would not recommend it as serious literature to the attention of public and critics. It was of inferior origin, would always bear the stamp of its provenance and was therefore to be shunned. Tatishchev and Kantemir were similarly persuaded. This is the attitude with which any attempt to deal seriously with folklore had to clash, a conflict which was not fully resolved until the nineteenth century.

The position of Tredyakovski's two greatest contemporaries, Lomonosov and Sumarokov, did not differ markedly from his own, though they did not share his historical interest in the poetry of the people. The efforts made by Soviet historians to show that Lomonosov, the son of the people, showed a positive interest in the literature emanating from his own social stratum, do not bear close scrutiny. His collection of proverbs and the finding of Slavic equivalents for Greek and Roman gods are insufficient evidence for a revision of the view that Lomonosov was indifferent, if not hostile, to folk art.[52] While Sumarokov, Russia's arbiter in matters of classical doctrine, agreed with Tredyakovski and Lomonosov in theory, in practice, he was much more susceptible to folk influences than they were. On occasion he was not above imitating the folk satire, and his fables contained expressions and materials which he should have shunned, had he been consistent. It was in his songs, however, that Sumarokov came closest to the language of the folk lyric, at times employing its modes, at others borrowing its language directly.

Sumarokov was not alone in his liking for the language of the folk song. Its style was reflected in many of the songs written by Popov, Dmitriev, and others. It is not surprising, therefore, that songs were the first form of folklore taken up by literary men and the public even before such interest could have been stimulated by Western writers. The collecting and publishing of songs of all kinds was rarely an indication of a systematic or theoretical interest in folklore. The love for song seems to have been common to all parts of Russian society throughout the century. The courts of Peter, of Anna, and Elizabeth were never without their contingents of native singers, dancers, and instrumentalists. The age of Elizabeth has even been called the "age of song," and the Empress herself sang folk-songs and composed in the popular style.

The cultivation of native music at the court of Catherine was a more studied affair, and she always kept at her court a number of *gusly* players, among them as official court musician, V. V. Trutovski. A songbook, published by him in 1776, contained much material of folk origin. The arranging, collecting, noting down, and publishing of folk melodies, without always distinguishing them too carefully from those of literary origin, continued throughout Catherine's reign. Her court conductor Kozlovski was one of the first Russian composers actually to go among the people, to listen to their songs as they were sung in market places and taverns and to note what he heard. The violinist Khandoshkin, son of a Petersburg tailor, was an equally indefatigable collector and popularizer of folk songs.[53]

The first printed songbook dates from 1759,[54] but the first to find a wide public response and to go through several editions, was Mikhail Chulkov's "Collection of Various Songs," published in four parts from 1774 to 1779. Chulkov's collection contains a total of 900 songs, all listed without any indication of source or authorship. This in itself makes it difficult to determine what proportion of the material is of folk origin. Blagoi's estimate of 400 songs of peasant, Cossack, or worker origin is in all likelihood somewhat too high, for it is based on Chulkov's rough division of his volume into literary and folk sections which he did not consistently maintain. The folk section, for instance, contains many lyrics composed by Sumarokov and Popov, because Chulkov considered them to have been written in the lyric style of the oral tradition. In spite of this occasional crossing of lines, the first section contains primarily literary products, love songs and pastorals, the second everything written in the style of the folk lyric, without specifying their origin.[55] The reverence with which later collectors approached and tried to preserve the original source materials was not yet part of Chulkov's method. He did not himself note down the songs he included, but relied extensively on manuscript collections which already existed or were prepared for him. In the brief preface to the first volume of his collection, he complained about the difficulty of transcription from the often defective and illiterate manuscripts available to him, and blandly announced that, where necessary, he had employed guess and correction to remove defects and obscurities.[56]

This somewhat high-handed attitude towards the sources characterized many of Chulkov's contemporaries. In view of this, it was significant that folk materials were included at all and set side by side with literary products. Not only folk songs, but proverbs, poetry, and epics were treated in similar fashion, doctored or "cleaned up." Even the *Igor Tale* did not escape this passion for "treatment," and to make it conform to the taste of the time its first editors and commentators, through a process of "ossianization," punctuation, translation, and explanation retouched it to meet their own aesthetic demands. A milestone on the road to greater faithfulness to the originals, which Chulkov and the compilers who came after him helped bring about by the very act of collecting, was the publication in 1790, of the "Collection of Russian Folk Songs" (*narodyne pesni*) by N. A. Lvov and Ivan Prach. Lvov thought that one of the main virtues of the book was its preservation of the character of the originals. "This collection," the editors announced, "has the merit of the original; its simplicity and integrity have been violated neither by musical ornamentation nor by corrections," and they hoped that the rich variety of folk melodies which their volume put before the public would serve to inspire and enrich the work of Russia's composers. Lvov, going even further, believed that a study of these songs in their unadulterated and unprettified form would shed much light on the national character. Since their authors were unknown men of the people, Cossacks, bargemen, laborers, soldiers, sailors, and carters, they were truly songs which the whole nation could claim as its own—they were popular as well as national songs.[57]

Songs, of whatever origin, were enormously popular towards the end of the century. They were so often reprinted and those of folk origin imitated, that they became truly a national art form. To meet the demand, Chulkov's compilation went through a second edition in 1776, the same year in which Trutovski's book appeared, and Novikov republished it twice in enlarged editions (1780–1781 and 1783–1787). The "New Russian Songbook" of I. K. Shnora appeared in 1791. It was followed a year later by a "Selection of Russian Songs" and Popov's "Russian Erato," by a new edition of Trutovski in 1795–96 and Dmitriev's "Pocket Songbook" in 1796.

In the complex of motivations which was responsible for the growing interest in folklore, the wish to discover a national heritage, to recognize and to define Russia's present through her antecedents, occupies an important place. In many instances, the historical interest in Russian "antiquities" was indistinguishable from what would today be called a folkloristic interest. In the absence of a sharp separation between ethnography, geography, and history, almost all the materials descriptive of Russia's past and present, contained information relating to folk customs, beliefs, rituals, and literature. Russia's remote areas, her outlying districts in time, in space, in social distance were all coming under observation, were described and brought to the attention of the country. It was a process of self-discovery, of filling out Russia's picture in all its details. It was also the achievement of national consciousness in the most concrete sense of the word, Russians getting to know their country and its features.

This discovery of Russia in all her aspects found its most literal expression in the reports of her learned travelers, geographers, and naturalists. Starting out to catalog the flora and fauna of little-known and remote regions of the empire, to collect physical and astronomical data, the work of these men had the effect of bringing to public notice the rich diversity of the Russian land. Men like P. B. Inokhodtsov (1742–1806) and N. Ya. Ozeretskovski (1750–1827), S. P. Krashenninikov (1712–1755), and I. I. Lepekhin (1740–1802), were not yet sufficiently specialized in their fields to restrict themselves to the recording of scientific data. They traveled across their fatherland with wide-open eyes, with wonder and curiosity. They observed and recorded local customs and folkways, historical monuments and tales along the Volga and the Urals, on Lakes Ladoga and Onega, in the environs of St. Petersburg and Astrakhan with the same thirst for knowledge and impartial accuracy they brought to the collection of plants and minerals. Neither literary doctrine nor social prejudice could keep their journals and records from noting the humble detail of everyday life in all parts of the country. Beginning with Krashenninikov's "Description of Kamchatka," (1755), they made a valuable contribution to the knowledge of Russians about themselves and to a more serious and tolerant attitude towards the lowly records of their culture. Most of these diaries appeared in the years from 1771 (Lepekhin) to the first decade of the next century and their publication coincided with the first decisive signs of that interest in folklore which they had helped to stimulate and nourish.[58]

Curiosity about the exotic and the wonderful and the wish to know more about the customs and practices which had remained untouched by the town, combined to call attention to parts of the national heritage which had never yet been the serious concern of writers and scholars. Journals asked their readers for contributions of folk tales and fables and included in their pages materials on old-Russian mythology, popular verse, descriptions of wedding and christening ceremonies. The collecting of riddles and proverbs became almost a national pastime. As was the case with songs, proverbs seem never to have gone out of favor among the educated classes, and a number of manuscript collections, dating from the early part of the century, are known. Proverbs also made their appearance in manuals of style, on the stage, in periodical literature, and in the dictionary of the Russian Academy. The first of many collections, the "4291 Old Russian Proverbs" of A. A. Barsov, a professor at Moscow University, appeared in 1770. Another, "Sayings and Proverbs of the Plain Folk" (1798), was distinguished for the faithful reproduction of its originals.[59] The most ambitious attempt of this kind was the collection made by the poet Ippolit Bogdanovich. Undertaken on the suggestion of the Empress Catherine herself, it was clearly intended to serve the purposes of official nationalism. Joined to a love for the familiar in everyday life and speech was a conviction that these sayings revealed those qualities of the national character which Catherine wished to see. To Catherine, definition of the national character had become particularly important since Fonvizin had first raised the question in 1783. The Empress, asked what constituted the national character, could only give a rather evasive and mechanical reply: "A quick and accurate understanding of things, exemplary obedience, and adherence to all the virtues given to man by his Creator." [60]

This, clearly, was not a definition of the characteristics which uniquely singled out Russians from all other people. It was a wish or a warning, not a description based on Russia's culture or history. In Bogdanovich, Catherine perhaps felt she had found a man who could answer Fonvizin's question more satisfactorily, yet in a spirit of loyalty and obedience to her ultimate purpose. The author of a verse treatment of the Amor and Psyche story into which he had introduced figures from Russian fairy tales did not disappoint the Empress' expectations. His proverb collection, published in 1785, could serve as a record both of the nation's genius and of the loyalty and piety of Catherine's subjects. These qualities Bogdanovich illustrated by dividing his material into several sections with titles supplied by him: duty to country and tsar, piety, respect for one's superiors, and forbearance were the Russian traits which Bogdanovich saw in the proverbs. He cited the fact that they had been handed down by word of mouth from generation to generation, that they were found in old manuscripts and current usage, among the plain people and the upper classes, as evidence that they truly reflected the nation's heart and soul. "I fondly hope," he wrote in his preface, "that the nation's own product, here appearing in print, will find favor in its eyes." [61] Since aesthetic predilections made it impossible for Bogdanovich to leave the proverbs in their pristine form the collection was as much his creation as it was that of Russia. Catherine, in any case, was pleased.

One form of folklore interest in which the national component was particularly strong was the discovery or creation of a national mythology. Russia's early mythologists, Chulkov and Popov in the eighteenth century, G. A. Glinka and A. S. Kaisarov in the nineteenth, wanted to discover an age of fable for Russia, a process which has been likened to the emergence of national states out of the Holy Roman Empire or the development of national languages with the decline of Latin.[62] Almost everywhere in Europe the gods and heroes of classical antiquity were losing out to local deities, legendary bards, and warriors. Fingal and Ossian, Perun, Votan, and Valhalla took the place of Odysseus, Homer, Zeus, and Mt. Olympus. Czechs, Russians, Norwegians, Germans, and Englishmen tried to discover their own pantheons, and in the tales, songs, and epics of their people the records of the lives and deeds of the heroes of old. Where these could not be found, the conviction was so strong that they must at one time have existed that writers did not fail to create them. Scientific accuracy was not yet part of the collector's code, as folkloristics or ethnography were not yet firmly established disciplines with a methodology of their own.

Invention and history, fantasy and folklore were rather

freely mixed in the mythological "researches" of Russian writers. The mythological notes to Chulkov's "Scoffer or Slavic Tales" (1766–1768) are an early example of the type of approach employed. The tales themselves were a curious assembly of comic and satiric essays, adaptations of Western tales of romance, chivalry, and magic, of sketches and tales of the author's own invention, some few of which had distant roots in Russian folk tales. However little they had in common with genuine folklore, Chulkov wanted the contents of his book to be regarded as "Slavic" tales, and the deeds of Russian *bogatyrs* as the equivalents of the Western romances and chivalry.

What Charles was for Western Europe, Vladimir the Great was for Russia. Like the former, this great Prince brought glory to his name through wars, victories, and the expansion of his lands. . . . It was this which caused Russian writers to select Vladimir's court as the locale for the wonderful exploits of our ancient heroes. As Roland, Oliver, Rinaldo, Amadis and others distinguished themselves by their incredible feats, astounding strength, and courage at the courts of Charles and Arthur, so Dobrynya Nikitich, Ilya Muromets, Churilo Plenkovich and others stand out among the mighty heroes of that time. In the Russian epic tales, just as in those of the French and the Italians, fairies and sorcerers play an important role; here too dragons are conquered, beauties liberated, and enchanted castles destroyed.[63]

The demand for a national pantheon remained unsatisfied by the bits of mythology which Chulkov had included in his tales. Both he and Mikhail Popov, author of a songbook and a collection of "Slavic Antiquities" (1770–1771), hastened to meet this demand. In 1767 Chulkov published a "Short Mythological Lexicon," followed a year later by Popov's "Short Description of the Pagan Legends of the Ancient Slavs." Neither of the two authors was especially concerned with accuracy but each wanted to supply the Russian public with its own mythical antiquity. Popov made a revealing confession of his aims and methods in a preface to the second edition

(1772) of his "Short Description." To scholars, he was sure, his sources would be known in any case, whereas "this work has been prepared more for the enjoyment of readers than for historical reference; and more for poets than for historians." A national literature needed a national mythology, but this did not, even in the eyes of Popov, justify complete fantasy. The first edition of his work contained indications of a some-what more serious approach, and mentioned the sources on which he had relied: "The ancient Slavo-Russian chronicle, the Russian history of the late Mr. Lomonosov, the history of the origins of the Slav people by Mavrourbin, Archimandrite of Ragusa; several Russian chronicles in manuscript, folk tales, songs, games and certain surviving customs." [64] Compared with the free play which Glinka still allowed his imagination in "Ancient Religion of the Slavs" (1801), Popov's was a relatively advanced position. The composition of a hymn to Perun, the Slavic Zeus, was only one of the ways in which Glinka filled what he considered "gaps and deficiencies" in the sources.[65]

Perun, Lada, Lel, Zimtserla, and Svetovid constantly gained in popularity, displacing Jupiter, Venus, Amor, Aurora, and Apollo from the Russian scene. Their discoverers and origi-nators kept them always before the public. In 1769, Chulkov again published mythological information in his magazine "This and That." In two later works, the "Dictionary of Russian Superstitions" (1782) and the "ABC of Russian Super-stitions" (1786), he included a great deal of material on Slavic deities and the rites connected with their worship. This vast store of ethnographic lore was still useful to scholars in the latter part of the nineteenth century. The Russian superstitions of Chulkov's titles included those of non-Russian nationalities as well and his "Dictionary" impartially described the rites and customs of Russians, Mordvinians, Bashkirs, Cheremiss, Kal-myks, Kirghiz, Chuvash, and Tatars alike. Although Chulkov paid tribute to the spirit of the century by expressing the pious hope that his little volume would help to drive these shameful superstitions from the face of an otherwise enlightened world, his real attitude was much more tolerant. "The polytheism, idolatry, and superstition of the ancient Slavs . . . are the same as among other peoples of the world, and error, therefore must be assumed to be the same everywhere. . . ." [66] His tolerance for the most part, however, stemmed from a recognition of the audience's taste for the strange, the wondrous, and the entertaining.

It was this which prompted the publication of the many "Russian Tales," "Genuine Russian Tales," and "Russian Narratives" which appeared and reappared after 1770. They were designed to meet the demands of a growing circle of readers of the merchant class and the petty gentry whose tastes had been formed by the popular chapbooks. Added to this basic commercial fact was the preference on the part of authors and readers alike for seeing their heroes and heroines, their sorcerers and demons, perform in native dress and on Russian soil. In addition to Western romances and picaresque novels and the classical and oriental tales which found their way into these collections, the writers turned also to genuine Russian folk sources and to Russian history and mythology for the local color which was so much in demand. V. A. Levshin in his "Russian Tales" (1780–1783) carried even further than Popov and Chulkov the Russification of Slavic mythology, and the invention of a Slavic historical geography.

Diffident about launching into the world stories which "could be heard in every low inn," Levshin sought to justify himself by pointing to similar French and German publications. His diffidence revealed a half-serious, half-apologetic attitude towards the stories which circulate among the people; a belief that in spite of their lowly origin, they might contain useful information about the manners and mores of the masses. Genuine folk motifs and materials were introduced together with the kind of fantastic contrivances which Chulkov and

Popov had used. The theme which runs throughout the collection is that of national pride. Russia too has her heroes and heroic legends which are in no way inferior to those of the West and their records will prove equally impressive. Only time was needed to revive the knowledge of Russia's ancient heroes, "of whom there must have been a great many among a people renowned in the world for its bravery. . . ." [67] The stories and poems of Levshin's "Russian Tales" were to prove the existence of chivalry in early Russia, and he described the orders of knighthood to which the bogatyrs belonged, their vows, their battles and conquests in an indiscriminate mixture of fact and fantasy. In the absence of a native literary tradition which Levshin could have made the basis of his tales, he was forced either to turn to the oral tradition or to Russify materials which had originated outside of Russia. He did both. Using the models, the stylistic example, the names, and places furnished by the bylina and the folk tale, he wove them, together with the picaresque and knightly tales of the West, into a whole which he further nationalized by a largely pseudo-Slav mythology, history, and geography.

The influence of Chulkov, Popov, and Levshin in calling attention to Russia's heroic age and in popularizing its tales and poems, soon made itself felt in the speed with which their themes, gods, and heroes found their way into literature. The charm which Russia's past exercised on Catherine and Krylov, Lvov, Kheraskov, Derzhavin, Radishchev, Zhukovski, and even Pushkin, was an early form of Russian romanticism. But for the time being the taste for "heroic songs" and "bogatyr tales," stimulated by Chulkov and Levshin had to be satisfied by invention. When Kheraskov (*Bakhariyana*, 1803) or Derzhavin (*Dobrynya*, 1804) inaccurately informed their readers that their subject matter was "drawn from Russian folk tales" or "all the events taken from history, folk tales and songs," they were not so much stating a fact as a program.

In 1795 these inventions were overshadowed by the discovery of a truly national epic. It bore all the characteristics of folk poetry which literature was striving so hard to imitate. The discovery of *The Lay of Igor's Host* was the culmination and the justification of the hesitant folkloristic and historical tendencies of the century. It was as pleasing to national pride as it was significant for literature and history. Count Musin-Pushkin, the Chief-Procurator of the Holy Synod, did not altogether stumble on the manuscript of the Igor Tale by accident, for he had long been interested in the collection and publication of Russian antiquities, an interest which the contemporary literary orientation had undoubtedly helped to form. Though not published until 1800, news of the Tale's existence soon spread, and Karamzin proudly made it known in the *Spectateur du Nord* of Hamburg in 1797:

> We have songs and romances which are two or three centuries old, where the most touching, the most simple expressions of love and friendship can be found. . . . We also have old romances of chivalry (whose heroes are, for the most part, the generals of Prince Vladimir, our Charlemagne), and fairy tales, several of which deserve to be called poems. But what may surprise you even more is that there was unearthed, two years ago, in our archives, the fragment of a poem, entitled the 'Song of the Warriors of Igor,' which may perhaps be placed side by side with the best pieces of Ossian, and which was written in the twelfth century by an unknown author. . . .[68]

In Prince Vladimir, Russia saw her Charlemagne; in the Igor Tale she had found her *Chanson de Roland*.

The "Russian Peasant" was an essential element in nineteenth-century discussions of Russia's past or present, her destiny, her mission, and her character. Whether he bore the conservative features of Konstantin Leontiev's "bearded Orthodox muzhik," who would defend and extend Orthodox tsardom; or served as the Slavophiles' embodiment of the communal spirit; whether he was Herzen's motive force of history, regenerating an exhausted Europe; the object of admiration on the part of Populists; or Dostoevski's God-bearing man, social and political thought was occupied with him to an extraordinary degree. Russians, insofar as they tried to arrive at a definition of the national character and its unique elements, had in one or another way to come to terms with the peasant as a phenomenon of Russian reality.

Out of these discussions there emerged a portrait which most often showed the Russian peasant to be a man of impetuous generosity, in love as in anger, of true radicalism and humanity, of deep religiosity and loyalty. All of these traits were in sharp contrast with the petty, formalistic, and accumulative instincts of Western man—bourgeois and peasant alike. The sources of this portrait were in many cases the result of a disappointment in the West and a vision held for Russia. But it had roots also in the eighteenth century, when the conversion of the contemptible serf into the symbol of national pride was first begun.

In the nineteenth century, a nationalist theory which would have denied rights of citizenship to the peasantry, and would have left a cosmopolitan upper class to be the sole carrier and expression of nationality, might have been conceivable, but not easily defensible. The empirical fact alone that peasantry and "people" were almost identical in fact and linguistic usage made that impossible. It is for this reason that any search for the sources of Russian nationalism must begin by tracing the changes which made it possible for the Russian folk and the Russian peasant to emerge as the truest embodiments of the national character.

The literature of sensibility which towards the end of the eighteenth century stressed the humanity of the lower orders reinforced an earlier, more political and utilitarian view, that the rights and duties of citizenship must be shared by all; that privileges, if they existed, could be justified only by special exertions on behalf of the nation. This view, not unnaturally, first appeared during the reign of Peter the Great who tried to implant firmly in Russian soil Western concepts of the state, of society, and of citizenship, and who in at least one regard created equality among Russians by imposing state service on all subjects alike. The idea of service to the state and society, of civic duties incumbent on all, was constantly propagated by the Emperor and his fellow-reformers. Peter himself ordered the translation of Pufendorf's "On the Duties of Man and the Citizen" and, characteristically, advised the translator to ignore the same author's treatise "On the Christian Faith." [69] The whole secularizing, statist trend of Peter's political outlook tended to favor the inclusion of the lower classes in his definition of subject and citizen. The peasants, equally with all others, were subjects of Peter's service state and as such took the subject's oath. The implications of such a view, which in Western Europe played a significant role in the development of revolutionary and liberal nationalism, did not come to fruition in Russia. The exclusion, in 1741, of serfs from the subject's oath,[70] the policy of Peter's successors towards the peasants, marked a retreat from the relatively advanced position of his time and illustrates the contradictions which in Russia made such a development impossible. But for all the deterioration in the legal and economic condition of the peasant, the view that he, like his master, stood in a direct relation to the state never disappeared entirely.

The premise of Peter's contemporary I. T. Pososhkov, that the *pomeshchik* was not the permanent owner of the serfs, that he was only their temporary master and that they had been entrusted to him for the performance of specific tasks, where-as their immediate and sovereign master was the Russian autocrat, was in substance restated whenever the legal and human condition of the peasant was defended. Nor was the basis of the argument which Pososhkov employed changed significantly. Since the peasant is not the master's property, but is only given to him in trust, by and for the sovereign and the nation, the master has no right to dispose of him as fancy dictates. He must deal with him according to the Tsar's will so that the peasants may be real peasants, not beggars, "for the well-being of the peasantry is the well-being of the kingdom." [71]

Whatever variations or more modern notes on this basic theme might be introduced, the transcendent welfare of the nation, overriding class interest, remained the most telling argument. When in May 1768, Catherine's Grand Commission debated a number of proposals dealing with runaway serfs, a deputy of the gentry of Kozlovsk, Grigori Korobin, opposed them on the ground that by threatening the peasantry with ruin, they equally threatened the state. Only there, said Korobin, does a society flourish where its members are satisfied with the arrangements under which they live. This is what makes for public tranquility, this is what fires the citizen's heart in the defense of his fatherland. "And since it is well known that the peasantry is the soul of society, consequently the whole of society must weaken if that soul be kept in weakness." [72] Although still confined to a small minority, there was a growing recognition that society had an obligation to those who bore the greatest share of burdens. [73]

Acceptance of the fact that "the same blood, the same bones, the same flesh" were to be found in noble and serf alike, [74] was remote from a conclusion which saw the peasant as the legal or social equal of the landowner. But sympathy for the peasant and disapproval of his excessive exploitation was neither insignificant nor insincere. If in much of eighteenth-century writing, the peasant remained a lesser brother, it was a fact of some importance that he was considered a brother at all.

In this respect, Russian thought was no more in conflict with itself than the more advanced thought of the West. If anything, Sumarokov, Fonvizin, and Shcherbatov were possibly more humane than Voltaire who, though willing to admit that "we are all human beings," could also deny that "we are all alike members of society." People (*populace*) to him meant rabble, oxen who need a yoke, a driver, and fodder.

The denial of equality, of full civil and human rights to the peasantry on the part of Sumarokov, Fonvizin, or Shcherbatov, must be viewed against the background of their exalted notions of the duties imposed by noble rank. To extend the rights of the nobility to the common people, when these had not yet developed a sense of their own dignity, would not have made sense to these writers. Their attempts to imbue the nobility with a consciousness of class, were designed as much to educate it as to protect the serfs. In the ideal society, in which every class is bred to its duties to the common weal, where legislation is based on natural law, class distinctions become less important, class lines are apt to grow less sharp. In Russia, however, the social orders must be kept separated. Here, the base people have as yet no noble feelings (Sumarokov), here only the gentry is honorable and born to serve (Fonvizin) and the lower orders must be kept from contact with education, lest they rebel against their lot (Shcherbatov).

This did not, as indicated, prevent these gentry spokesmen from lashing out with vigor against the misdeeds of their own class. Inordinate pride, sloth, abuses of power, exploitation of serfs, were frequent targets. Indirectly, at least, these criticisms amounted to sponsorship of their inferiors. In the description of a dream, "The Happy Society," which appeared in Sumarokov's magazine "The Diligent Bee" (December 1759) and was most probably written by him, a society which did allow of greater tolerance was depicted. "People there are neither of noble nor of mean birth and excel on the basis of rank which they receive for their worthiness, and the son of a peasant has as much right to become a great lord as the son of the first magnate." [75] Similarly, in the happy "lands beyond the sea" of his "Chorus to a Corrupt World," the peasants are not skinned by their masters, nor are they sold and gambled away. "Beyond the seas there are no idlers, all work and all serve the fatherland." [76] In Shcherbatov's own land beyond the sea, the kingdom of Ophir, the government and laws of the country can be freely discussed by all citizens and their opinions will be heard with respect by their rulers. For preserve us, says one of the officials of the kingdom, from the false belief that all understanding is found in the heads of a small number of people of high rank. The ruler and his advisers are accessible to people of all stations, at all times, and the great courtiers are so devoid of arrogance that every citizen may demand to see them at will.

The reiteration of the theme that the greater the noble's worldly position, the greater his obligation to defend and protect his inferiors, shows how painfully conscious Shcherbatov and Sumarokov were that the Russian gentry had not yet made *noblesse oblige* its guiding principle. There was also the underlying fear that unless their class proved itself worthy of its privileges, it might well lose them. What is a noble, asked Shcherbatov in a "Letter Addressed to the Nobles who rule the State," but a man who by birth, by his deserts or by chance has been raised above all his follow-men, brought near to the throne and enriched with the nation's treasures? His elevation, the Prince warned, signified that he who was raised must excel in virtue, not in rank alone, work for the general good and repay Tsar and people with service, honesty, and the protection of the people's interest.[77]

The concern that each class should live up to its social obligations and that "all callings and classes are alike necessary to the state and must find a lawful existence," [78] was uppermost in the minds of Sumarokov's generation. The next generation, which made its debut in the intellectual life of the country around 1770, differed in its attitude towards the people. This was the period of Catherine's early liberalism, of the satirical journals, of new and powerful foreign influences bringing echoes of the enlightenment and of freemasonry, the age of Novikov and Radishchev. It was the generation which read Diderot as well as Voltaire, and showed a willingness to evaluate man in human and moral terms, not alone for his service to society. Virtue, delicacy of feeling, uprightness, honesty in dealing with one's fellow-men now became as important as the civic virtues—duty, honor, service. The latter had always been thought of as the ornament of the nobility at its best, whereas the private virtues might flourish just as well in the narrower sphere of merchant, artisan, or peasant. As the ode and the classical tragedy began to give way to more intimate poetic forms in literature, so a warmer, more emotional tone began to appear in the approach to the common people.

The change was not a sudden one, and the apotheosis of the people was still in the future. The first new notes which presaged it could, however, be heard in the early years of Catherine's reign. In 1769 a weekly edited by Novikov and F. A. Emin (one of the first exponents of Russian sentimentalism), raised the issues posed by the relations of the classes in a lengthy article which tried to define what the essential quality of the plain folk was. Its author, pretending belief in the absolute inferiority of the lower classes, sought the reason for their benighted state. It was only too obvious: they live in hovels, rise early, plough the fields, mow, drain swamps, dig canals, build houses and, in short, supply every want of their betters, just as work horses or oxen do. Consequently, they have no aspirations higher than those of animals and lack the capacity of reason. By way of contrast, comfort, luxury, abundance, and leisure surround their well-born masters day and night. They can give real meaning to their lives and raise it above mere brutish existence, thanks to the reason with which they are so richly endowed. Reason helps them to devise new refinements, launches them into excess and manifests itself in the latest fashions, a new carriage, a stylish *kaftan*. The evidence then was incontrovertible; reason cannot be found among the lowly. But the more important question still remained to be asked.

Do the people have virtue? I do not know . . . since those who sing the praises of virtue in lyrical tones have never written an ode in honor of the peasant, nor of the nag with which he plows. But the people are patient and forbearing. They endure hunger, cold, heat, the contempt of the rich, the pride of the mighty, the landlord's depredations and the hostility of his steward. . . . Though it may be admitted that they are forbearing, I do not yet dare impute this to virtue, for virtue the nobility appropriate as theirs alone. Thus all I can do for the people is to call forbearance a good quality. For plain folk are irrational, just, faithful, and pious . . . without reasoning why or weighing possible benefit. Whereas noble folk never exert themselves without calculation.[79]

The writer finally turns to an anatomist for an answer which will decide what differences exist between men of low and of high birth. The anatomist finds the peasant's brain as well equipped for thought as that of the noble which is filled with trivialities. The people are equally endowed with reason, though prince and master assert the opposite. May the truth, still hidden by prejudice, but glimpsed by many, be revealed to those who oppress their fellow creatures.

Reason and good sense were qualities which the enlightened mind valued above all others. In this instance, the anatomist's microscope furnished the proof that the lower classes partook of them, but for Novikov no such naive, positivistic proof was alone valid. His impassioned *cris de coeur* on behalf of an oppressed peasantry made the possession of a soul as important a touchstone of man's humanity as the quality of reason. "He is the owner of two thousand souls," he wrote, "but is himself without a soul." That, by and large, was the conclusion at which he arrived about almost everyone of the nobles who mistreated their peasants and traced their family trees to the beginning of the universe. They hated all those who could not prove their aristocratic blood at least five hundred years back and bore such names as Lacksense, Hundredsnake, Honorlost, and Frivolous. Baseness was not a result of birth but of behavior, of a disposition of heart and soul over which the individual could exercise some moral choice. If the peasant had been depressed into base inhumanity, the fault was not his own, but that of the master who had tyrannized his fellowmen, abused virtue, and shown more love for horses and dogs than for human beings.[80]

It was not difficult to conclude from this, as later generations did, that the oppressed were less debased by their sufferings than the oppressors were by inflicting them. Misfortune had stripped its victims of the vanities and illusions of success and left them purer, more Christ-like, more humane. Every humanitarian or philanthropic instinct of the eighteenth century seems inevitably to point to such a conclusion. "Low, base," wrote Fonvizin in his satirical "Russian Dictionary," "means that a man is low in station, but base in soul. A man of low estate may have the noblest soul, just as the greatest lord may be the meanest man." [81] To the egalitarianism of civic duty there was now added an egalitarianism of moral obligation which could proclaim that a simple peasant is more estimable than a depraved prince, or that the peasant soul is as great as that of the greatest ruler, perhaps greater. "I have heard," sings the Rozana of Nikolev to the gentleman who pursues her, "that you love but for an hour while for peasant hearts, love knows no end." [82]

The strongest impulse for the idealization of the peasant came near the end of the century from the literary current known as sentimentalism. However remote it may have been from the peasant's real situation or character, however abstract its personification of rural virtue, it came closest to a declaration of the peasant's superiority in constancy and depth of feeling. It is not merely the repeated assertion that "peasants too have hearts," that "every peasant woman too knows how to feel," or that "peasants too know how to love," [83] but it is the implication, most likely unintended, that emotion among the poor runs deeper, stronger, and longer. Karamzin's "Poor Liza" (1792),[84] the most famous of all the Russian Héloises, is a case in point. The daughter of a "well-to-do villager," she lives quietly with her mother in the environs of Moscow, near the Simonov monastery. Impoverished by the death of her father, a sturdy, upright peasant, Liza does all within her power to comfort her mother who is inconsolable — "for peasant women too know how to love"—and to support her. Only fifteen years old, she spares neither her tender years nor her beauty: weaving and knitting, picking flowers in spring and berries in summer and selling the produce of her labor in Moscow. Bringing to town an armful of lilies of the valley, she is stopped one day by an elegant young gentleman. Demanding whether her flowers are for sale, he vows that the five kopeks she asks for them are less than she deserves. Liza modestly refuses to take more money for them. They part with the understanding that Liza, from now on, will sell her flowers only to the young gentleman. Liza returns to town next day with the most beautiful flowers she can find, and all day long refuses to sell them. When by nightfall, her young gentleman has not come to fetch them, Liza, true to her promise throws them into the Moscow river. "None shall own you," said Liza, feeling a sadness in her heart. The failure of Erast to keep his promise, Liza's abandonment of the flowers, her sadness, are the first forebodings of doom and of the tragic roles the two lovers are fated to play.

The next day, Erast appears at Liza's home. His modesty

and beauty completely win over her mother. "How good and kind he is, if only your bridegroom were like that. . . . But mother, how could that be? He is a barin." Young Erast is a rich landowner of good mind and heart, but weak and frivolous. Unable to find pleasure and diversion in society, he hopes to find relief from *ennui* in simplicity and isolation. The two fall violently in love. Liza breaks her engagement to the son of a rich peasant and Erast promises to marry her. Soon he tires of his pastoral idyll, and sees Liza less and less frequently, until finally he tells her that he has been called to active war duty. Liza believes him and bids him a tearful farewell. Some two months later she sees him driving by in a carriage and runs after him into his house. Erast receives her coldly, tells her that he has gambled away most of his estate and is going to marry a rich widow in order to pay his debts. He gives Liza a hundred rubles and has her escorted out of the house by a servant. Liza, in desperation, returns to the scenes of their happiness and drowns herself. Her mother, hearing of her daughter's fate, also dies. Erast is unhappy and oppressed by a sense of guilt for Liza's tragic end.

The discovery that peasants too know how to love, so often considered the central theme of Karamzin's tale, is only a casual addition to the character sketch of Liza's mother. It was a truth which had already been proclaimed by other, though perhaps less popular, authors. Much the most important achievement of Karamzin's sentimentalism is the creation of two literary archetypes, each fashioned by a distinct environment, whom the Russian reader was by now trained to identify. Erast is not only the younger brother of the gallants and worldlings of an earlier generation, a man who has been briefly stirred to sensibility, he is also the ancestor of the superfluous men of a later period who have not the strength to love or to live what they know to be the better life. He is without the lasting conviction of the courage which led him, momentarily, across lines of birth and class to seek strength and purity in the embraces of a peasant girl. Unable to follow his better feelings, for he is not evil, he falls back into the patterns which his upbringing and his environment have traced for him. Erast is incapable of giving himself fully. Karamzin makes that clear. Society, the habits of his class and station, have too strong a hold on him. On first meeting Liza, he cuts short their interview because the passersby are beginning to take notice, to laugh at the young barin talking to a peasant girl. He does not want Liza to tell her mother of their love, betraying an uncertainty about its permanence from the start.

Liza has no such doubts, or at least they do not lead her into a cautious reserve. Of the two, she alone, the peasant girl, knows how to love. There is no afterthought to her love. It is pure and steady, of one piece with the rest of her existence, which is composd of affection and work for those dear to her, both deeply rooted in her way of life. It is simple, God-fearing, and industrious, a Russian life; and, in fact, Karamzin in later editions, called the story of "Poor Liza" a Russian tale.

Although she is neither the first nor the last soulful heroine of the literature of sensibility, Liza was to become the most famous. Young men and women shed copious tears over her fate, went on sentimental pilgrimages of their own to the monastery near which she lived. They sought out the places where she and Erast had pledged their love, the pond where she had drowned herself, and in homage to her memory carved their initials into the birches on its shore. To the melancholy delight of her admirers, the events of Liza's life were repeated by an increasing number of Beautiful Tatyanas, Poor Mashas, Unhappy Margaritas, and Seduced Henriettas who appeared in print in the early nineties of the century.

In "Frol Silin, a Charitable Man," Karamzin, a short time before the appearance of "Poor Liza," had created the male counterpart of his heroine. In giving Frol pronounced Russian features, Karamzin intended to show that Russians knew how to appreciate the unsung deeds of little people. "Let Virgil sing the praises of the Caesars! Let the golden-tongued flatterers praise the generosity of the mighty, I want to laud Frol Silin, a simple peasant. . . ." What was it that Frol Silin had done? Why had Karamzin suggested that a monument be erected to him? In a time of famine he had been charitable and had helped his fellow peasants. The most enlightened nation of Europe, Karamzin said, has built a temple to honor the memory of her great men. To this temple, Frol Silin, a true benefactor of mankind, should be admitted as Russia's representative.[85]

Newspapers and magazines were filled with praises of the virtue and goodness of the simple people. "Russian Anecdotes," short sketches reporting deeds of love for humanity and fatherland on the part of soldiers and coachmen, peasants and burghers, were a prominent feature of the "St. Petersburg Mercury" and other journals. They bore such titles as "The Qualities of a Great Soul," "A Soldier of Sensibility," "Love for the Fatherland," "The Coachman," and "The Heroic Deed." These stories were designed not only to stress the sensibility of simple people but to show that they who were capable of such feelings were Russians.[86]

In his "Russian Pamela, or the History of Maria, the Virtuous Peasant" (1789), Pavel Lvov wanted to show that Russia too had "tender hearts, great souls, and noble sentiments in people of low station." In a characteristic line of reasoning which has ever been dear to nationalists, Lvov went a step further and claimed for Russia a greater number of Pamelas and Héloises than other countries possessed. In comparison with the West, Russia had preserved the purer morals of an earlier age. His Pamela is a woman without blemish, who had learned from her father that true education is an education of the soul, that it does not consist in idle chatter or modish pursuits. Pamela actually marries a gentleman, whose weakness, like Erast's, leads him to abandon her. He returns to her and to happiness, rejecting the cynicism of a friend who is without respect for virtue, man, or God. Pamela's incredible virtues provoked the skepticism of Lvov's readers and in the preface of a similar novel, published in 1790 and called "Roza and Lyubim, a Village Tale," Lvov defended his peasants with humanitarian and patriotic fervor. Only a lack of patriotism, he implied, could inspire doubts that peasants like Philip, Pamela's father, could be found in Russian villages. "I am astonished," he wrote, "how many sons of our sacred Russia can think that we have no such great souls, quick wit, and tender feelings in people of low origin." [87]

The extension of this literary convention to politics and social life was an almost foregone conclusion; the worship of the plain folk an almost inevitable outcome of the contempt in which it had been held. A peasantry less enserfed, less dehumanized, more like its ruling class than the Russian, could not so readily have been exalted as a national symbol, for it would more insistently have demanded recognition of its true character and needs. That was to happen towards the end of the nineteenth century. In the meantime, the question asked by one of Lvov's characters about men who are alike in soul and feeling—"in what, then, are we unequal"— was answered, in favor of the peasantry: in our Russianness.

## CHAPTER V

# The Uses of History

The close connection between the writing of history and the growth of nationalism is a commonplace in studies of either subject. Historiography played a major role in molding national consciousness and national aspirations at least as far back as the Renaissance. Just as they had once sought justification for dynastic or particularist claims in the antiquity and descent of their patrons, the writers of history could with equal ease provide impressive genealogical trees for whole nations when the nation-state became the focus of political thought and endeavor. The history which took for its subject the national community and the history which sought to call such a community into being—the national and the nationalist schools—both flourished most widely in the nineteenth century.

The eighteenth century appears at first to have been inhospitable to national and nationalist history. For the men of the Enlightenment, history was too often a record of stupidity, cruelty, and fanaticism, broken infrequently by periods in which the light of reason shone brightly, held high by men of taste and power. This overestimation of their own age on the part of the eighteenth-century rationalists caused them to apply their own standards of reason and progress to other historical periods. Oversimplified views of causality, a neglect of process and continuity led later generations to view them as antihistorical, narrowly rationalistic, and incapable of understanding the values intrinsic to other ages. The widely accepted nineteenth-century dogma of constant change and growth in a vital interplay of forces was, it is true, foreign to most historians of the eighteenth century, but they did not totally lack the historical sense. There has been a reappraisal of their attitudes to history and a more favorable verdict has been rendered.[1]

Limited as it may have been, the historical literature of the Enlightenment yet managed to overcome the narrow preoccupation of earlier writers with political history. It began to inquire into the manners and morals, the spirit of an age and to extend its range of interests to commerce and customs, letters and laws. Nor did it altogether neglect its civic and patriotic duty. Bishop Burnet wanted the study of history to inspire men with a zeal for the public; and Bolingbroke, expecting from it an improvement in private and public virtue, hoped that history would keep men's minds free from a ridiculous partiality in favor of their own country and a vicious prejudice against others; while creating in them a preference of affection for their own. There were, moreover, counter-currents to the prevailing emphasis of the age. In Italy, Gianbattista Vico was willing to concede to less enlightened ages worth and value of their own, each epoch playing an essential role in the preparation of the next. In Germany, men like Justus Moeser and J. G. Schmidt, in their studies of local history brought to light regional peculiarities which did not conform to the dominant standards of the age. Towards the end of the century, the strange and the novel, as well as the ancient, gained new respect and new meaning.

For Russians it was from the start difficult to share the enlightened bias of their Western contemporaries. They were always painfully aware of the fact that the Russian present was not nearly as enlightened as that of the West. To look back on their past, which still surrounded them at every step, as evil and barbaric would have been a denial of their

national identity. The impossibility of such a denial was force-
fully brought home to them by the condescension with which
most Westerners wrote about Russia. Looking down from the
heights of their achievement on this country still ridden by
priestcraft and superstition, Western historians saw in Russia
an earlier stage of history which they had long surpassed.
Goaded by Western slurs to the defense of their fatherland,
Russians tried to prove that their country was not as backward
as generally believed and that their past had been glorious. As
a result, even the most rationalistic of Russian historians
brought to their task a greater sympathy for the life of the
past than would have been likely in the West. Unable, with
full conviction, to hold up the Russian present for comparison,
Russia's defenders turned to her past with an understanding
born of hurt pride and necessity. The basic motive, then, for a
concern with history seems to have been the search for a
school of instruction and inspiration; its purpose, to show
Russians what a glorious future a glorious past promised them;
to show that Russia, no less than other countries, had produced
great men and that she was no Johnny-come-lately in the
family of nations.

A strong motive for creating a general awareness of the
national past was a dissatisfaction with the products of non-
Russian historians. These were felt to be hostile, ill-informed,
or lacking in true feeling for Russia and her fate. This was
Tatishchev's complaint about Poles and Germans as it was
Boltin's, Radishchev's, and Karamzin's. "Russia did not nourish
him," the latter wrote about Levesque, "no Russian blood
flows in his veins—can he speak about Russia with the same
kind of feeling as a Russian?" [2] Russians constantly complained
about being misunderstood and slandered abroad, a fact which
helps to explain extensive governmental sponsorship of historical work as well as the nature of some of the results. When
Lomonosov was told to write his history in an "artistic style,"

when the Academy instructed G. F. Mueller not to bother
with tedious researches and source materials, but to "write
history," the purpose was not to satisfy scholarship but a public
opinion which wanted to see tangible evidence of national
greatness. It is this alone which can explain the official support
and public acclaim given to works which were of dubious
scientific value.

In addition to these general causes which turned Russians
to the study of their history, there were at various times
throughout the century specific reasons which prompted historical research and historical mindedness. The development
of Russian historiography, as a factor of national consciousness, reflects closely the general evolution of Russian thought.
Three fairly distinct stages in this development may be noted.
In the first period, which coincides with the first third of the
century, a concern with history is primarily an outgrowth
of Peter's wish to create among a population which was indifferent or hostile to his work attitudes of civic pride and
responsibility. No less important in the Tsar's eyes were the
uses to which history could be put at home and abroad, serving
as justification for military and diplomatic action. Even the
most practical concerns of this period helped to foster the
study of history, for the government's need to know intimately
all phases of Russian reality inevitably led Peter and his collaborators from statistical and geographical to historical inves-
tigation, to the first attempts at orderly collection of the
sources and their description.

The middle decades of the century, almost entirely taken
up with disputes on the origins of the Russian state, illustrate
the degree to which academic and personal issues had become
questions of national pride and integrity. The Bironovshchina
had made Russians particularly sensitive to any real or presumed slight to the national honor, with the result that history
as scientific pursuit became almost an impossibility. It was this

period which left to later generations the irritating legacy of the "Norman controversy." It also produced the first projects for an institutional approach to the study of history.

The last stage proceeds to the solution of disputed questions —Russia's backwardness, her immaturity, her dependence on the West—with greater moderation and sophistication than had been the case in the preceding period. With Boltin, Russian historiography reached a new complexity by turning from a preoccupation with national origins to social and cultural history. It found more effective ways than mere protestations of national excellence to prove that the Russian past, in spite of similarities with the history of other European countries, revealed an independent devlopment which made it unnecessary to speak in terms of superiority or inferiority. The standards of comparison which had been set were no longer accepted indiscriminately. As the quality of historical work improved and government sponsorship increased, history became also a popular literary form. This fact insured that in future debates about Russia's fate, the record of her past would become the indispensable basis of discussion.

Russian historiography received its strongest impulse in the first decades of the century from Peter the Great. Contemporaries speak of the love and the curiosity with which the Tsar would peruse historical tracts and documents, a matter of literary taste which undoubtedly had its utilitarian side. For the "civil history" of Western origin which Peter had Gavriil Buzhinski translate not only entertained its readers, but also directed their thought into political channels, caused them to think about "nations and their origins, about settlements and migrations of populations, about the affairs of war and peace, the rise and fall of kingdoms." Peter's own interest in these matters had always been great. Perhaps he thought that to acquaint his subjects with them might make them more state-minded, more sympathetic to his goals. In 1711, his curiosity about the historical origins of the Slavs and their language grew so intense that he requested the Russian ambassador to Austria to ask for enlightenment on this point. At Vienna, Baron Urbich turned to Leibniz, who supplied him with a treatise on the subject which was sent on to Moscow.[3]

To Peter, it was a matter of course that a modern, secular state have a full record of its past and a native school of historians who could be called upon to support the political claims and intentions of the ruler. The Academy of Sciences which Peter had planned was to include a historian among its members so that the Tsar might avail himself of his services at any time. He was also of the opinion that Russian history should be written by Russians, for Dutchmen or Frenchmen, lacking access to the sources, were in no position to do justice to the subject. Most importantly, he believed that history would educate his subjects to the tasks of citizenship, and it is for this reason that Peter repeatedly and energetically called for a narrative record of the Russian state, "not of the beginning of the world or of other states." His own reading of the chronicles had taught him to recognize their value as source materials and had led him to think of their publication as early as 1703. But his practical sense also made him realize what an unmanageable job the writing of a full scale Russian history would be. The task given to Fedor Polikarpov in 1708 was limited to a more recent period of Russian history, beginning with the reign of Grand-Duke Vasili III. Even the more modest plan was difficult of achievement, and in 1712 Polikarpov had to be reminded that His Majesty was still waiting for his Russian history. A sample of the work was finally completed towards the end of 1715, but altogether failed to satisfy the Tsar. "I know," he said, "that the raw materials for a Russian history lie buried in cloisters and monasteries throughout the country. To save them from destruction, to give a talented historian the opportunity to write a true history of old Russia, that has long been my intention; but I have always been prevented from carrying it out." [4]

In December 1720, Peter issued a decree which was to make this intention a reality, a step of inestimable value to future historians. The decree instructed all governors and vice-governors to examine old letters-patent, original documents, and historical texts in every monastery, diocese, and cathedral, to copy them and to send these copies to the Senate. A decree of February 1722, went further. It provided that messengers be sent out by the Holy Synod to collect chronicles, chronographs, military and genealogical records in the provinces, to bring them to Moscow for copying and to deposit the copies in the synodal library. Though the results of these appeals remained for the time being meager—Pekarski notes that no more than forty manuscripts were reported to be in the Synod in 1730—they made clear the government's interest in materials of this kind and undoubtedly contributed to their more respectful treatment.

The comprehensive history for which Peter had clamored and for which he had begun the collection of materials never appeared during his lifetime, but the need for such a work was felt by others as well. A. T. Mankiev, secretary of the Russian ambassador at Stockholm, composed "The Kernel of Russian History" while a prisoner during the Northern War. He was inspired, Mankiev said, by Peter's deeds. Dedicated to the Tsar, his work was throughout patriotic in tone and intention. Unlike the *Sinopsis* of Innokenti Gizel (Kiev, 1674) which had relied heavily on Polish and Lithuanian sources, Mankiev tried to keep his work free of Polish data and to supplant them, wherever possible, with information gleaned from the

Russian chronicles. Full of anti-Polish and anti-Swedish sentiment, especially in the narration of the Time of Troubles,
Mankiev's "Kernel" carried the record of the Russian state
up to the year 1712. This was a period in which Russia's renewed brilliance and power contrasted comfortingly with the
description of her decline under the Tatars with which the
major portion of the *Sinopsis* concluded. This rebirth of Russia,
as Mankiev called it, was the work of Peter the Great, a
monarch whose deeds of glory and bravery excelled those
of Nebuchadnezzar, Cyrus, Alexander, and Ulysses. There
could be no doubt in Mankiev's mind, as there had not been
in Gizel's, of the etymology which happily derived the tribal
name of all the Slavs from the word glory (*slava*), and he
rejected with violence the notion that the Italian word *schiavo*
or *sclavo* had originated as a designation for Slavic prisoners
of war.* Not published until 1770 the "Kernel" remained for
many years the fullest and most accessible guide to Russian
history, though works of greater merit had already appeared.
Its patriotic tone and the fact that it dealt with the relatively
recent past insured its popularity; it was republished in 1784,
1791, and 1799.[5]

Disappointed in his hopes for a history of Russia, Peter
wanted at least to have as complete a record of his reign as
possible, and on a number of occasions he suggested that a
history of the Swedish War or of his entire reign be undertaken.** One of those entrusted with these labors was Peter's

* The debate over the etymology of the word Slav was still going on
in 1840 when Yakov Tolstoy, a Russian emigré in Paris who was expiating
a liberal past by furnishing reports to the Russian police, engaged in a heated
polemic with the French historian Alphonse Rabbe. The latter, Tolstoy
felt, had made too much of the similarity between *esclave* and Slav. The
Russian word for slave, Tolstoy pointed out, was *rab*.

** Of some moment, in Peter's mind, was foreign opinion of Russia and
her government. One of the "historians" employed by him to write on the
Swedish war and his reign was a Baron van Huyssen who acted as a kind
of public relations officer for the Tsar. An important part of his job was
to refute slanders circulating in Western Europe about Russia and her

collaborator in church matters, Feofan Prokopovich (1681–1736), Archbishop of Novgorod. Fully sharing the Emperor's pragmatic approach to the writing of history, Feofan did not need to be convinced of its didactic value. He preached the necessity of bringing to light the forgotten deeds of the fatherland so that enemies and friends alike might learn of Russia's valor and her sons be inspired to glorious deeds by the example of their ancestors. He was the first Russian author to employ a theme from Russian history in a dramatic composition (the tragicomedy "Vladimir," performed in Kiev in 1705) and the first to introduce into a course of rhetoric a section dealing with the writing of history. He also turned his talents to historical composition and compiled a "Genealogical Table of the Grand-Dukes and Tsars of Russia to Peter I" (1717) as well as a "Short History of Peter" (date unknown).[6]

Feofan felt that the main reason why Russians knew so little of their past was the lack of trained writers whose main occupation was the compilation of an historical record. As long as government clerks or archbishops only occasionally, and on the urging of higher authority, devoted themselves to history, the result would necessarily be spotty and unsatisfactory. The sustained effort necessary for an intimate familiarity with materials and methods had not yet been made and could not be made so long as the occupation with history was an amateurish, part-time affair, called forth by the immediate needs or wishes of government. The study and writing of history as a long-range enterprise, which alone could assure a permanent historical culture, did not really begin in Russia until it was undertaken by German scholars who devoted themselves to it entirely. But there was one man, a practical administrator of Peter's school, Vasili Nikitich Tatishchev

---

political intentions. One of the targets of the Baron's polemical activity not incorrectly called him "His Tsarish Majesty's Pasquillant." (Pekarski, *Nauka i literatura*, I, 65.)

(1686–1750) who came as close to fulfilling the requirements
of scholarship as was possible for one so deeply engaged in the
everyday business of government.

The factors which induced Tatishchev to add history to
his many other pursuits reflected, as did Peter's own activities,
the practical needs of the times and the wish to bring to his
countrymen a record of their past greatness. "The cause for
my undertaking this labor was Count Bruce," Peter's artillery
expert, under whom Tatishchev had served. Bruce was the
first Russian to attempt a full geographical survey of the
empire, a work whose usefulness to a well-ordered state was
fully appreciated. When the pressure of other work forced
him to abandon his geography, it fell to Tatishchev to carry
it on alone. In the process he became convinced of the impossibility of doing so without a wider and more accurate
range of historical information than was available. But his main
reason for the continuation of his historical work was the wish
to "pay proper tribute to the eternal glory and memory of . . .
Peter the Great . . . as well as to honor and glorify my beloved
fatherland." [7] Although Tatishchev did not actually settle
down to the writing of his history until 1729, the decade which
elapsed since he was first entrusted with Bruce's task was filled
with the preparatory steps of collecting and sifting the necessary materials. Intensive study of the sources, visits abroad,
contact with foreign scholars and their work, impressed him
with the confused state of knowledge on the antecedents of
the modern Russian state. He therefore saw it as his main duty
to bring order into all this confusion, to cleanse what had been
written about Russia of impurities and inaccuracies caused
by prejudice and ignorance.

In Tatishchev's eyes, the writing of a Russian history was
preeminently a Russian task. For in spite of the danger of
partiality, it was the only way of avoiding yet greater partiality and of making certain that "the lies and fables invented

by our enemies, the Poles and others, for the sake of disparaging our ancestors, may be laid bare and contradicted." Even an unprejudiced foreigner, "through a lack of comprehension of many circumstances," and an unfamiliarity with the language, was likely to err. A Russian history, written by Russians, was a necessity not only for an accurate knowledge of their own history but so that all of Europe, "the whole learned world," might be informed of the true state of affairs.

> European historians accuse us of having no old history, and of knowing nothing of our antiquity, simply because they do not know what historians we possess. Though some have made a few extracts, or have translated a passage here and there, others, thinking that we have none better, despise them. Some of our own ignorant writers agree, while those who do not wish to trouble themselves by looking into the ancient sources or who do not understand the texts have, ostensibly to give a better explanation but in reality to hide the truth, invented fables of their own and have thus obscured the real facts. . . .[8]

Tatishchev's hope of having an English translation of his "Russian History" published by the Royal Society of London, through the good offices of Jonas Hanway, an English merchant he had met at Astrakhan,[9] was part of a larger ambition which he shared with Peter—of presenting to Europe a favorable picture of the state of learning and civilization in Russia.

When Tatishchev finally submitted a first draft of his history to the Academy of Sciences in 1739, it was fully as cumbersome as the title it received on publication: "The History of Russia from the Oldest Times, Collected and Described by the Indefatigable Labor of Thirty Years by the sometime Councilor, and Governor of Astrakhan, Vasili Nikitich Tatishchev." Aside from the fact that publication did not begin until 1768–69 (for the first volume; the remainder appeared in 1773, 1774, 1784, and 1848), the very scope and bulk of the work would have made it inaccessible to all but the most dedicated students of their country's history. The specialists of the

Academy, among them Lomonosov and Mueller, utilized the work in manuscript, so that it did not remain altogether without influence even before publication. Due primarily to Mueller's efforts and the interest of the Empress Catherine most of the "History" was published in the eighteenth century, enabling Shcherbatov, Boltin, and others to benefit by the labors of its author.

Its very virtues—extensive reproduction of the sources without substantial alterations of style and language—condemned it to a cold reception on the part of the general public, which preferred to take its history with considerable literary embellishment. Tatishchev had explicitly disavowed any intention of entertaining or edifying his readers, and had decided to let the old writers and records speak in their own way. As a factor which helped shape a historical awareness among the larger public, it can consequently have been of only limited importance. It is significant primarily for calling attention, among an audience which already shared Tatishchev's interests, to national history and its sources and for demonstrating that national consciousness need not be identical with a narrow-minded xenophobia. To the historical discussions of later generations it contributed the statement of a number of controversial issues which agitate Russians to the present day. These were the questions of the ethnic origins of the Russian people; the foundation of the Russian state; the degree of enlightenment among the ancient Slavs; and the problem whether there was, historically speaking, a best, a traditional form of government for Russia, prescribed for her by history.

In his exposition of the tribal history of ancient Russia, which occupies chapters nine through thirty of part two of his first volume, Tatishchev showed himself free of the cruder forms of academic nationalism and refused to follow the time-honored custom of tracing the descent of various peoples from the sons of Noah. Instead, he took up the history of those peoples, particularly the Scythians and the Sarmatians, whose past had an immediate relevance to the origins of Slavic and Russian history. He dealt extensively with their divisions, migrations and relations with one another; speculated at length on their origins and names; and connecting the ethnographic picture of the Russia of his time with that of antiquity, concluded that two main groups constituted the ethnic stock of old Russia: the resident Slavs, whom he derived from the Scythians, and the immigrant Russes, whom he traced to the Finnish Sarmatians. He cited Herodotus and Strabo, Pliny the Younger and Claudius Ptolemy, Constantine Porphyrogenitos, and the Russian chronicles for the information they contained on the territory and the peoples of ancient Russia who march past the readers' eyes in a bewildering array of names and facts.

Tatishchev accepted the Norman theory of the foundation of the Russian state and incorporated into his text its first scientific formulation, G. S. Bayer's *De Varagis* (chapter 32). Though he regarded Varangian rule over the Slavs as rightful and politically beneficial—Rurik, according to Tatishchev, had received his power from Gostomysl, the last of the Slav rulers of Novgorod—he found that it had weighed heavily on the native Slavs and viewed it as an interruption of their organic cultural development. It was this, perhaps, which led him to reject the hypothesis of a Slavic origin for the Varangian princes, whose home he placed in Finland. In a subsequent chapter devoted to the Slavs, Tatishchev established that they had settled in their present habitations long before they were mentioned by Roman or Byzantine writers. They were a people as old as any other, whose ancestors were the Amazons (or *alazony*), a Slavic tribe whose Greek name means brilliant or glorious (*slavny*). For all his critical acumen, Tatishchev also fell victim to the etymological habits of the age, especially where these reflected credit on Russia's antecedents. Another such instance was his explanation of the Slavic origin of the name *Moisei* (Moses) as a composite of two Slavic words spoken by Pharaoh's daughter on finding the basket of reeds: *moi sei*—he is mine. Beyond appearing to prove the wide extent of Slavic influence in biblical times, this derivation also lent support to his belief in the great antiquity of the Slavs which compared favorably with that of the ancient Hebrews and Egyptians. Tatishchev's description of the Slavonic language as a kind of *lingua franca* of the Byzantine Empire has been mentioned; its spread to non-Slavic peoples was evidence of a political and cultural renaissance, the resumption of a development interrupted by the Varangians. The linguistic vitality of the Russian Slavs also enabled him to contrast the growth of their culture and power with the decline suffered by other Slavic nations.[10]

What was the reason for this difference in development? Was it the greater endowment of the Russian Slavs, was it fortune or geographical accident? For Tatishchev, the confirmed opponent of the oligarchs in 1730, the answer was supplied by Russia's political history, where periods of strength and greatness were inevitably those periods when a strong sovereign ruled, while weakness and disunity were the outcome of dynastic or aristocratic division. This conception was implicit in the periodization employed, and was spelled out in the chapter which dealt with the origins of civil society and of monarchy. The division of Russian history into three periods was designed to show the permanence and the benefits of undivided authority, to demonstrate "how much more useful to our state monarchy is than all other forms, and how it increases the wealth, the power, and the glory of the state, while others diminish and ruin it." [11] The first period of Russian history, ending in 1132, had been one of absolute rule. It had been confirmed, not begun, by Rurik who merely inherited it from the legendary princes `of Novgorod. The second period, from the death of Mstislav II to Ivan III (1462), had been one of weakness and decline, the rule of local princes who had lost sight of the common welfare, an age in which the rise of an aristocracy was accompanied by the disintegration of the body politic. The last division, beginning with the accession of Ivan III, represented the full restoration of monarchic power, the shedding of the Tatar yoke, the return of unity and prosperity. In reverting to the problem of government in a later section of the first volume, Tatishchev restated his opposition to the elective-aristocratic principle because it had led not only to the decline of Russia in the second period of her history, but to the fall and the enslavement of the Assyrian, Egyptian, Persian, Roman, and Greek monarchies as soon as the power of their rulers had been limited. The lesson which history, and most immediately Russian history, had to offer was clear. Tatishchev, and in his view Peter, had mastered it.

Progress, in Tatishchev's scheme, could be quite objectively measured by determining which of the three stages of enlightenment a nation had achieved. The invention of an alphabet, the acceptance of the Christian religion and its teachings, and the introduction of printing were the three way stations to the attainment of universal reason. Which of these had Russia passed? How did her rate of progress compare with that of other peoples? The question was an important one to Tatishchev, and in surveying his evidence one feels an unconscious selectivity at work which favored answers saving to pride and patriotism. The first fact to be established was the antiquity of letters among the Slavs, to refute the assertion of those (among them Bayer) who had assumed their late development. "As far as the art of writing among the Slavs in general, but more specifically among the Russian Slavs, is concerned, the notion, spread by foreign writers, that they had no written records before the time of Vladimir [980–1015] is incorrect.

Writing was known to the Slavs long before Vladimir. . . ." [12]
The existence of an old-Russian law (the *Russkaya Pravda*),
dating back even further, bore this out. Having enjoyed the
benefits of literacy, the Slavs must also have had historical
records, now lost, which were employed in the writing of the
ancient chronicles. Even Tatishchev could not deny the fact
of paganism in ancient Russia, but its admission was made
easier for him by a relativism which lessened the burden of
backwardness and ignorance in the absence of a higher moral
standard. "Not knowing evil, it is difficult to arrive at a correct
understanding of good, just as it is difficult to recognize white-
ness without a notion of its opposite." [13] Even his best en-
deavors on behalf of the Slavs could not, however, make him
accept the legend that their conversion had been effected by
the Apostle Andrew, come to Kiev for that purpose. Enlightened skepticism here proved itself the stronger instinct. The
introduction of printing to Russia went unmentioned. Perhaps
the very existence of printing presses satisfied his third criterion.

Tatishchev's rationalism, his utilitarian approach to the study
of history which led him to look on it as a science of experience, his attempts at scholarly objectivity which often failed,
earned him the reproaches of the nineteenth century in the
person of Sergei Solovev. To have so limited, so pragmatic
a view of history's function seemed to Solovev the abandonment of a greater duty: "Unable to achieve an understanding
of history as the science of national and human consciousness,
Tatishchev and his contemporaries could define but poorly the
meaning and the uses of national history." [14] If by this is
meant that Tatishchev wrote pragmatic rather than philosophical history, that his work lacked a comprehensive *Weltan-
schauung*, then the charge must be conceded. But Tatishchev
did make a contribution to precisely that "science of national
and human consciousness" of which Solovev spoke. To ac-

quaint Russians with their past, to set them wondering about their identity, their state, and its fortunes, was an indispensable step towards a greater awareness of themselves as citizens of the world and of their country. All of Tatishchev's writings, even the most narrowly utilitarian, had that purpose, though the means he employed were not those of the nineteenth century.

The postulates on the ethnic and political origins of the Russian nation which Tatishchev had advanced in his "History," especially his acceptance of Bayer's Varangian theory, went unchallenged or unnoticed when he first formulated them. In 1749, however, when they were substantially restated by Mueller, they were attacked as a form of *lèse nation* and became the object of a furious controversy whose echoes reverberate to this day. The fact that so remote a period and so esoteric a subject could arouse public controversy is in itself a measure of the growth of national consciousness in Russian society. It is a measure also of the unreadiness even of educated Russians to recognize the needs and methods of scholarship. Although it is possible that Mueller and A. L. Schloezer held to Bayer's original thesis out of a sense of Germanic superiority, it is unlikely in view of the available evidence. It is much more reasonable to suppose that a mixture of personal and national pride led their opponents to denounce Mueller and Schloezer as slanderers of Russia.

Gerhard Friedrich Mueller (1705–1783),[15] the son of a Westphalian *gymnasium* principal, came to Russia at the age of twenty in search of a career which he began as librarian at the Academy of Sciences. To this post there were added the duties of editor for the "Commentaries," then published by the Academy as a supplement to the "St. Petersburg Gazette." A combination of private and professional circumstances, possibly the friendship of Bayer, induced him to make the study of Russian history his lifework. He served history with devotion and singleness of purpose, to the neglect of any other subject. If this immersion in historical materials led to the narrowing of Mueller's own outlook, it also stood Russian historiography in good stead, for it was the beginning of the most systematic collection of sources which had so far been undertaken. Mueller's industry and his attachment to his chosen field and home spared him the charges of disloyalty which were leveled at the "academic Varangians" in later centuries,[16] though they did not exempt him from the enmity of his contemporaries.

Mueller's first project was the publication of a historical journal which served as guide and clearing house for the dispersed and unorganized researches into the country's past. The *Sammlung Russischer Geschichte*, the first publication of its kind, began to appear in 1732. There he planned to publish (in German and Russian) historical treatises and documents as a preliminary to the writing of a comprehensive national history. The guiding purpose, as Mueller stated it, was to collect the materials for such a work and to encourage those who were laboring in isolation. Another goal was to acquaint foreigners with those facts and documents of Russian history which were so far unknown or had not yet made their way into print. Mueller shared the view that ignorance or ill-will had caused too many mistakes in the works of foreigners writing on Russia, and he made the discovery and correction of these mistakes one of the cardinal duties of the new publication. He himself supervised only the first three numbers of the collection but his initiative carried it through the preparation of five more. After that time it ceased publication until 1758. The reason for the suspension of the *Sammlung* after

1737 was Mueller's absence in Siberia and his participation in the second expedition of Captain Bering to Kamtchatka. His Siberian stay gave him an unequaled opportunity for a survey of local archives which yielded up unsuspected treasures for the study of Russian history in the sixteenth and seventeenth centuries. For ten years, from 1733 to 1743, Mueller traveled the length and breadth of Siberia, wherever there were settlements, administrative or military posts, collecting and copying chronicles and documents with untiring industry. He brought back with him thirty-eight portfolios of material which were of intestimable value to all students of Russian history.

A year after his return, Mueller submitted to the Academy of Sciences a project for the establishment of a historical section. Headed by an official historiographer, the new section was intended to overcome the shortcomings of isolated, individual efforts. He clearly felt that Russian historical research stood in need of governmental sponsorship. Other governments, Mueller pointed out, had recognized the value of history and had opened their archives to scientifically trained persons, while Russians still relied on foreigners and their falsehoods for knowledge of their own history. The new department was to be composed of a director, two adjuncts (of whom one had to be a native Russian), a secretary, copyist, and servant.[17]

Though Mueller had undoubtedly struck the right patriotic chords in his proposal, it was turned down. His continued membership in the Academy was made contingent upon his becoming a Russian subject, a condition to which he agreed after some hesitation in January 1748. The contract which Mueller and the Academy had concluded in November of the preceding year went beyond the former's proposal in one respect: it stated that the position of official historiographer to the Russian government ought rightfully to be held by a "native Russian and loyal subject." In view, however, of the services already rendered by Mueller (and prompted, presumably, by his resolve to become a Russian citizen) an exception was made and his appointment as professor and historiographer approved. The earlier plan for the establishment of a historical department in the Academy was also realized at this time. But Mueller's own role in it was severely restricted by the supervisory functions lodged in the Chancellery of the Academy, and by the subsequent creation of a "Historical Assembly." The members of this Assembly virtually acted as censors over all materials prepared for publication by Mueller's department, and even the historiographer's personal correspondence with foreign scholars had to be conducted via the Academic Chancellery.

The sources of the hostility and suspicion with which Mueller was met by superiors and colleagues alike were basically of a personal kind, but it was inevitable that questions of loyalty and national honor should also be raised. The foreign complexion of the Academy, almost a microcosm of the government in the thirties, readily lent itself to exploitation in disputes which were not necessarily the result of conflicting national loyalties. During the first seven years of its existence, the Academy had no Russian members at all, until the mathematician Adadurov was appointed an adjunct in 1733. He was followed in 1742 by Teplov (a botanist), Truskott, the geographer, and Lomonosov, the first Russian to be a full-fledged academician. After 1745, when Tredyakovski and Krashenninikov became members, the number of Russians gradually increased, though their scientific contributions and their weight in the administration remained relatively insignificant. The first four presidents of the Academy were without exception Germans. Johann Schumacher, its permanent secretary for over thirty years, outraged Russians and Germans alike by his high-handed and dictatorial methods. Shortly after the accession of the Empress Elizabeth, a Russian Councillor, supported by others, thought the time ripe for a complaint about Schumacher who had been the Academy's virtual ruler in the absence of a president. Schumacher was denounced for embezzlement and hostility to Russia, for preferential treatment given German students and professors, and for failing to carry out one of the Academy's fundamental purposes—the training of Russian scholars. His arrest and replacement by Andrei Nartov were only of short duration, and he was restored to his position in 1744.[18]

No improvement resulted in the relations of his administration with the professorial staff, native or foreign. The quarrels continued, as did Schumacher's hostility to all things Russian. The only tangible results of his temporary eclipse were the promulgation of a new statute for the Academy and the nomination, in 1746, of a Russian president, Count Kyrill Razumovski. Though he was much in favor at Court, Razumovski was only eighteen years of age and relatively uninterested in the organization entrusted to his care. As a consequence, Schumacher and his son-in-law I. A. Taubert remained the Academy's actual directors. The new statute went some way to insure the independence of the academicians and to safeguard the national pride and interest. From now on the teaching and research functions of the Academy were to be more strictly separated and each of the ten academicians was to work together with an adjunct of Russian birth. Latin and Russian were designated as the official languages of discourse and instruction. As if to lend emphasis to the new course, the young president, on his first official visit to the Academy, addressed its members in Russian.

For Mueller, the return of Schumacher meant an unending series of petty quarrels. His adversary was only too willing to employ every weapon at his disposal, including the charge of behavior prejudicial to the good name and best interest of Russia which had earlier been raised against Schumacher himself. Lacking the support of the secretary, Mueller was a particularly vulnerable target for attacks from all quarters. His plan for the establishment of a historical department, in the form in which he had proposed it, was turned down; repeated requests for financial help were ignored, as were his suggestions that the Academy acquire Tatishchev's library and manuscripts. He was accused of trying to slander the name of the Academy abroad, and virtually of spying when he was found to be in possession of a genealogical table of Russian rulers.

Typical was an incident involving Peter Krekshin, who was preparing a history of Peter the Great, and whom Mueller had generously supplied with information drawn from foreign sources. Learning that Mueller had expressed himself unfavorably about the quality of his work, Krekshin knew no better way of avenging himself than to denounce Mueller to the Senate. One of the academician's manuscripts, the denunciation stated, contained matter humiliating to Russia's grand dukes. The success with which the sanctity of the nation and its heroes could be invoked is shown by another attack staged against Mueller in the Historical Assembly, to which fell the task of examining his Siberian History. The majority of the Assembly's members held Mueller to have erred seriously in stating that the Cossack leader Ermak had condoned the brigandage committed by his men in the conquest of Siberia. Lomonosov in particular was outraged at the suggestion that Ermak or anyone under his command could have had base motives for so noble a deed. Mueller was advised to be more discreet in his discussion of the Cossacks' role, but he insisted on the accuracy of his sources and refused to alter them. Rather, he said, would he omit mention of the entire episode.[19]

Compared with the storm which broke over Mueller's head in 1749 his censure by the Historical Assembly was only a minor skirmish. The issue which formed the substance of the

later controversy—the origins of the Russian nation—lent itself
too readily to nationalist exploitation. In early 1749 it had been
decided that Mueller and Lomonosov should deliver the fes-
tival orations at a ceremonial session of the Academy to be
held on the Empress' name-day. Mueller, with more courage
than foresight, chose to talk about the origin of the Russian
people (*De origine Gentis et nominis Russorum*). As the date
of the session approached, he had not yet submitted his speech
as he had been instructed to do. The Academy's secretary then
prevailed upon its president to postpone the session so that
Mueller's oration might be reviewed in advance by members
familiar with its subject matter.

Their reaction was violent, because the "entire speech showed not a single event which might redound to the glory of the
Russian nation." [20] The majority of those who read his dissertation felt that Mueller had only recorded what might serve to
discredit the Russian people—defeats in battle, robberies,
plunders, and other excesses. What seems to have rankled
most was "the carelessness with which he stated that the
Scandinavians with their victorious weapons subjected all
Russians to their sway." [21] The Norman controversy here had
its first public unveiling, in the midst of the national revival
stimulated by the overthrow of Biron and the accession of
Elizabeth. It transcended purely academic concerns and became inextricably linked with questions of national honor
and independence. In the Academy, where Mueller had
enemies not only in Schumacher's Chancellery but also among
his colleagues, its usefulness was immediately recognized.

In this instance, neither Mueller's claim to scientific detach-
ment, nor his countercharge that his critics were determined
to find fault with him in any case, were of any avail. After a
full-scale examination of the thesis by Lomonosov, Krashenninikov, and Popov, it was condemned as prejudicial to Russia.
Mueller was subsequently tried, and his rank and salary re-

duced.[22] This time, recognizing the strength and determination of the forces arrayed against him, Mueller bowed to the inevitable. Only a year after the disciplinary action against him, his professorship was restored. Eventually, whether from caution or conviction, he even gave up his adherence to Bayer's theory of the Scandinavian origin of the Varangian princes and moved closer to the position of Lomonosov, who held that they were of Prussian (therefore of Slav) origin.[23]

The written opinion which Lomonosov submitted in 1750 may be regarded as the start of his own historical researches. It is an indictment not only of Mueller, but also of his teacher Bayer, and a plea for a return to the *Sinopsis* of Innokenti Gizel as the purer source for the history of ancient Russia. Five of the points of the indictment against Mueller were central to Lomonosov's argument: the fact that Mueller did not trace the Russians and their name to the ancient Roxolani who had settled in the area between Dnepr and Don; his denial that the Varangians were of Slavic race and tongue; his attempt to prove that the Russian name stemmed from a Finnish designation for the Swedes—Rossaleina; his ridiculing of the favorite etymology for Slav (from *slava*—glory), and finally, the political dangers inherent in a theory which ascribed Swedish nationality to Rurik and his descendants and so late a beginning to the Russian name and nation. Summarizing his findings, Lomonosov reported that no amount of partial correction could make Mueller's thesis acceptable, and that it had to be abandoned *in toto*. Least of all could it be presented in a public session where it might give offense to a Russian audience.[24]

The involvement of the nation's honor in what were essentially private and professional differences was an element of real importance in the minds of Mueller's adversaries. Conscious of the low esteem in which they were held by Europe, with sharp memories of internal weakness and foreign domination, the discovery that foreigners of Scandinavian origin had created their first political organism came as a severe shock to their Russian self-respect. The most recent memories served to make it especially unpleasant. Scandinavians meant Swedes, and the Swedes had for almost a century been bitter enemies of Russia. In the midst of the fierce struggle in which Peter the Great had engaged them, their role as invaders and despoilers of Russia in the Time of Troubles had been recalled. After the victorious conclusion of the Northern War, they were potentially still the most threatening enemy, capable of denying Russia her European role. It was equally offensive that Russia's first rulers were not of Slavic, but of Germanic stock, and the prominence of Germans in the government, the armed forces, and in the Academy had created resentments in which personal and public motives became easily fused. The echoes of this conflict reverberate to this day, and the question of the ancient annalist—Whence is the Russian land? (*otkuda est poshla russkaya zemlya?*)—has rarely been answered dispassionately.*

* A Soviet historian, M. Tikhomirov, reviewing Rubinshtein's "Russian Historiography" in 1948 (*Voprosy Istorii*, no. 2 (1948), pp. 94–98), criticized him for his unpatriotic appraisal of Lomonosov's contribution to Russian history and for overestimating the work of Bayer and Schloezer. "This question," wrote Tikhomirov, "was given an unexpectedly sharp turn in the middle of the eighteenth century, and the vehemence displayed by Lomonosov in his fight with the German academicians had nothing in common with the vehemence of a scholar who is resentful because his views do not find acceptance. It was not Lomonosov, but the German academicians themselves who invested the question with such bitterness. This was connected with the important political events of the first half of the century .... Is it surprising then, that special interest in the 'Varangians' was shown by those academicians who had been invited from Germany by the self-appointed 'Varangians' of the eighteenth century? For the German academicians, proof that the eastern Slavs in the ninth and tenth centuries were real savages, saved from the depths of ignorance by the Varangian princes, was necessary to support their own rule in a country whose people had long had a great culture of its own. And the German academicians, without delay, carried out the orders given them by the highly-placed German functionaries." Thus, the reason for Bayer's and Schloezer's adherence to the Norman theory was their devotion to German interests. Mueller,

The storm which threatened Mueller in the years 1749–1750 did not end his career, nor did it settle the question of the beginnings of the Russian state. The center of the storm, to judge by his activity, was barely disturbed by the controversy which raged around him. By 1753 he had completed twenty-three chapters of a Siberian history; in 1754–1755 he edited the Academy's *Novi Commentarii*, founded the first major review "Monthly Essays" (*Ezhemesyachnye Sochineniya*) in 1755, and in 1758 resumed publication of the *Sammlung Russischer Geschichte*. The monthly review, although a magazine of general character and content, reflected the interests of its editor and frequently contained materials relating to the history and geography of Russia. With the resumption of the *Sammlung*, many of the articles which first appeared there were translated into Russian and placed in the review.

By far the most ambitious undertaking of these years was Mueller's "Essay on Modern Russian History." It dealt with the period from the accession of Boris Godunov to the election of Michael Romanov, the Time of Troubles, which no native writer had yet dared tackle. Muller stressed the fact that no Russian had written on Russia in a foreign language and he attributed to this the inaccuracies and prejudices in the works of foreigners. Fully aware of the dangers he was courting, the more so since he was writing in German, Mueller avowed that

---

though denied merit equal to that of Russian historians, happily found himself excluded from the censure visited upon his more talented and famous colleagues, possibly because he never left Russia, possibly because in later years he moved closer to Lomonosov's position. The reason for Tikhomirov's sharpness, at least, is clear: it is the "anti-cosmopolitan" campaign conducted at the time of his writing in the Soviet Union. It was also the cause for the condemnation of Rubinshtein's book. *Voprosy Istorii*, no. 11 (1949), pp. 3–12, called on Soviet scholars to unmask "all manifestations in the works of the foes of the USSR, foreign pseudo-scholars and renegade White emigrés, of the Indo-European theory of the origin of peoples, the Norman theory of the origin of the Russian state, fascist views on the alleged organizing cultural role of the imaginary Goth 'state,' false and unfounded contentions of a lack of independent development on the part of the Russian people. . . ."

the choice of these parlous times as his subject had not been
a voluntary matter; it had imposed itself as a duty, so that the
record of the Russian past, which Tatishchev had ended with
Fedor Ivanovich, might be carried to a more recent and
happier era.[25] When part of the "Essay" appeared in a Russian
translation it provoked an immediate and angry response from
Lomonosov, with whom Mueller's relations continued to be
strained. Lomonosov complained to Razumovski that Mueller,
in addition to his many other faults, was much more intent on
seeking out spots on the robe of Russia than on discovering her
many true beauties. The very publication (in German, at that)
of an article dealing with the darkest portion of Russia's past
would damage Russia's reputation in the eyes of foreigners.
It was clear proof of malice on the author's part; otherwise
Mueller would have chosen a period in which it was possible
to see good and evil in equal measure. To make matters worse,
Mueller had revived his theory of 1749, "that accursed dissertation," which he had stolen from the "pedant Bayer," and
was again trying to give it currency in learned circles.[26]
Mueller's honest efforts once more earned him a reprimand
from the Academy and he was instructed to cease publishing
such improprieties as had been contained in the "Essay."

Whatever his personal shortcomings may have been, and his
proud and masterful nature led to quarrels with even his closest
associates, Mueller's services to Russian history are beyond
question. The "Monthly Essays" continued to widen the historical horizon of its readers. It gave scope to local and regional
history and many documents and texts, among them Tatishchev and Mankiev, would have been lost but for Mueller's
care. From his appointment as director of the archives of the
College of Foreign Affairs in 1766, until his death in 1783,
Mueller devoted himself exclusively to archival work, to the
publication of its results and to the training of younger men in
this important field. To this end he resigned his hard-won

appointment as historiographer, and suggested to the Empress Catherine that Prince Mikhail Shcherbatov be appointed in his place.[27]

It is impossible to be certain of the motives for Lomonosov's implacable hostility to Mueller. That one of its sources, perhaps the major one, was a clash of personalities compounded by professional jealousy (Lomonosov was undoubtedly the poorer historian), seems borne out by the fact that both of the antagonists also quarreled with almost every other one of their colleagues, irrespective of nationality. But Lomonosov's spleen, which unhappily vented itself on Mueller as a most convenient target, was also the product of a lifelong, patriotic indignation over Russia's neglect of her scholars and scientists.

Lomonosov's own career had begun in the academic gymnasium at St. Petersburg, to which he had been assigned because of his knowledge of Latin, the only language in which the foreign academicians could discharge their duty of transmitting to young Russians their skills and learning. Unwilling or unable, because of their ignorance of Russian or the inadequate preparation of their students, to train a native crop of teachers, the foreigners retained a virtual monopoly of learning in the first half of the century. One way to circumvent this monopoly was to send young Russians abroad for their studies. After only eight months in St. Petersburg, Lomonosov was dispatched to the University of Marburg, where he became a student of Johann Christian Wolf. Wolf was more than a teacher to the young Russian. He was his idol and the embodiment of all that was glorious and valuable in the life of a scholar. Wolf was honored, he was rich, he was a baron and *Geheimrat*, the friend of princes and a German patriot. Comparing his own position in Russian society with that of his teacher in later years, Lomonosov could not fail to notice how small the prestige and the rewards of scholarship were in his own country.[28] It was not unnatural, nor entirely unjustified, that he should see in the reputation enjoyed by foreign scholars a slight to his own merits and the neglect of native talent. It helps to explain his attitude towards Mueller, towards Taubert ("in other countries professors are given high rank, but booksellers and printers . . . are not so rewarded"), his attempts to have Russians supervise the administration of the Academy, and the wish to make science accessible to his countrymen in their native tongue.[29]

Lomonosov's occupation with history was also inspired by the desire to show that Russia need not rely on foreigners alone for knowledge of her past. His scientific interest in this field was limited to its connection with the history of the Russian language. An additional motive for the pursuit of history must have been Mueller's dissertation of 1749. Its critique, written in 1750, is Lomonosov's first known work on a historical problem and may well have been the beginning of his own researches. A review of his activities for the year 1751 mentions that he had been reading "in order to collect material for the writing of a Russian history." The Nestor chronicle and the first volume of Tatishchev which was still in manuscript at this time, were among the works from which he made extensive excerpts and notes. He was similarly occupied during the next two years, and for 1754 reported that he had already completed a history of the Slavonic nation to the time of Rurik. By the following year he had written about the reigns of Rurik, Oleg, and Igor. To deepen Lomonosov's involvement with history, there was an imperial commission for the writing of a Russian history (1753), and the task of supplying Voltaire with materials for a study of Peter the Great. By 1758, Lomonosov's "Ancient Russian History," carried up to 1054, was presented to the Empress and the order given for its printing; publication, however, was delayed until 1766.[30]

The factors which had played so large a role in Lomonosov's

occupation with history also determined the character of the result. The official commission which had asked for fluency and artistic style insured its conformity to current literary tastes. The great variety of Lomonosov's other interests and duties left only a minor portion of his time and energy for the "History" and was perhaps repsonsible for its relatively low level of scholarship. And his awareness of history as an instrument of national consciousness, so fully displayed in his disagreements with Mueller, assured the usefulness of his work as a text of inspiration and example.

The introduction set the tone. Telling his readers that Russia's great past had too long remained in oblivion, Lomonosov affirmed that there was abundant testimony to its greatness, and that this evidence compared favorably with the annals of other nations. If ancient Russia had not had as many or such skillful chroniclers as Greece or Rome, this did not mean that she was plunged in total darkness. "There is much proof that the extent of ignorance in Russia was not as great as represented by many foreign writers," and even if Russia had entered upon the scene of history after the two great peoples of antiquity, her deeds and heroes were worthy of comparison with them, not cause for self-abasement. The parallel with Roman history was carried further and furnished the rationale for the divisions Lomonosov employed in his own narrative. In his scheme, the Roman period of kingly rule corresponded to the reign of Russia's first autocratic princes; Rome's republican government had its parallel in the principalities and free cities of Russia's intermediate period, while the empire found its counterpart in the Muscovy tsardom. There was this difference to be observed, however: Rome had been raised to greatness by a republican government, whereas "the dissidence of opinion which freedom brought to Russia almost caused her total ruin; autocracy, her strength from the beginning, restored and increased her and made her illustrious. We are confident of the welfare of our fatherland, seeing in the rule of a single man the pledge of our happiness." [31]

All of the first part of the "Ancient Russian History," a little more than a third of its entire contents, was devoted to Russia before Rurik and to those questions which had been at issue between Mueller and Lomonosov since 1749. Lomonosov's own views on the origin of the Slavs and the Russian state may be summarized as follows: the Slavs, a people of many branches and wide dispersion, had come to the notice of foreign writers relatively late, hardly before the reign of Justinian. This was not, however, sufficient reason for dating their existence from their appearance in the sources. "Peoples do not take their beginning from a name," and the first and most obvious proof of the Slavs' antiquity was their greatness and power, maintained for more than 1,500 years. It was impossible, therefore, to assume that they had suddenly appeared upon the scene of history. Their ancestry could be traced back to a time before the destruction of Troy, when the Enety, a Slavic tribe, came from Asia to settle on the shores of the Adriatic. At the same time, other migrants came from Asia Minor via the Caucasian chain to the northern shores of the Sea of Azov and the Black Sea, and these too were ancestors of the Slavs, called Vendy, Venety, or Anty. For Lomonosov, the antiquity of the Slavs was adequately established by history and he decided not to judge on the tradition which derived them from a grandson of Noah. [32]

Another problem was the ancestry of the Eastern Slavs, more particularly of the Russians and the origin of their name, which Mueller had held to be Finnish. Lomonosov believed that among the Sarmatians (Slavs, according to him), between Black Sea and Baltic, there lived the tribe variously called Roksi, Roxolani, Rossolani, Rossi, or Russi, and that these were the most likely ancestors of the Russians. Their name was derived from Rha, the ancient Volga, along which they had lived and which they left (though possibly under another name), to migrate to the shores of the Baltic. There they had mingled with the Kurlanders, kinsmen of the Ross-Varangians. The latter, who had given to the primitive Russians their rulers and their state, had the same ancestors as the Prussians of the Baltic littoral—were in fact the same people. "Since the ancient language of the Ross-Varangians was the same as Prussian, Lithuanian, Kurlander, or Lettish, it must have come from the Slavonic as one of its branches." [33] The Scandinavian origin of the Varangians need not then be accepted if Rurik came from Prussia and if the Prussians were Slav. What is more, and here he was on firmer ground, Lomonosov doubted that the Varangian name could be assigned to any given people. He surmised that it was rather an occupational designation, applied to men of various tribes and tongues who had banded together for piracy.

Another result of Lomonosov's readings and researches was the "Short Russian Chronicle," written in 1759 and published in 1760.[34] Divided into three sections—an introduction which dealt with Slavic history before Rurik and sounded the same themes as the History, a chronological table with brief summaries of all reigns to Peter, and a genealogy of Russia's rulers —the "Chronicle," by virtue of its brevity and compactness, could serve as a historical handbook and introduction and seems to have been so used. But in the effort to make Russians aware of their history, Lomonosov did not confine himself to historical texts. Every literary genre, above all the ode and the epic poem, were vehicles particularly adapted to his talents. Inscriptions and dedications, eulogies and heroic poems invoked great Russian deeds and names. But over all, there towered the heroic figure of Peter the Great, the culmination of all Russian history so far, shedding his glory even on his lesser descendants.[35] In returning time and again to the theme and person of Peter, Lomonosov identified himself with the reformer-

Tsar and looked upon his own labors in the arts and sciences as a replica and continuation of Peter's activity. Isolated as much by his choleric temperament as by the lack of interest shown by a society which preferred elegance to power, Lomonosov looked back with nostalgia to a period in which the nervous vitality of the Tsar had set the tone and pace of all activity. There, he must have felt, he would have found his reward, and holding up to later generations the accomplishments of that reign, he wanted them to see how far short they fell of that ideal.

Lomonosov embittered the very last years of his life by another of the academic-political conflicts in which his career had been so rich. It was an almost exact repetition of the Mueller affair, carried on this time against August Ludwig Schloezer. A protégé of Lomonosov's old enemy Mueller, and a young scholar who was subsequently to become one of the founders of modern German historiography, Schloezer came to St. Petersburg as a tutor for Mueller's children. Unlike his sponsor, he was a man of considerable education and clearly defined scholarly interests. His occupation with history and philology, after he left Mueller's employ, was a logical outcome of these interests. His friendship with Taubert helped him to obtain a position as tutor to Count Razumovski's children and an adjunctship in the Academy. There, almost every facet of his background and personality—the connection with Mueller and Taubert, nationality and profession—pointed to eventual collision with Lomonosov. It occurred in 1764, only three years after Schloezer's arrival in Russia. The occasion was his request for a leave of absence in Germany and submission of a research project in Russian history.

Lomonosov, as one of the Academy's senior members, was asked to pass on the young German's request and refused to approve it. The reasons for his decision seem curiously remote from the real issues and almost border on the pathological.

Schloezer, in drawing up his plan of research had failed to consult either Lomonosov or his works and had taken excerpts from Russian state documents which Lomonosov feared he would publish abroad to the detriment of Russia's interests. Whatever the merits of this curious argument, Schloezer's request was denied. But in January of the following year, Schloezer was appointed academician and professor of history on Catherine's order, in spite of Lomonosov's view that the Academy lacked the vacancy and Schloezer the experience for a professorship. Lomonosov, ill and bitter, poured out his bile in a memorandum which described Schloezer's appointment as an insult to all Russians connected with the Academy. To admit such a man to government archives and libraries would have, he warned, the direst consequences for Russian security.[36] Three months later Lomonosov died.

The threat to the security of the Russian state posed by Schloezer's activities was unreal and a grotesque exaggeration of Lomonosov's fears. Real enough, however, was the blow national sentiment sustained as a result of Schloezer's researches, which provoked the anger of nationalists and historians of later generations.[37] Lomonosov could not have known of Schloezer's eventual conclusions, but what he knew of his associations and the direction of his thought told him that they would not be flattering to Russia. He had already had a sample of Schloezer's philological method from the latter's Russian grammar, which related such purely Slavic words (or so they seemed to Lomonosov) as *korol* and *knyaz* (king and prince) to the German *kerl* and *knecht*. Had he lived long enough to await the maturing of Schloezer's views on early Russian history his fears would have been confirmed.

In 1767 Schloezer returned to Germany, only two years after having received the coveted professorship in which he agreed to serve a minimum of five years. His major work in Russian history from then on was dedicated to a restoration of the original Nestor chronicle, which he believed had existed. His studies of the Russian chronicles (of which a first fruit was the *Probe Russischer Annalen*, 1768) led him to confirm by the use of Russian sources what Bayer had tried to establish without them: the "Norman" theory, which Schloezer not only accepted but developed further. His "Nestor," which appeared first in Germany in 1802, kept alive the question which had become an issue of national policy in 1749.

Having always insisted that the historian must be free of favor to king, country, and religion, Schloezer revealed to Russians who would have it otherwise the indisputable record of their beginnings, now verified by the most advanced techniques of scholarship.

May patriots not be incensed, but their history does not go back to the Tower of Babel; it is not as old as that of Greece and Rome; it is younger even than that of Germany and Sweden. Before this period [the calling of the Varangians] all was darkness, in Russia as well as in adjacent regions. Of course there were human beings there, but God alone knows whence and when they came. They were a people without government, living like the beasts and birds of their forests, undistinguished in any way, having no contact with the Southern nations, which is why they could be neither noticed nor described by a single enlightened South European.[38]

In this setting of primitive savagery, which placed the ancient Slavs on a level with the American Indians before the coming of the white man, there was neither possibility nor proof of civil society, of law, of learning, or of trade. Like the Iroquois or Algonquins, Schloezer wrote, the peoples of the Baltic shores had neither the goods, the money, nor the literacy which would have enabled them to trade.[39] In all the Russian North, up to the middle of the ninth century, there was not one settlement which could properly be called a town. "Savage, coarse, and dispersed, the Slavs began to form themselves into communities under the influence of the Germans, whom destiny had appointed to sow the first seeds of civilization in the North-Western and North-Eastern Worlds." [40]

No matter how great Schloezer's devotion to historical truth, it is only natural that Russians would consider such language condescending and intemperate, a sign of German haughtiness. Schloezer did not look upon Russians and their past as contemptuously as his critics made out,[41] but he thought of Russian historians as lesser examples of the species, possibly a reflection of his unhappy experiences. His condemnation of their provincialism and backwardness (he found even Mueller to be thirty years behind the times) appeared to them to grow out of a general theory of Russian backwardness. What kind of people were these, he exclaimed, who prided themselves on their knowledge of Russian history? "Men without any formal training, men who read only their chronicles, not knowing that outside of Russia there was a history also, men who knew no language but their own." Of all the Russian writers whom he had come to know personally or through their writings, only Boltin (who differed with him on many important points) came anywhere near meeting his professional standards. "I was at least a scientific critic . . . I was in this respect the only one in Russia." [42]

The patriotic prefaces which preceded every Russian work and endlessly remarked on the uses of the history of the fatherland only provoked Schloezer's laughter and made him think that he had been transported back to the sixteenth century. History was not history if its inspiration was anything but the impartial search for truth. "Love for the fatherland, wrongly understood, makes impossible the critical and dispassionate treatment of history . . . and becomes ridiculous." Lomonosov thought otherwise. "If literature can move the hearts of men, should not true history have power to stir us to praiseworthy deeds, especially that history which relates the feats of our ancestors?" [43] Under the circumstances, the question was a purely rhetorical one; not only had history that power, it had also that duty. It is in their differing approaches to history, not in their nationalities, that Lomonosov and Schloezer were most sharply at issue.

It is true that there was no scholar in Russia during the entire century who could measure himself with Schloezer in terms of achievement or expertness. His knowledge of history, of ancient and modern languages, his mastery of the methods of textual criticism, of historical geography and linguistics, gave him an undoubted advantage over his Russian colleagues. It is a fact which no history of Russian historiography as a scientific discipline could neglect, but it is only a fact. In that complex of emotions and passions, of resentments and fears which is national pride and sentiment, fact plays a minor role. The professional competence of a historian is of less weight as a factor of national consciousness than other, not so tangible elements. Viewed from this vantage point, all Schloezer's skill and objectivity were less important than the impact of his conclusions. It was these that were resented, not his method. Gizel, Mankiev, Lomonosov, and others, though they might lack the critical apparatus of scholarship, did not upset beliefs that had been cherished for centuries; and when they combined literary skill with patriotic fervor they made history come alive.

The last stage of Russian eighteenth-century historiography, which developed new and sophisticated answers to the challenge of the West, is dominated by the figure of Ivan Boltin. Though intrinsically far less interesting than the work of Boltin, the "Russian History" of Prince Mikhail Shcherbatov must be discussed briefly to show the distance which his generation had traveled since the disputes of Lomonosov and Mueller agitated the Academy of Sciences. Shcherbatov and Boltin were men of the world, men of undoubted standing and importance, and they were less easily shaken in the conviction of their own and their country's merits than was Lomonosov. Shcherbatov was not deficient in that quality of patriotism which Lomonosov considered such an essential tool of the historian's trade. It was a quality, however, which characterized the sum total of his activities; it did not obtrude as a disturbing element in his work and his personal relationships. Nor was he capable of identifying his person and his fate with the welfare of Russia as closely as Lomonosov had done. He was, it is true, deeply perturbed by the unsettling effect which a superficial Europeanism had had on the social and political life of his country, but it was a concern which grew out of a complex of ethical and class values which were as much European as they were Russian.

It was therefore impossible for Shcherbatov to see in the question of Russia's origins quite so burning an issue as had Lomonosov. To recognize the value of speculation on the origins of the Russian people before Rurik was one thing; to lose oneself in the morass of ethnological and linguistic guesswork which it entailed was another. On this particular question, Shcherbatov limited himself to a résumé of foreign writers. He began his own exposition of the course of Russian history with the coming of the Scandinavian princes, the first events recorded by the Nestor chronicle and other native sources. In relating the calling of Rurik and his brothers by the people of Novgorod, Shcherbatov was equally unmoved by the question of their ethnic identity. To him it was clear that the Varangians were of Germanic stock, for the names of Rurik and his immediate successors were very much like Germanic names. This fact did not, however, prevent him from assuming that one reason for the choice of the Scandinavian princes had been their kinship with Gostomysl, the last elected ruler of Novgorod. Although this would show that they had come to rule over Russia not by conquest but by right of legal succession, it would also make it doubtful that they were Germans. It might be, Shcherbatov agreed with the *Sinopsis* and Lomonosov, that the Varangians came from Prussia, but this did not lead him to conclude that they were Slavs.[44]

In discussing the level of culture which prevailed in Russia at the beginning of her history, Shcherbatov made no attempt to push the frontiers of civilization further back in time than seemed to him warranted by the evidence. Of the five conversions, beginning with the apostle Andrew, which Russia supposedly had undergone, he accepted only two as having had any impact on the beliefs and customs of Russia: that of the Princess Olga and the acceptance of Christianity by Vladimir. Of these, only the latter firmly established the true faith among Russians, and succeeded in softening the savagery of their unenlightened, pre-Christian state.[45] In that state, Shcherbatov found them no less primitive than had Schloezer, a marauding, warring, and nomadic people, whose habitations were hardly deserving to be called towns. "Though Russia had towns before her baptism, they were little more than crude shelters . . . and the people, and more especially the most noble among them, spent their time warring and raiding, living out in the open fields and moving from place to place." [46]

Nor did he feel the need to insist that letters and literacy had come to Russia before Christianity, so that on most of the issues which were in dispute between the so-called slanderers of Russia and her defenders, Shcherbatov was found most often among the former. It was the skepticism of the enlightened, the suspicion of impure motive unbecoming the reasonable man, not lack of patriotism, which kept Shcherbatov aloof in the battle of contending loyalties. When he did feel called upon to arbitrate between differing interpretations of an event, he made the decision on the basis of what right reason knows and reveals about the weakness of men.

And so . . . I conclude that if the campaign of Svyatoslav was not as disastrous as the Greeks would have it, neither was it as glorious for him as our writers report; for following the sources, one must take care not to fall into the partiality for either side which each of them had for their own country.[47]

Shcherbatov's "History" was not a success in spite of the fact that he incorporated into his narrative the sources he had used, including important government documents to which Catherine had given him access. "The History of Prince Shcherbatov," said the Empress, "is boring as well as heavy; his head was not fit for this work." [48] It was an impression which others shared, for the work lacked the life, the passion, and the literary qualities which had assured the success of lesser efforts. It was the absence of these qualities, not its inaccuracies, that accounts for the lack of enthusiasm with which the work was received by the general public. In fact, the "History" is perhaps the least historical of Shcherbatov's writings. Its abstract, categorical explanations of events, cast for the most part in terms of individual psychology, appear in no way rooted in the particular historical experience of the Russian state or people. Law and government, Shcherbatov believed, were the forces which shaped the manners and morals of society and they, in turn, were shaped by the ruler's personality and intelligence. Such a view was bound to lead to a neglect of the "organic" elements of history, to substitute individual motivation for historical process, biography for social history. It is no accident that the main divisions of Shcherbatov's work correspond to the lives and reigns of princes and tsars, and that in all its vast bulk little more than ten pages are devoted to a survey of the "conditions of Russia, her laws, customs, and government."

It was in the "Corruption of Morals in Russia" (ca. 1786–1789) and in other writings that Shcherbatov addressed himself to the history of Russian society. There he described changes in behavior and morality not only in terms of individual passion or depravity but also developed broader historical views. Central to these is the assumption of a sharp break in Russia's past with the coming of Peter. Though he held this rupture responsible for many of Russia's ills, it was impossible for him to go back to the ignorance, superstition, and coarseness which the reforms had driven out. But with these simplicity, loyalty, and faith had also disappeared; without them, without the fear of God, which had been one of the main features of Russian history before Peter, no state was safe. In its reliance on a newly-created service gentry, the state which Peter had fashioned made it impossible for these virtues to flourish.

The relationship of mutual trust which had bound monarch and aristocracy together had been destroyed and with it the soil for civic and private virtue. Shcherbatov did not suggest a return to the traditions of Muscovy, and his vision of Russia's future derived for the most part from his imagination. In the imaginary "Kingdom of Ophir" where monarch and hereditary nobility, each confirmed in their rights and duties, worked together, he saw the best guarantee of the common weal. In the history of Russia the early part of Ivan the Terrible's reign had been such a period when tsar and boyars were in harmony. But when monarchy turned to despotism and raised its creatures to share the seat of government, not only the boyars but all Russia suffered. The one principle, therefore, which history and an enlightened intelligence revealed was that no reform, no introduction of foreign techniques, must take place at the expense of the union between monarch and nobility. In departing from that principle, Peter had abandoned the tradition which had ever been Russia's strength and greatness. To its restoration, Shcherbatov devoted a great part of his energy. Some time between the years 1770 and 1775 Shcherbatov made the acquaintance of a man who was well aware of his extensive knowledge of the facts and materials of Russian history. Nicolas-Gabriel LeClerc (1726–1798), by profession a doctor, but a man of many parts, twice during his life visited Russia for extensive stays and held a number of important and rewarding posts. Physician to Count Kyrill Razumovski during his first sojourn, LeClerc, on his second visit which lasted approximately from 1769 to 1775, was at one or another time personal physician to the Grand Duke Paul, Director of Sciences in the School of Cadets, Professor and Councilor of the Academy of Arts, Inspector of the Pavlovski Hospital in Moscow, and an honorary member of the Academy of Sciences. A writer with a wide range of interests, LeClerc conceived the plan for a history of Russia and he approached Shcherbatov for advice and guidance. The prince generously offered his help and prepared for the Frenchman an extensive sketch or "conspectus" of the history of Russia from Rurik to the time of Fedor Ivanovich, and also supplied him with information on the history of the arts and the gentry. The personal relations of the two men were friendly, even cordial. Yet Shcherbatov, like every Russian who read the finished product of LeClerc's facile pen, was shocked and hurt by the unflattering picture it gave of the country which had received its author so hospitably and showered him with honors. When Shcherbatov opened the book with which he was so closely associated, it struck him as an "unjustifiable mixture of absurd slanders and lies," and though admitting his personal acquaintance with LeClerc, he stressed that he had always been convinced of the Frenchman's ignorance of Russian and the carelessness of his method, now so fully demonstrated in the History.[49]

LeClerc's ambitiously titled "Physical, Moral, Civil, and

Political History of Ancient and Modern Russia" (six volumes, Paris, 1783–1794), provoked similar reactions from the Empress Catherine, from her favorite Potemkin, and from Major-General Ivan Nikitich Boltin (1735–1792), a member of the War Office where Potemkin had presided since 1786. Boltin, whose wide reading in Russian history had so far been prompted by curiosity alone, was roused by LeClerc, and possibly by the urgings of Catherine and Potemkin, to put his extensive knowledge to use and to refute the Frenchman wherever possible. In causing Boltin to abandon his self-imposed silence, in forcing on him a degree of professionalism, this "impudent libeler and downright liar," [50] as Boltin angrily called LeClerc, in some sense atoned to Russia for his sins.

The condescension with which LeClerc approached his subject, the conviction of his own merits and of the superiority of the culture he represented, were indeed cause for anger. He did not merely repeat views, such as Schloezer's, that Russians before the coming of the Normans had lived in primitive barbarism, for which there was some scientific basis; he went further, and saw almost all of Russian history in the light of that original defect. Russia emerged from his pages as Europe's last fortress of ignorance and despotism, the grave-yard of individual liberty. LeClerc read into Russia's past all the "Gothic" and medieval horrors that were the *bête noire* of the enlightened mind and that clashed less with the realities of the age than with its ideals. Even now (according to LeClerc), the Russians were half-pagan, superstitious, and priest-ridden. The clergy, usurping the functions of civil government, exercised rights over life and death; all-powerful patriarchs, such as Nikon, had enjoyed undue influence in the state; before the time of Peter there had been no civil law whatever. Unlimited in their power, the country's rulers may do as they wish; the condition of the country, therefore, depends on their qualities of character or their whims. More concerned with their own safety and comfort than the welfare of their oppressed subjects, they have given no incentives for an increase of population, which remains inadequate for the size of the empire.

This was the work which, "for the sake of truth and father-land," Boltin set out to refute—the "lies and libels . . . the partiality with which the author distorts accepted facts, the insolence with which he speaks of matters totally unknown to him, the absurdity of his judgments, the emptiness of his argumentation and the gross errors of every kind." [51] It is remarkable that the heat with which Boltin entered the lists against his adversary was not sustained; the two volumes of his "Commentary on . . . the History of M. LeClerc" were, by and large, a reasoned and balanced examination of the Frenchman's text. Together with the "Critical Comments . . . on Prince Shcherbatov's History," they are the reflection of Boltin's historical method and thought, which he never de-veloped in a history of his own. From these works it is possible to determine not only Boltin's position on specific questions, but also the sources on which he drew.

It was not the emotion of patriotism alone that informed Boltin's criticism. It was also an insistence on the historian's duty to mankind, on freedom from bias for country and friends which Schloezer could not have formulated more severely. Above all, the historian must bear in mind that he is a human being, that he is writing about men like himself. Impartiality, on the other hand, does not mean an indiscrimi-nate recital of the facts.[52] The historian should approach his task with a purpose or conceptual scheme and arrange the data at his disposal in some conformity with that scheme, so that they may yield an internal unity and consistency. LeClerc had imposed some kind of unity and consistency on Russian history and in doing so had done violence to fact. For him it was the stamp of backwardness, the tyranny of the rulers and

the servitude of the ruled that formed, the connecting link
between the stages of Russia's past. In debating with him,
Boltin could not escape the search for a principal, unifying
characteristic of his own. To do so was not solely a response to
the challenge of LeClerc. To an equal degree it was the independent application of the teachings which Boltin had imbibed
from his models, from Montesquieu, from Voltaire, from
Raynal. It was the first appearance of philosophical history
in Russia.

In direct antithesis to the method of Shcherbatov, which
offered explanations of individual acts and events, philosophical
history tried to define the character of nations, the distinctive
features of their spiritual and social life. These it sought to
derive from the influence of climate, of political institutions,
and of religion. Boltin ascribed to climate, the "major role
in the formation of the mind, the heart, and the soul of man . . .
while other circumstances, such as the form of government,
education, etc., only further . . . or hinder its action." Viewed
apart from climate, government and education exercise no
independent influence of their own; their action on the nature
of man and society is secondary. "It is easier for manners and
morals to fashion the laws [i.e. the action of the state] than to
be fashioned by them; the latter is impossible without coer-
cion." [53] To assume otherwise, to conclude that state or
church, laws or institutions play the dominant role in shaping
men and their societies is to fly in the face of nature. Virtue
does not depend on the degree of enlightenment institutions
have brought to a country, nor is an advanced civilization the
root of corruption and immorality. Neither LeClerc nor Rousseau is right. "The nature of man remains always one and the
same; virtue and vice belong to all ages and to all nations." [54]

In this shift of the ground on which the discussion "Russia
*vis-à-vis* Europe" had so far taken place, Boltin proclaimed
Russian man the equal of all others. At the same time, in his

insistence on the primacy of climate, the door was left open for a delineation of the unique elements in Russian character and experience. Where heretofore every instinct had been to say to Europe "we are like you," Boltin gave to national consciousness a less imitative argument and freed it of the need to deny its otherness, its peculiarities. As human beings, he said, we are indeed like you; as Russians we are different in some ways and proud to acknowledge the fact. It is wrong, therefore, for Europe to apply to Russia standards derived from a different geographical and historical setting: "to judge Russia by comparing her with the other states of Europe would be to clothe a full-grown man in garments measured for a dwarf." [55]

There are two basic positions then from which Boltin proceeds to the solution of the controversial questions which had been debated throughout the century. First stands the basic similarity of human nature. Character and conduct are alike under similar conditions, so that it is impossible to exclude Russians from the operation of nature's laws. They are no more and no less tainted with defects than other peoples. But there were also undeniably different ways in which nature and history had left their imprint on Russia for all times. Combining these two approaches in varying proportions, stressing differences as well as similarities, Boltin expounded his own views on the issues raised by LeClerc and Shcherbatov.

The most fundamental of these was LeClerc's assumption of the backwardness of ancient Russia, the description of her early state after the manner of Schloezer. As the inevitable corollary of that thesis there followed for LeClerc Russia's delayed development in the modern period. The rationalist's bias for his own age was displayed in all its superciliousness even where he found cause to praise. His eulogy of Peter the Great, part of a speech delivered on his election to the Academy of Sciences, must have been as offensive as his history to a Russian audience.[56] For in praising Peter, LeClerc depicted

Russia in the preceding period as weighted down by ignorance and coarseness. Peter alone had raised his people from their low state, he alone had led them into the light, towards Europe, and ended their isolation. The most confirmed partisan of the reforms could not accept this blunt division of Russian history into two periods, of which one alone deserved the attention of the present; least of all Boltin who was aware of the complexity of a past which did not admit of such crude treatment.

Subject to the same laws of development as other societies, Russia could not for long have remained in primitive stagnation, unmoving and unmoved. From the very beginning of her history, Russia had traded, warred, and treated with the Greeks of Byzantium, a complex and advanced civilization. On the basis of his study of the treaties concluded between the early Kievan princes and the Byzantine state, Boltin arrived at the conviction that Russians then enjoyed the benefits of stable government and unalterable law. Far from being savages in the wilderness, they were highly skilled in trade, in navigation, the arts and crafts; lived in a complex society in which each estate had well-defined rights, prerogatives, and distinctions and where law and justice were accessible to all.[57] This was hardly the picture of a primitive culture, and by Oleg's time the Russians were no longer nomads. They had abandoned their nomadic way of life some centuries before his conquest of Kiev, witness the many towns which attest to the successful existence of a stable social order over a considerable period of time. The publication in 1792, by Boltin and others, of the *Russkaya Pravda*, a collection of medieval laws, also served to discount the barbarism of medieval Russia. Here was a document which need, experience, and the complexity of human relationships had produced. Parts of it would do honor to a modern legislator, and if it had aspects of severity which the eighteenth century found harsh or brutal, one had only to look at comparable evidence from Western Europe to see that its laws were not more humane and possibly less so.[58]

In this fashion, the concrete internal evidence supplied by the facts and documents of Russian history itself made answer to LeClerc. But there was also the other part of Boltin's approach, the comparative method which helped him keep the balance which other defenders of Russia had so often lost. If, in the question of the towns for example, one posited the existence of urban settlements and trade, one could yet not assume an urban or cosmopolitan culture. For the attainment of these, history required many centuries. In the entire region stretching from the Rhine to the Baltic, there had not been a single town before the ninth century, and as late as the 1300's there were few such in Europe (mainly in Italy) fully deserving of the name. Nor was medieval France more advanced in the justice she dispensed, relying more often on the law of custom, the decisions of elders and popular tribunals than on the written codes. In sum, "the way of life, government, gradations of rank, education, and justice were the same among Russians of the period as they were among the primitive Germans, Britons, and Franks before their first organization into communities." [59]

For every phenomenon of Russian history a parallel could be found in the history of the West. Was Christianity in Russia marked by superstition, hypocrisy, and sanctimoniousness? Boltin would not deny it, but it was the age which was receptive to them, not a particular country. In reply to LeClerc's remark that the Russian clergy perpetuated ignorance and superstition for the sake of power and profit, he noted only that it was better for a people to be superstitious under an ignorant clergy than to be enslaved by an enlightened one, that it was easier to stamp out primitive beliefs than to liberate man from the tyrannical power of the hierarchy. There was no doubt about the target of this observation: "A blind guide—that is the old Russian priest, but a seeing guide—that is the Catholic cleric." [60] The contrast was between ignorance and malevolence. It was also one of the reasons why

Orthodoxy was preferable to Catholicism. Even though the Eastern Church was the source of many superstitions which still survived, she had remained true to the ancient rites and teachings. Catholicism, on the other hand, had moved far from the true bases of faith, and in raising high the power of the Popes of Rome had created a Christian Dalai-Lama. Ignorance, Boltin seemed to feel, since it was more likely artless, was preferable to craftiness. Even if one agreed with LeClerc that learning had been neglected in ancient Russia, this had been no bar to virtue and wisdom. Some of her princes had displayed these qualities to an exemplary degree, in an age when all over Europe knowledge had been in a mournful state. The present has not the right to proclaim its superiority over the past and though it is possibly more enlightened, the hearts of men in olden times were purer and their morals better than ours.[61]

Surely LeClerc could not be right in saying that from 865 to 1620 the Russians were the unhappiest people in the world. If it was true for them, it was true also for all other nations, because the parallel extended to almost every period and every sphere of life. The division of the Kievan state into near-independent principalities, the hierarchy of prince, boyar, gentry, and serf, and the tyranny of Ivan IV had their counterparts in the history of the West. With this belief in the essential unity of all historical development, the question of how and when the Russian state had come into being, what was the genealogy of its people, was less important to Boltin than it had been to some of his predecessors. To lose his way in the uncharted wastes of prehistory (Russian history began for him with Rurik) was not to his taste. Who the ancestors of the Russes were he did not decide with finality, and he ridiculed the pretensions of those who believed in their direct descent from Noah and his grandsons. The Norman question Boltin resolved in line with Mueller's thesis, believing Rurik to have been a Varangian Prince of Finland.[62]

In a theory as insistent as Boltin's on the right of a people to its own character and customs, a right limited only by the overriding laws of nature and history, one would expect to learn how these, in interaction with environment and experience, had given rise to peculiarly national ways of life. Although Boltin warned frequently against the introduction of innovations which would be in conflict with traditional, national values he never spelled out in detail what these values were. Nor did he make any claim for their unchangeable and inviolable nature. There was, he held, a unity of custom, a permanence of law and belief which could be followed through all of Russian history up to the time of Peter; but Boltin never pointed to a specific phenomenon of Russian life, as the true nationalist must, never proclaimed: this is the principle, the essence of our being which must not be touched. It is this above all which separates him from the Slavophiles whose view of the Petrine reforms he shared in important respects. Boltin does not idealize the past in any of its aspects. He does, however, demand that posterity deal gently—in practical as well as in intellectual terms—with those of its features which by their very survival have passed the test of history. No mere act of will on the part of a ruler, no decree of government can change the customs of thought and practice which have been centuries in the making.

The period of Tatar domination served Boltin as important illustration of a point which was basic to all of his thinking. Russia may have been beaten and reduced to political impotence, but she never was conquered. The thought, the dress, the language, the manners and morals of her people were, with minor exceptions, untouched by Tatar rule and preserved their distinctive quality. Whatever changes did take place in the national character were of a superficial kind.[63] Russia's physical features and her historical experience made it impossible for the effects of a foreign rule imposed from above to penetrate to every level of society. A people's way of life is something so deeply rooted that it can change only slowly and gradually. It is a lesson which every true statesman must master, a lesson which Peter and other advocates of Western ways had often neglected. "Changes of the principles of national life, of the people's patterns of thought must not be introduced by force; it must be left to time and circumstance to bring them about." [64] To force the pace of reform, as Peter had done, led either to blind, unreasoning resistance (as from the Old Believers) or to those grotesque distortions of Westernism which had characterized the young men sent to study abroad. It was best not to insist on an empty conformity and to allow some latitude of ritual and belief where these did not conflict with the obligations of a good Christian and citizen. Of what possible benefit could it be to force the Don Cossacks to shave their beards against their wishes? Was it not better to respect custom, even prejudice, so long as it did not challenge the bases of authority? Neither beard, long cloak, old prayer books, nor making the sign of the cross with two fingers had any power to influence the disposition of a man's heart or soul. [65]

To believe otherwise would give unwonted preference to externals, and while neglecting substance stress ritual at the expense of belief, training before education. It was the failure to realize this distinction which had marred some of Peter's best efforts, and the most profound change in Russian manners and morals occurred when he sent young men abroad to study or had their education placed in the hands of foreigners. Boltin dated from that time a waning of patriotism, of attachment to the faith and the traditions of the fatherland. In his impatience to raise Russia to Europe's level, Peter had lost sight of the differences between education which addresses itself to the moral nature of man, and instruction which is but the acquisition of technical competence. Not having acquired at home a firm grounding in the former, the young men came back caricatures of what they had been and of what they wanted to be, grotesque testimonials to the wisdom of older days, when a mature mind and firm grasp of the laws and morals of the fatherland were the prerequisites for foreign travel. Only too late did Peter recognize "that in order to gain the desired end, one must begin with a good education and end with foreign travel." [66]

The undiscriminating introduction of novelty was harmful not only to morality; it had a deleterious effect also on the physical stamina of Russians for it caused the abandonment of traditions which climate and conditioning had created. "Many have observed that when we gave up the habits of our ancestors and began to live in the foreign manner, we became weaker, more easily fell prey to sickness, and less often lived to a ripe old age: I believe that the main reasons for this are the abolition of the custom of the bath and the introduction of French cooking." [67] To Boltin's quite modern perception a culture was all of one piece. Destroy the old-fashioned bath-house, accustom stomachs to the refinements of French cuisine and you destroy vital elements of culture which have enabled Russians to adapt to the rigors of their climate and to use to best advantage the products of their soil.

"Accept us as we are," Boltin seemed to say to Russia's critics, "for we cannot be anything else." There was never, as there must be for the true nationalist, the willful assertion, that Russians *must be* something else than other Europeans. They were neither a world unto themselves which could go back only to its own past for guidance, nor were they destined to copy all that the West had evolved out of its experience. Imitation or isolation were terms in which Boltin did not, and could not possibly have posed the problem of Russia and the West. He was a Westerner and a modernist who could view the period of Catherine's reign as Russia's golden age.

But he was also a conservative who could cherish what was vital in the past, "organic" as it was later called. He was not a Slavophile, but there can be little doubt that in the more discriminating attitude which both he and Prince Shcherbatov brought to the study of Russia's modern history, there were sounded notes which recur as major themes in the Slavophile doctrine. Boltin's thinking though national was not nationalistic.

From a purely academic point of view the achievement of Russian eighteenth-century historiography may well appear meager. Where the work of Lomonosov and Shcherbatov was not sufficiently critical to serve as the basis for a further development of the discipline, the products of better research or better minds failed equally to found a scholarly tradition in which successive generations refined the work of their teachers. This is not to say that a man like Boltin was unaware of what his predecessors had done—he relied on Tatishchev to an extraordinary degree—but even for this most gifted of the writers of history there was lacking the autonomy of motive, the strict definition of purpose, and the institutional resources which together establish history as a science and academic discipline. Important beginnings were made, but even the very best of these came too late to bear fruit within the century. The value and the subtlety of Boltin's work found their greatest appreciation much later, when new trends created a greater receptivity for his views. It would be an unjustified limitation, however, to apply only professional standards to the writings of Russian historians in the eighteenth century or to ignore other writers. In studying the formation of a historical consciousness, which was also the consciousness of a common national past and fate, the contributions made by amateur antiquarians and archivists, publishers, and litterateurs cannot be neglected. Their work was as much the result of an increased awareness of national history as a factor in its growth.

By any other criterion, F. A. Emin (1735–1770) and I. P. Elagin (1725–1794)[68] hardly belong to the history of Russian historiography, for nothing was further from their minds than a detached, scholarly study of the evidence. They both belonged to what Sergei Solovev aptly called the "rhetorical school," and their purpose was to edify and to entertain, or simply to make a quick "killing" in a favorable literary market. This was most true of Filip Aleksandrovich Emin, an adventurer of obscure antecedents, a Polish Catholic who turned Muslim in Turkey and Orthodox Christian in Russia and was not above exploiting a shrewdly-gauged public demand for national history with literary embellishment. A journalist of quick perception and ready pen who had learned how to assess and meet public taste in Western Europe, Emin arrived in Russia in 1761 and quickly learned the language and customs of his new homeland. He soon set about the composition of a historical work and as early as 1767 the first volume of his "Russian History" appeared. Its subtitle left nothing to be desired and promised everything: "The Lives of all the Russian Rulers from the very Beginning; All the great Deeds which are worthy of eternal Remembrance of the Emperor Peter the Great and his Successors; Including a Dsecription of the Golden Age in the North in the Reign of Catherine the Great." Brought up to the year 1213, the work was as rich in invention, dramatic narrative, and dialogue as it was unmindful of the rules of historical composition. There was no indication of sources, little adherence to those that were used, references to some which did not exist, and a fertility of imagination which carried poetic license to new heights. Facts and speeches were simply invented, and it deterred Emin not at all that a speech of Gostomysl to the people of Novgorod which adorned his narrative was not to be found in any of the chronicles. If Gostomysl, he argued, had not in fact uttered this speech, he must have said something very much like it.

Elagin's "Essay on Russian History," (1790) which he wrote towards the end of his life as a diversion in his retirement had all the literary flourishes and inaccuracies of Emin's opus. Elagin, who prided himself on the beauty of his style, had been in charge of the Petersburg Theater in the years 1766–1769 and it may well be that the dramatic quality of his "Essay" is a reflection of tastes and habits developed during that period. He was most anxious to avoid the boredom which other historians had induced, and thought a historical narrative ought to be brief and to the point, to teach wisdom and statecraft, not lose itself in an uninspiring recital of facts. In the life and institutions of pagan Novgorod, Elagin saw significant similarities with the ancient history of other states. Dictatorship and senate, priesthood and *magister equitum*, all had their equivalent in Novgorod, and he implied that the mythology and superstitions of ancient Russia were no more and no less reprehensible than those of ancient Egypt, Greece, or Rome. Emin, on the other hand, had with uncharacteristic delicacy skirted the whole topic of the religious rites and customs of the ancient Slavs for fear that their description might be offensive to the enlightened and Christian eyes of his readers.

One of the most important stimuli to historical interest during the last third of the century came once again from the monarch. As in the case of Peter, Catherine's sponsorship and her participation in this field had public as well as private motives. Her lively intellect, her close contact with the opinion of educated Europe, her keen awareness of the value of a good "press" at home and abroad, the wish to be regarded as a true successor of the great tsars, the hope of reconciling a disaffected and critical opposition—these were the factors which made the Empress historically conscious. In 1763 she restored history, which had been neglected in the reforms of 1747, to a place of first importance in the curriculum of the Academy, and after her accession both Mueller and Schloezer fared better than they had previously. The former was summoned into the Empress' presence in October 1764, asked about the state of his researches, requested to supply Her Majesty with volume nine of the *Sammlung Russischer Geschichte*, and instructed to assist Muennich in the preparation of his memoirs. Schloezer was appointed to the coveted professorship in 1765.

By an expression of interest or requests for historical data, by encouragement or subsidy, Catherine supported the work of Boltin, Shcherbatov, and Golikov (a Kursk merchant, author of "The Deeds of Peter the Great"), the researches of N. N. Bantysh-Kamenski in the Moscow archives, and the publication of historical monuments by Count A. I. Musin-Pushkin. Volume IV of Tatishchev's "History" was printed at her expense, and the publication of Novikov's "Ancient Russian Library" was made possible by her financial support as much as by materials which government archives supplied on her instruction. By a decree of 1784 Catherine established a historical commission and appointed two professors of Moscow University, A. A. Barsov and Kh. A. Chebotarev to serve on it under the chairmanship of Count A. P. Shuvalov.

It is possible that Barsov and Chebotarev were in this fashion rewarded for helping the Empress in the writing of her extensive "Notes on Russian History," with which she filled the pages of a new magazine in the years 1783–1784 (*Sobesednik Lyubitelei rossiiskigo slova*). The magazine had been called to life by Catherine herself but failed to have the success and the contributors for which she had hoped, so that the "Notes" alone bore the burden of affirmation with which the magazine was to have met criticism of the Empress and her regime. Without scientific or literary merit, the "Notes" (subsequently republished in a special edition) were little more than literal extracts from the chronicles. With these, Catherine as the guardian of the national honor, wanted to reply to Russia's foreign detractors. Comparing Russia's history with that of the West, the unprejudiced reader would discover that the human race had everywhere the same passions and desires, and that for their achievement it had often employed the same means.[69] It was a position which brought her much closer to that of Boltin, and one which was much more readily defensible than blind praise, but it was not informed by his knowledge nor inspired by his historical insight. In Catherine's case it was too much tied to the monarch's personal prestige and the magnifying of her role.

A few years later, perhaps under Boltin's influence, Catherine herself had come to recognize that too great an emphasis on the role of the monarch could only damage the national reputation. When a French emigré, Senac de Meilhan, in 1790 proposed that he write a history of Russia in the eighteenth century, Catherine imposed on him the absolute condition not to "assert that Russia before Peter the First had had neither laws nor institutions, since the opposite was true." Russia, she continued, had been on one level with the rest of Europe; only the turbulent years of the late sixteenth and early seventeenth centuries had held up her progress for some forty or fifty years. In warning the Frenchman against painting the history of pre-Petrine Russia all in black, which he undoubtedly would have done in order to underscore more emphatically the successes of the eighteenth century, the Empress warned implicitly against an overestimation of her own role. "One must never forget," she admonished de Meilhan, "that on every reign there lies the imprint of its time, and that the spirit of the times can open up for us views which we have never expected." [70] In this fashion, Catherine was brought by an identification with the nation she ruled to minimize somewhat both her own role and the achievements of the present, to speak of a "spirit" or "imprint" of the times which might not, after all, be identical with the spirit or imprint of the ruler.

In a not dissimilar way Novikov, seeking to counteract the immorality of foreign influence, and blocked from attacking its true source, had been led to look for an indigenous way of life and values in Russia's past. His shift from a satirical attack on the evils of the present to a search for the moral values of the past, could and did find the Empress' support. From about 1773 on, Novikov began an extensive publishing activity which was devoted primarily to works of Russian history, geography, and literary history. He issued some thirty titles, of which the "Ancient Russian Library" was the most famous as well as the most valuable. It was the first regular collection of sources printed in Russia and the first exclusively devoted to archival materials and literary monuments. It contained materials on geography and ethnography and Novikov enlisted as collaborators such men as Mueller and Shcherbatov. Encouraged by the reception of the first ten volumes of his collection, all of which had appeared by the end of 1775, Novikov in 1776 planned publication of a "Treasury of Russian Antiquities," of which one volume appeared; it was subsequently incorporated into a second edition of the "Library" (1788–1791). In a preface Novikov voiced the hope that the readers of the "Library" would delight in the greatness of soul and the unaffected simplicity of their ancestors and would come to cherish this heritage. Though useful to know the manners, the morals, and the customs of other nations, it was much more useful to be informed about one's own ancestors; if it was praiseworthy to love and to do justice to foreign achievements, it is shameful to hold one's fellow-citizens in contempt.[71]

The work of the newly-founded Russian Academy (1785) also helped to make the distant past appear in a more favorable light. From the very beginning, history had together with language and literature been one of the Academy's primary concerns, and the collection and publication of the "treasured memorials of the deeds of our ancestors" [72] was one of its foremost tasks. Those who were closely associated with the work of the Academy, men like Count A. I. Musin-Pushkin, Boltin, and Shcherbatov, did not need to be reminded of the importance of historical research and would make sure that in this regard the Academy lived up to the expectations of its founders. Nor were these disappointed. The publication, in 1792 and 1793 respectively, of the *Russkaya Pravda* and the *Dukhovnaya* ("Testament") of the Grand Duke Vladimir Vsevolodovich, were events of first importance for Russian historical science. But at the time they were acclaimed as more than that—testimonials to a Russian civilization now conclusively shown to be of more ancient date than the reforms of Peter.

Boltin and Musin-Pushkin were to a high degree conscious of this aspect of the documents which they had published and in their prefaces and notes they stressed the wider significance of their discoveries. Provided with translations into modern Russian, both texts aimed to give samples of the manners and the thought of old Russia, and finally to lay to rest the slander that "our ancestors . . . had been a savage, nomadic people without commerce or enlightenment;" to show, on the contrary, that "the venerable customs and morals of our fathers . . . have been perverted by fashionable French education." [73]

There are numerous milestones, beyond those already mentioned, to mark the change in attitude which led articulate Russians to revalue past and present. In a more critical approach to the reforms and person of Peter, the basis was laid for an idealization of the past. The Princess Dashkova, in disputing with Count Kaunitz at Vienna the opinion that Russia had been called to life by Peter, was not content to introduce some balance into the foreigner's views. She had also to assert that long before Peter "the arts had taken refuge and were cherished in Russia" and that "we can boast of historians . . . who have left more manuscripts than the historians of all the rest of Europe put together." [74] The unknown author of "Thoughts about Russia" (1792 or 1793) saw in the popular assemblies of Moscow's Red Square a kind of civic club or Athenian stoa where the lessons of citizenship were imparted to the young—a scene of primitive democracy on which the patriarchal tsars of pre-Petrine Russia looked with interested benevolence. From it they derived a direct knowledge of the needs and feelings of their people. [75]

The bricks for the construction of a romanticized view of the past were at hand. Only the cement of a comprehensive philosophy was lacking to bind them.

Although his most important work, the "History of the Russian State," belongs clearly to the next century, Nikolai Karamzin, in his person and his thought exemplifies to an extraordinary degree the way stations which Russian national consciousness passed at the turn of the century. Born in 1766, well educated for his time by extensive reading in the literature of Russia and Europe, Karamzin never shared the antihistorical bias of some of his contemporaries, nor did he ever think of his country with anything but pride. But in his youth he had felt that a gulf of centuries separated old Russia from Europe, and only with the coming of Peter had that gulf been bridged. His first historical speculations on that subject were recorded on the occasion of a meeting with the French historian Levesque, whose acquaintance he made in Paris in 1790. Levesque was the author of a history of Russia which the young Russian traveler, in spite of its shortcomings, found to be the best he knew.

There was still a need, Karamzin felt, for a good Russian

history written with philosophical spirit, critical discernment, and nobility of style—a history that could compare with the works of a Tacitus, a Hume, a Robertson, or a Gibbon. That no such work existed could in no wise be the fault of the subject, for there was much of interest to Russian and foreigner alike, much that was attractive and powerful, in the history of his country. Russia, too, had her history as well as her heroes. She had her Charlemagne in Vladimir, her Louis XI in Ivan IV, and her Cromwell in Godunov. In Peter the Great she had a monarch whose equal no other country could boast. Levesque's failure to recognize Peter's true stature, his denial of genius and originality to the Tsar whom he saw mainly as an imitator, convicted the Frenchman of mediocrity and ignorance in the eyes of Karamzin. He defended his hero, but his defense was conducted in the characteristically cosmopolitan tones of the Enlightenment.

Even Russians, wrote Karamzin, had charged Peter with imitation. For himself, he had never been able to listen to them with anything but distaste. For what other way but that of imitation should or could have been chosen? "Is the way of enlightenment not one and the same for all nations? All enter upon it, one after another."

The foreigners were more advanced than the Russians, so that they had to borrow and learn from others and to utilize foreign experience and methods. Is it reasonable to go searching for something that has already been found? Should Russia then not build ships, not have a standing army or establish an Academy because all these are foreign achievements? Does the people exist which has not borrowed from others? And does one not first need to catch up if one wants to advance?—Well, it was answered, it still was not necessary to imitate slavishly, to accept from the foreigners those things one could easily have done without. And what are those things? Perhaps they speak of our dress and beards? Peter introduced German dress because it seemed to him an improvement; and he ordered the shaving of beards because they are uncomfortable and ugly. The long Russian cloak is too heavy

and is a hindrance in walking . . . and as far as the beard is concerned, it is fitting only for a savage.[76]

To Karamzin, as much as to Boltin, a culture was a whole
whose isolated parts could not be moved without affecting
their totality. It was precisely for this reason that Peter had
been right in attacking beard and kaftan with as much vehemence as state and church. It was done in order to create a
precedent, to make way for other incomparably more important and useful foreign innovations. The old inborn obstinacy
of the Russians had to be crushed in order to make them pliable
and receptive to instruction. All the sad Jeremiads about the
corruption of the national character, about the loss of a truly
moral national philosophy, were dismissed by Karamzin as
jest or as grounded in a lack of insight. "All that is national is
nothing against the Human. The main thing is to be men, not
Slavs. What is good for Man, cannot be bad for Russians, and
all that Englishmen or Germans have invented for the benefit
of mankind belongs also to me, for I am a man." [77]

Here indeed is a different Karamzin from the one who
subsequently blamed Peter for depriving Russians of their
Russianness. His conception of borrowing is too elevated to
be put on one level with that foppish Westernism of dress and
speech against which Novikov warred so persistently. Opposed
as he was to that kind of imitation, Karamzin yet remained
unmoved by the plaints of those who traced to the reforms
a lowering of the moral qualities of Russians. Progress imposes
iron laws. The beard and the kaftan must yield to it no less
than the crossbow. Before long, however, Karamzin arrived
at a position where, like Shcherbatov and Boltin, he felt constrained to defend ancient customs as an integral part of the
national heritage which must not be swept away by a flood
of innovations, and as a result he appraised the work of Peter
in a different light.

The circumstances and the motives of this change of perspective on the part of Karamzin, his intellectual biography for the two decades which separate the appearance of the first of his "Letters of a Russian Traveler" (1791–1792) from the "Memoir on Ancient and Modern Russia" (1811) cannot be traced here in detail, beyond indicating that the events of European politics, the influence of romanticism, the discovery of the literary charms of the Russian past, and his growing conservatism all played a role in his conversion to a new viewpoint. As early as 1802 Karamzin posed the problem and indicated the nature of its eventual solution in an article entitled "Of Love for the Fatherland and National Pride," and even before then, in the historical tales *Natalya* and *Marfa Posadnitsa* he consciously returned to the times when Russians were still Russians, dressed in their own fashion, walked in their own way, and spoke in their own language as their hearts dictated. However remote, however crude others might find those times, Karamzin for his part professed to love them, to retreat to them, to find there his "bearded ancestors," to talk with them of the events of past ages and the "character of our dear Russian people."

In 1803 the passion for the past received official sanction. Karamzin was appointed historiographer and began that gigantic task, the writing of his "History of the Russian State" which was interrupted only by his death in 1826. The attraction of a world which Karamzin had himself felt so strongly was conveyed, as no Russian had been able to do before him, to a wide circle of readers. For a great many literate Russians of the first half of the nineteenth century, Karamzin—thanks to the excellence of his style and the vividness of his narrative— became the guide and mentor in the exploration of the past. When the first eight volumes of the history appeared in 1818, memories of the Fatherland War of 1812 were still fresh and the patriotic sentiments to which it had given rise helped to assure a warm reception for Karamzin's work. It sold 3,000 copies during the first month of publication, and Pushkin recorded that even society ladies who were not in the habit of reading books now took up the history of their fatherland as if it were the latest fashion. "It was a new discovery for them. Old Russia, it seemed, had been found by Karamzin as America had been discovered by Columbus, and for some time there was talk of nothing else." Another contemporary and friend of Karamzin's, the poet Vyazemski, called him the Kutuzov of the postwar years, the man who had saved Russia from oblivion, called her to life and "showed us that we do have a fatherland, as many of us found out in the year twelve." [78]

Much more clearly and directly than he could have done in the "History" which dealt primarily with the events of the political past, Karamzin expressed his feelings and thoughts in the historical reflections contained in the "Memoir on Ancient and Modern Russia." Here he was not restrained by the needs of pragmatic exposition and could give free reign to a speculative synthesis which with vast sweep embraced the whole of Russian history. The starting point for him as for so many of his predecessors was the fact of Russia's possession of a highly developed material and spiritual culture at the very beginning of her existence as a state. Neither internal dissension nor foreign invasion had been able to destroy forever the creative features of the national character which had revealed themselves at such an early stage and they, together with the wise policy of her rulers and the institution of autocracy, had succeeded in creating a new empire which was a synthesis of all that was best in Slavic, Germanic, Mongolian, and Byzantine life. In spite of Tatar domination, Russia had not been hermetically sealed off from the rest of Europe, and had made her own such achievements of the West as gunpowder and printing. There were great libraries which could rouse the envy of Europe; famous Italian artists practiced their skills in fifteenth-century Moscow and Ivan IV created an army such as Russia had not seen until then. At the same time, the country carried on an extensive foreign trade and the eyes of Europe were upon her. These acquisitions had been made in the course of time, born of the need to close the gap with the West which Tatar rule had caused. They were transformations of Russian life which went on gradually, quietly, almost imperceptibly, like a natural growth, without upheavals or the use of force. Borrowing, but as if reluctantly, all that harmonized with their life, Russians fused the new with the old.[79]

It was Peter who had willfully and needlessly destroyed that union and with it the unity of the nation. Peasant, burgher, and merchant from now on saw only a German, a foreigner, in the noble. The dignity and respect which the boyars had enjoyed were undermined; old offices and functions were given new and foreign names and the capital was removed to St. Petersburg. Russians, as a result, became citizens of the world but ceased to be, in some ways, citizens of Russia. Whatever positive results the work of Peter had, however necessary it was, his passion for all that was new and foreign went too far. It had led Russians themselves to share with ignorant foreigners the belief that Peter alone was the creator of Russia's present greatness. Peter had neither created all, nor had he changed all. The Muscovite Tsars had prepared the ground for him, had created the means without which he would have failed, without which he could not have given Russia a fleet, an army, science, and laws. But with these Peter had also brought contempt for the national spirit on which the moral power of the state is based. By uprooting old customs and holding them up to ridicule, he had debased Russians in their own eyes and weakened their attachment for the fatherland. Beard and kaftan, Karamzin now believed, were no obstacles to progress. "Two states can stand on one level of progress without enjoying a similarity of customs. One state may borrow from another useful knowledge, but not its manners. These must change naturally; to prescribe such change by law is unjustifiable violence, even for an autocratic monarch." [80]

Had the reforms then disrupted the unity of the old and the new once and for all; had the organic development of the national life been interrupted for all times? Karamzin believed that it had, that the past could not be retrieved, that Peter had made Europeans of his subjects and that it was fruitless to try and be anything else now. To complain of it was useless. The unity of spirit between the old and the new Russia had been broken and with a mighty hand Peter had set his country on a new road.[81] Yet there was hope for the future, for this need not mean the loss of national identity, of a unique national spirit or the abandonment of all efforts to preserve what still remained. Peter had not succeeded in changing all that was most basically Russian and national. Literature, in particular, gave proof of the survival of distinctive and creative traits which had their sources in the native soil, the Russian heart, the Russian mind. "Having appropriated the taste of the French, we also possess our own. . . . There are sounds of the Russian heart, the play of the Russian spirit in the creations of our literature which will unfold yet more richly in the future." [82] If the lessons of the past were heeded, if history, "that sacred book of nations . . . the mirror of their deeds and being . . . this testament to posterity," [83] were only consulted, Russia need not surrender the essential features of her character nor suffer damage in her civil polity whose miraculous harmony must be preserved from all violent change.

Karamzin's profound respect for the national past and its integrity expressed a social conservatism which feared a radical change in the institutions of his country. It also reflected an awareness of the unique elements in Russia's historical experience—an awareness which others shared and which had been growing throughout the century. This made it possible for Boltin or Karamzin to do without the crude efforts of men like Lomonosov and Tatishchev to prove Russian equality with the West. They felt no need to disprove the Norman origins of the Russian state. It was enough to show that the course of development had not been substantially different for Russia than for other countries; that there were certain native impulses at work in Russian history which gave it a degree of continuity and refuted the charges of dependence. There was imitation, as there must be for all peoples who do not want to live in backward isolation. But there was also originality and uniqueness, prerequisites for the existence of a national character.

## CHAPTER VI

# The Search for a National Character

One result of the spread of a historical consciousness was that the discussion "Russia *vis-à-vis* Europe" was now conducted more often in historical terms. A sense of history and a perspective of time allowed Russians to add a new dimension to the evaluation of their own culture, to abandon that rather shaky ground from which they asserted defiantly that their political and cultural life was not substantially different from that of Europe. This very defiance had had the effect of pointing up the stark contrast with observable reality and of impressing further with their own backwardness those Russians who were in a position to make comparisons with the West. History was of some help in this impasse. It demonstrated that the course of human development was everywhere the same, but that its speed and individual stages were not at every point strictly comparable. It showed that Russia's history could boast of features which other countries did not enjoy and that it was foolish to claim for her an absolute identity with the West. The study of history and a sense of history, particularly towards the end of the century, deepened and refined the dialogue between Russia and the West and even entered the vocabulary of nonhistorians. Yet the earlier, more naive attitude survived and continued to proclaim: we too are part of Europe, and are like Europe in every way. Asking Russians to look into their own culture and past for unique objects of attachment and pride was all well and good; the instinct to claim similarity with Europe was still stronger than the attitude which demanded recognition of Russia's difference. These superficially different attitudes sprang from identical motives— the wish to establish Russia as an equal in the Western family of nations, to show that Russians were "real Europeans," not a peculiar people to which standards relevant to all the civilized world were inapplicable. In the end, the conviction won out that it was difference and uniqueness—a national character—that best supported this claim.

A touchingly naive instance of the desire not to seem inferior in the eyes of Europe is related by the Princess Dashkova. Putting up at a Danzig inn for a couple of nights, she was horrified to see that its large dining room was almost completely dominated by two paintings depicting battles lost by Russian troops "who were represented in groups of dead and dying, or on their knees, supplicating mercy of the victorious Prussians." The Princess was scandalized that this evidence of Russian pusillanimity and defeat should be so openly displayed for all to see, and she upbraided the Russian *chargé d'affaires* for allowing such an "abominable monument of our disgrace to exist." That gentleman assured her that it was quite outside his province to influence the art work in Prussian inns, so that the Princess took it upon herself to redress this grievous slight to the national honor. She and a few companions barricaded themselves in the dining room, and with the help of paints and brushes regained these lost battles for Russia by "changing the blue and white of the conquering Prussians into the red and green uniforms of our Russian heroes." [1] This redemption of the national honor was not much more than the prank of a spirited young woman; but it reveals the deep sensitivity of many Russians in the face of a Europe which seemed still to deny them recognition.

To gain that recognition had been the hope of many Russians since the beginning of the century. For Peter, too, one of the basic goals of his activity had been to prove to

Europe that the country over which he ruled was not as backward as generally believed. Not the least of the functions of his projected Academy was "to gain for us trust and honor in Europe, to show . . . that in our country, too, we work for science, and that it is time to stop regarding us as barbarians who hold all learning in contempt;" and on one occasion Peter advertised to a fellow-monarch the talents of a Russian painter as proof that Russia too produced good masters.[2]

In large part, Peter's efforts to launch Russia into Europe politically and to bring European techniques and manners to Russia, were themselves responsible for creating an awareness of the gap which separated the two worlds. An accompanying feature of Peter's reforms had been a national inferiority complex, and subsequently few chances were missed to overcome it by pointing out that Russia's shortcomings were apparent rather than real. The triumphal processions with their themes reminiscent of the glories of antiquity, poems and plays celebrating military victories, the comparisons of Russian monarchs with the heroes of antiquity, were to reassure Russians about their standing in the world. In this sense, even the work of court poets and dynastic adulators was of importance, for pride in the monarchy and the Tsar could stand for a national pride whose other elements had not yet been developed. Until folklorists and writers, historians and artists could discover or create objects of national reverence, the monarch was made to serve as the symbol of national strength and greatness.

One of those who contributed to the elevation of the monarch as the personification of the nation was Feofan Prokopovich. He did so in terms which were designed to stimulate and to gratify national pride. Eulogizing the late Tsar Peter in a memorial oration of 1725, the Archbishop reviewed the ruler's services to the Russian fatherland in the fields of economics, state organization, and international politics. Peter had raised Russia's standing and reputation in international affairs, and thanks to his labors Russia had stepped forth as a strong power which had defeated Charles XII, a monarch considered invincible. Now the world began to respect Russia, to reckon with her, to recognize her might. Now Russia too had a fleet and an army, and with these instruments fashioned by Peter she had conquered for herself the rank of a major European power, had raised herself in the eyes of the world from "shame, contempt, and impotence to glory, respect, and might." [3] As Peter had wanted, all eyes were turned to Europe, seeking Europe's approval, respect, and acceptance.

The image of the newcomer trying to force his way into society is not remote, for the very terms in which Peter's contemporaries described their changed relation with Europe suggest it. In an address celebrating the peace of Nystadt, Chancellor Golovkin offered the imperial title to Peter, and thanked the Tsar for having brought his subjects "out of the shadows of ignorance onto the theater of glory of the whole world . . . out of nothingness into being and into the society of political nations." In almost identical terms, Peter's biographer Krekshin addressed him as "our father . . . [who] has brought us out of nothingness into being." [4] This newly found existence which Peter had made possible for Russians, and which in some minds contrasted as sharply with their former isolation as did being and nonbeing, was to be played out on the European stage. On this Western ground, national feeling could flourish as well as it could on native soil. Acceptance of Peter's Western orientation, though it clashed sharply with isolationist and conservative instincts, did not necessarily mean the abandonment of national interest or identity. It could mean, as it did for his followers, the heightening of Russian prestige and power. Though the instruments for this extension into the international arena—a modern army, navy, and bureaucracy—were essentially European, the goals which they were to achieve were felt by Peter's partisans to be purely Russian.

It was a point of considerable pride to many Russians, one might say of national pride, to be thought good Europeans, no longer to be looked down upon as crude barbarians, to have gained the notice and respect of Europe. Where Fonvizin, typifying a later stage in the devleopment of national consciousness, would proclaim Russians to be "bigger people than the Germans," his older contemporary I. I. Neplyuev could still find cause for pride in the fact that Russians too were people. "This monarch," he wrote of Peter, "brought our fatherland into comparison with others; he taught [others] to realize that we too are people—in a word, whatever you see in Russia began with him and whatever will be done in the future will draw on this source." Now Russia was met with respect and wonder as an equal in the community of nations, no longer regarded as one of those Indian, Persian, or other exotic states, no longer ridiculed, no longer formless.[5]

This feeling of pride was reflected not only by Peter's biographers and admirers, by court preachers and poets; it found expression also in the popular stories which were perhaps the most widely read literature of the early part of the century. The sailor Vasili Koriotski, hero of one of these tales, is referred to as a "Russian sailor;" yet his country of origin is "Russian Europe." In the person of Vasili, the Russian who is also a European, his country had entered European society; the fact that this Russian adventurer could woo and win a Florentine princess and be received on terms of almost perfect equality by the Holy Roman Emperor was as much a tribute to his country as to him. Equally gratifying to the readers of his exploits must have been the fact that after his European triumphs he decides to return home to father and fatherland. The Vasili who could be considered a serious contender for the hand and inheritance of a princess had gained this right, as literary convention demanded, by overcoming insurmountable obstacles and vicious enemies, by courage, prowess, and skill.[6] These very same qualities had also won for

Russia entry into European political society and they were stressed throughout the century as an important basis for national pride and foreign recognition.

The power of her arms and the respect they commanded from friend and foe were Russia's strongest claims for recognition. With the weapons Peter had fashioned, Russia extended her rule, her influence, and her greatness. Her poets, from Tredyakovski to Derzhavin, sounded this theme with varying degrees of skill and emphasis. But in their eyes it was not the naked power of arms and numbers alone that these victories revealed: it was the lion-like courage of the Russian warrior, the nobility of the country which had nourished him, the excellence of military organization which betokened similar capacities in other fields, and the greatness of spirit which defended Christian Europe from the infidels. Now, after having demonstrated their greatness on the field of battle, their divine election to martial might and glory, it was time for Russians to scale new heights. This was the task proclaimed for his countrymen by the jurist S. E. Desnitski in a public lecture at Moscow University (1768). His subject was the study of jurisprudence, but in a lengthy introduction he reviewed Russia's successes in the arts of war, rated her conquests higher than those of Greece and Rome, and saw them as heralds of yet greater triumphs in the arts of peace. "Worship at different shrines now, Russians! The Russian Minerva is creating a new Olympus where your deeds, needed for the fatherland's peaceful glory, will bring honor to your names. . . ." [7]

No one identified his person and his fate more closely with this newly found national pride of place than did Lomonosov, and all of his work was deeply imbued with a sense of Russian greatness and destiny. Russia's might and the respect to which this entitled her among the nations of the world—these were the themes which Lomonosov never tired of stating. "The

Russian Empire, by the wealth of its internal resources and its great victories is the equal of the first European states and even exceeds many of them." Its troops have defeated Turks, Swedes, and Prussians and have extended Russian power and influence to China, to Japan, and even to distant America. Europe no longer looks down upon Russia, no longer disposes of her as if she were an impotent colonial dependency; it is Europe now that looks attentively to the East for help and leadership.[8] It was of equal importance that the world recognize Russia's claims in the arts and sciences. Here it was more difficult to point to past achievement and Lomonosov pictured in his mind's eye a future in which the Russian land would give birth to its own Columbus, its Platos, and Newtons. To some of his contemporaries, Lomonosov had already fulfilled Russia's great promise. They acclaimed him as greater than Virgil (Plavilshchikov), a Russian Malherbe (Sumarokov), "this Pindar, Cicero, and Virgil, glory of Russians, inimitable, immortal Lomonosov" (Derzhavin). Novikov found noteworthy the fact that Lomonosov had finished a mosaic depicting the feats of Peter the Great with native materials and masters, "without any foreign help whatsoever." [9]

For the moment, alas, the most convincing and dramatic evidence of Russian greatness still came from the battlefield. In 1760, after defeating Frederick the Great at Kunersdorf, Russian troops entered Berlin in dramatic emphasis of their new role in the European concert of powers. Other victories followed in quick succession. Those of Rumyantsev in the war against the Turks, the naval victory at Chesme, which seized the Russian imagination with particular force, the fall of Ochakov, the capture of Izmail by Suvorov, victories in Poland and Italy, and the defeat of the Swedish fleet in the short war of 1789 were cause for pride and poetry. They were also the real ingredients of Russia's military and political importance. The literary monuments to these events viewed them as signs of moral fibre and the favors of Providence. This was particularly the case in Derzhavin's poetic celebration of the "Capture of Izmail." God's will had guided the Russian sword and Russia's martial spirit had marched hand in hand with Christ's religion. Not only in her fight against the enemies of Christianity, but also in combating the armies of revolutionary France, had Russia warred for the peace and well being of all Europe.

In other areas of life, particularly in literature and the arts, few Russians felt the time had come to measure their achievements with those of the West. At times they might indeed mistake their Lomonosov for a Pindar, their Sumarokov for a Northern Racine and turn with Bogdanovich away from Greece to hail the coming of the golden age in Catherine's Russia. For the most part, however, they still looked to the future. Karamzin, for instance, was too much the man of the world, had too intimate a knowledge of Western life and letters not to be aware of the limitations of Russian literature. But where he was critical of past and present, he was also full of high hope for the future. "Oh Russians," he wrote in 1787, "the age is near when in our land too poetry shall shine like sun at noonday. . . . Soon all the nations shall come North to fetch their light." [10] It was necessary for the realization of this hope that Russians should cease to pay exclusive attention to the products of French and English authors and begin to read and support their own. By 1802, when Karamzin formulated this as the most important condition for the success of Russian literature, Russia's right to enter the republic of letters as an equal was for him no longer dependent on future glories. Past successes had proved the great talents of Russians, and he asked his countrymen to cherish what they would have others respect.

These frequent declarations of equality with the West in politics and poetry had their counterpart in the most mundane pursuits where national consciousness was often nourished by the vital sources of economic rivalry. There must have been a good deal of this, unrecorded by writers or historians, among tradesmen and artisans who felt they were being displaced by foreign competitors. Though the contribution which the economic envy of inarticulate and unknown men made to the debate with Europe was small enough, it could be taken up by others who had broader perspectives and wider goals. Beginning with Pososhkov, the realization that Russians could do as well what foreigners were now given excessive wages and unusual privileges to do, led to conclusions which were inevitably broader than mere calculations of profit and loss. There was also economic nationalism in the mercantilist sense,[11] but when a Russian master or artisan could replace a foreigner this meant more than a saving of specie; it was proof of the existence of native talent. "Many Germans have greater learning than we do," Pososhkov conceded, "but our minds, thanks be to God, are no worse than theirs . . ." or: "Our Russians have hands just as the foreigners do, and the foreigners did not come from heaven but are just such people as we are."[12]

If belief in oneself was to be preserved and strengthened, it was necessary to reduce the foreigner, unquestionably the possessor of advanced techniques, to proper proportions, to strip him of the attributes of the extraordinary, to show that he did not "come from heaven." Ya. P. Kozelski, author of texts of philosophy, arithmetic, and mechanics, fought the notion that a people's possession of an advanced technology and science was a sign of intellectual excellence. This would be true only, he argued in 1764, if a mastery of the sciences were inherited. Since it can be gained only by application and long years of study, it makes no difference whether a man is born in France or Tatary. Similarly, the "first Russian arithmetician and geometer," as Tredyakovski called L. F. Magnitski, emphasized the fact that the "Arithmetic" which he published in 1703 was a product of the "native Russian mind, not the Germans' doing." [13]

Novikov repeatedly deplored the lack of confidence which Russians expressed when they preferred the foreigners' products to their own. If Russians arts and crafts were not yet the equal of those in the West, the fault was not intrinsic to them, lay not in any presumed inferiority. Having a wealth of human and material resources to draw upon, Russian artists and craftsmen suffered from a lack of recognition at home, from the snobbishness of a class which refused to concede that anything home grown could compare in quality or beauty with that which was of foreign origin. His story of the bridge builder who is thought to be German or French is a sermon on a theme dear to his heart. "Go home, you blockheads," the bridge builder shouts to some bystanders, "or I shall beat and skin you; I am a Russian. And also let me tell you that a Russian head is often better than a foreign one, but it grows dull from neglect." [14]

All that we have, our history and our heroes, our language and our Gods, our manufactures and our towns are fully the equal of anything that Europe has to show. Whatever standard of measurement was applied, it was always done with a backward glance at Europe. Even in the possession of knaves and scoundrels (engaging ones, however) Russians would yield nothing to Europe. "We have and have had great swindlers, thieves, and robbers," just as we have had great artists and generals. [15]

For Catherine, the question of Russia's Europeanness at first admitted of no doubt. The country she ruled and into which she wanted to introduce principles of government derived from the most advanced Western thinkers must necessarily be a European state. She proclaimed this conviction in the first chapter of her "Instruction" to the Grand Commission on the drafting of the laws. To Prince Shcherbatov the proposition was questionable and although he expressed his disagreement with the Empress in geographical terms—"it is impossible to call all Russia a European state, for many of her provinces are in Asia"—his doubts extended also to the advisability of imposing laws which conflicted with native beliefs and practices.[16] The Empress herself soon realized that to call Russia a European state was at best oversimplification and that the living and often intractable reality she had to deal with was much more complex. Although it was clearly necessary to go beyond the formulation of the "Instruction," she was reluctant to do so.

In refuting the Abbé Chappe d'Auteroche's *Voyage en Sibérie* of 1768, Catherine stated categorically that few countries had been so much maligned and slandered as Russia. Prejudice and ignorance alone, she wrote in her "Antidot" (1770), could have led to the conclusion that Russia was on a lower level of culture than the other nations of Europe. Conscientious examination and philosophical reflection would show that Russians stood on approximately the same height. The principle that they were the same as men everywhere, neither altogether good nor altogether bad, assured a similarity of cultural and political development—Russian equality with Europe. Catherine would not retreat from this position and although her argument occasionally betrayed her doubts, she remained essentially committed to the proposition she had expressed in the "Instruction." For 700 years the course of Russian history had run parallel to that of Europe; only an occasionally unsettled state of affairs in the seventeenth century had caused her to fall back somewhat.[17] Armed with the conviction that wise and enlightened legislation would overcome any historical lag, Catherine could reduce to insignificance every unpleasant fact which the Abbé or others might bring forward.

With great intellectual agility Catherine would occupy whatever ground seemed most advantageous at a given moment. If Russian peasants were said to be badly off, she would point out that their situation in most cases was better than that of peasants elsewhere. If the accusation charged that Russia was governed by an arbitrary bureaucracy in the name of a despotic ruler, Catherine would insist that there were few countries in the world where law was so widely respected as in Russia, none in which life and property were better protected by the laws and where these were in such perfect harmony with the monarch's will. As if dimly aware of an argument which made a virtue of the absence of formal law, she was also ready to point out that in fact, as well as in law, Russians were as free, if not freer, than other peoples; that their laws, though many and detailed, were simpler and easier to understand than those of any European country. In spite of the dominance of the monarch's will, Russia had a tradition in which all citizens were educated to public responsibility and shared in it. The positive elements of the national character had made the Russians more tolerant, humane, cooperative, and honest than the most elaborately contrived system of laws could have done. "Pay heed, M. Chappe, soon you will have nothing but the shadow and the substance will be ours." [18]

There was yet one other point on which Catherine felt it necessary to take issue with the Frenchman. He had asserted that climate and geography were responsible for the Russians' lack of genius and imagination, but that they were possessed of excellent imitative capacities. This imitativeness was considered an outstanding national trait by d'Auteroche and others. Russians themselves might claim it as proof of a quick and adaptive intelligence, but Catherine regarded it as a slander on the national character. She was not unwilling to have it known that Western ideas of law and government found their widest application under her aegis; but when a somewhat similar idea was stated critically, she was quick to take offense. All virtues have their source in the human heart, and human capacities being everywhere the same, no one has the right to accuse us of being copies.

There is much that is contradictory in the Empress' polemic with the French Abbé. It was not effective as an antidote and failed, because of its inconsistency, to come to grips with the problem of similarity and uniqueness. Catherine wanted Russia to be recognized as enlightened and European and also to be measured by other than European standards. In spite of her plea for the autonomy of Russian mores, Catherine proclaimed the similarity of Russia with the West, always taking Western standards as the basis of comparison. In the end, her tract turns out to be little more than an elaboration of the paragraph in the "Instruction" which had stated that Russia was a European country.

On occasion, however, Catherine had been driven by the illogic of her position to claim difference, otherness, as a value. In doing this, she answered the challenge of the West in a way that implied abandonment of the "we too" argument. This new reply, which held that the absence of certain Western achievements need not mean inferiority in a different setting, made possible an even more advanced position. It enabled those engaged in the debate with the West to leave the ground which the West had chosen, to proceed to the attack and to proclaim the superiority of the Russian way of life. No longer were Russian customs and traditions considered best for Russia; in certain of its aspects this way of life was absolutely superior to that of Europe. The point was rarely made quite so bluntly, but a number of writers came close to it.

Fonvizin, discovering that life abroad is no better than in Russia, and finding that no amount of formal freedom can guarantee true liberty of person or conscience, postulated a

Russian greatness of heart which other peoples lack. In a similar way Boltin, questioning the meaning of "liberty" for the European peasant who is economically and socially disabled, gives his reader the sense that he thought Russian serfdom superior to any other arrangement under which most European peasants live. "For that liberty which makes one people happy, leads another to unhappiness and ruin. Our peasants could not bear the Prussian form of freedom; the German kind improves their position not at all, from the French variety they would die of hunger, and the English kind would bring them to the abyss of misery." [19] Unlike his Western counterpart, the Russian peasant enjoyed the fruit of his labors, secure in the knowledge that it would not be taken from him by the state, nor did the increase of his well-being make him fear new exactions. Boltin admitted that there were brutal and inhuman masters, yet he believed that the majority of Russian peasants lived in peace and contentment. Each family had its own property which, though not guaranteed by law, belonged to it by a custom which had the full force of law. The landlords, with few exceptions, treated their serfs humanely. Why then introduce into a way of life which was alike considerate of human and property rights, legal and economic relationships which elsewhere seemed to destroy both? For the Russian peasant the improvement of his condition lay not in a freedom which he did not seek, but in an extension of the positive features of Russia's agrarian system which was by any test superior to that of the West.

No longer content to view themselves with Western eyes, Russians, in their search for national identity, asked ever more insistently what the definitive features of the Russian way of life were, in which of them the national character most clearly revealed itself. The question had been at the basis of every articulate confrontation with the West, but towards the end of the century, as imitation and unreasoning protest lost in force and appeal, it was posed with greater immediacy. The search was for a determining principle, as Karl von Moser called it,[20] a principle by which he believed all nations were motivated: obedience in Germany, freedom in England, trade in Holland, the honor of the King in France. The Russians could not be sure what their determining principle, their national spirit or character was; nor were they entirely certain that the search for it should be their goal. For having once found it, it might well serve to separate them from the West of which they wanted so desperately to be a part.

Nonetheless, beginning with Fonvizin and Novikov it became a matter of real concern to Russians first of all to establish that in the possession of that most elusive quality—a national character—Russia did not yield to any other country, and in the second place to determine what that national character was. The term itself, and the more frequent use made of it in the last third of the century, are indicative of the growing preoccupation with a guiding principle which would inform all aspects of the national life and would serve as a standard by which reality could be measured. Even the Empress Catherine had paid tribute to the notion of a "people's cast of mind" (*obshchee v narode umstvovanie*). She had derived it from the influence of faith, climate, laws, traditions, and customs,[21] but it was a fashionable obeisance paid to her Western mentors rather than a serious belief in a basic and abiding set of features distinctive of Russian man. When Fonvizin asked her for a definition of the national character, Catherine stated that the outstanding Russian traits were exemplary obedience, virtue, and quick understanding.[22] This definition satisfied neither her questioner nor future generations. It may be, of course, that any definition of national character is only a projection of wishes and ideals rather than an accurate interpretation of reality. But if it is to have any success at all, the definition must correspond fairly closely to some image people cherish of themselves, and this Catherine's triad failed to do.

Though there was no agreement as to what the features of the national character were, the conviction was widespread that it did exist and the search for it continued. To Novikov it was inconceivable that the Russians should not have a character of their own. To believe that the influence of foreign ways had been so profound as to obliterate all traces of the national character would be absurd. "As if nature, which has arranged all things with such wisdom and which has given to each country its own climate, gifts, and customs, were so unjust as to deny Russia alone a character unique to her people and had fated her to wander about the world, to borrow, bit by bit, the customs of other nations and from them to fashion a character which belongs to no one, least of all to Russia." [23] The journalist Klushin also assumed the existence of a national character when he introduced into his journal, the "St. Petersburg Mercury" (1793), a department of "Russian Anecdotes" designed to illustrate the "national traits." [24] And the poet N. A. Lvov, in the preface to his "Collection of Russian Songs" (1790), expressed the hope that they would be of some value for philosophy which seeks to deduce national character from folk songs. "In the minor tones . . . of these drawn-out songs typical of Russian music, philosophy will ultimately see that tenderness, that sensitivity of the Russian people and that disposition of the soul to melancholy which produces great people in all races." [25] These were the same tones heard by Radishchev on his "Journey," the songs which revealed to him the soul of the people and a musical disposition on which he was prepared to build governments.

A national soul, a national way of life, a national character, some timeless quality of heart and mind which was so deeply a part of every Russian's being that it needed only to be called to life, had to be presumed if the many appeals for a return to the true bases of national life were to have any meaning at all. Sumarokov and Kheraskov, Fonvizin and Novikov, Karamzin and the Princess Dashkova, though they were unable to define the national character in detail, were at one in the belief that there had been a time when Russians had lived in harmony with it, when they had not been torn by conflicting fashions and loyalties. When the Princess called upon Russians to be Russians, and Karamzin expressed his love for the days when Russians were Russians and talked of the "character of the glorious Russian people," they had before them, as did Shcherbatov and the author of the "Thoughts about Russia," the image of a nation which was simple and unspoiled, straightforward and honest, loyal and God-fearing. It may have been a bit coarse, this people, but the absence of polish and elegance was possibly an added guarantee of genuine sensibility and a generous soul.

Little by little, new features were added to the national portrait, new details to the general sketch that was already in existence. Each new feature was a positive contribution that marked Russians off from other peoples and their deficiencies. Lvov not only gave voice to his relief at being liberated from an infatuation with the West, but also helped to define a more conscious attitude towards it, a kind of Russophilism which became quite common in the nineteenth century. "In our young years," he wrote, " we look toward a foreign land as if it were heaven. I have let myself be captured by its glitter. But from beyond the sea I have always looked towards home." Why was the attraction of the new, the distant, and the brilliant never strong enough to keep him from turning and looking back? Because in the strange environment there was lacking some quality of warmth and friendship which to him spelled home. This is a human enough reaction and one which is not unusual for a homesick youth. But to Lvov, in retrospect, it appeared that these qualities which he missed were peculiarly Russian and characteristic perhaps only of Russia and her people.

It seemed to me as if there were no real joys where they cannot be shared, where the creative spirit of Russian happiness cannot release itself. . . . The gigantic spirit of our ancestors appears in other lands to be an unnatural exaggeration. And how could it help being so? In foreign lands all goes according to plan, words are weighed, steps are measured. There one sits hour upon hour; then begins to think. Having thought, one rests. Having rested, one smokes a pipe, then, thoughtfully, goes to one's work. There are no songs, no pranks. Among us Orthodox, however, work is like fire under our hands. Our speech is thunder, so that the sparks fly and the dust rises in columns.[26]

Spontaneity of feeling and behavior was for Lvov the trait which endeared his countrymen to him, the trait he missed most in the more convention-ridden, ceremonious life of the West. Believing that creativity would be stifled by the more deliberate approach to life and art, he also advocated for Russian poetry that it emancipate itself from the constraining influence of classical canons, that it turn from the iambic and trochaic meters of the West to the freer rhythms of folk-poetry. His view that Russian poetry would have a greater harmony, variety, and expressiveness in the tonic verse form, that even a native epos could be written entirely in a "Russian" style, marks him as a nationalist of a rather advanced type. Here is a man who is not merely conscious of his Russianness and defiantly insists on it, but one who has developed for himself an explanation of the sense of otherness which made him long for home when he found himself among strangers. Lvov named the quality which was distinctly Russian and found it in art as well as in life. Discovered there, it must also be carried back into both. He came as close as anyone in the eighteenth century to the discovery of a determining principle of national life, and elevated spontaneity to a position of eminence from which it was not soon displaced. The tenderness, sensitivity, and melancholy that spoke to him in the Russian songs which he so assiduously collected, were virtues subsidiary to the one he considered paramount. In this regard too, many seekers after the Russian soul followed in his footsteps.

Much more polemical in tone and decidedly more ambitious was the attempt made very near the end of the century by the actor and journalist Plavilshchikov to provide a definitive treatment of the problem of national character. His article on the innate qualities of the Russian soul[27] is more of a panegyric inspired by a fervent and rather public patriotism than the reflection of a serious debate between the author and his readers. Tone and content, indiscriminate praise for all that is Russian and abuse for all Russia's detractors suggest the patriotic pamphleteer, not a man engaged in a search for the human and cultural values which he would like his native land to typify. Though it must seem as if Plavilshchikov's method consisted of simply ascribing all the known virtues and talents to his countrymen, those which he chose to stress and linger over made him a contributor of important features to the collective Russian portrait which was emerging.

He was provoked, Plavilshchikov told his readers, by the disparaging remarks of a Frenchman in a company of foreigners and Russians. The conversation had turned to the question of national character, its definition and the fact that the term itself was of Graeco-Latin origin. That it was not translatable into Russian suggested, perhaps, that Russians, being without the word lacked that for which it stood. This was the view of the Frenchman, who held that his hosts were without a character of their own, monkeys who knew only how to copy the behavior of others. The young Russian fops who were present, as if to confirm this, hastened to agree with him and even to thank him "as for the revelation of the secrets of alchemy."[28] Plavilshchikov, angered by such shameful talk, hastened home to compose his refutation. In it he carefully avoided not only the term "national character," for which he substituted "innate qualities," but all other non-Russian words. The linguistic purity of his article was in itself to stand as proof of the self-sufficiency of the culture which he was defending.

Plavilshchikov had no doubts that there were native Russian qualities. If this were not so, Russia could not have been the envy, the delight, the astonishment of the world. "All Europe, the seat of learning and of taste, must render Russia her due; it is delighted by her virtues, which do not exist elsewhere." [29] Since these virtues were not found outside of Russia, they could hardly have been the result of imitation. Therefore, in the sphere of morals as in the arts of war and peace, Russia was no mere student copying the ways of her teachers: there was an element of real creativity in the national make-up which transformed even the passive experience of learning from others into an active intellectual process. This capacity for creative adaptation, which must be carefully differentiated from mere imitation, distinguished the Russians from all other peoples and accounted for their superiority. The students, beginning with Peter, outstripped their masters who remained imprisoned in their narrow world of fixed and ossified knowledge. Only a people coming like the Russians with a fresh and unburdened mind to the study of things could go beyond the eternal repetition of dead learning. Once more we are told that the world is wrong if it believes that backwardness is a burden and a hindrance. It is, on the contrary, evidence of originality and freshness of mind as yet undamaged and unrestrained by rule and repetition. Virgin soil yields rich harvests; the untutored mind takes flight with ease.

In those countries where the sciences have been at home for a long time and where they are widely practiced, the man of natural genius cannot make as much of a mark as in Russia, for with the capacity to understand, he who has imagination can create new fields for himself. . . . This leads to new, heretofore unknown discoveries in the arts and sciences.[30]

Frequently, the discoveries of more advanced minds are made independently by Russians, without benefit of instruction. There is thus no harm in admitting a lower level of culture, for it makes all the more remarkable what self-taught Russians have achieved, astounding the world and widening immeasurably the frontiers of future possibility. What must the prospects of a nation be in which untrained and illiterate peasants perform scientific miracles? "One of our peasants has made a tincture which all the learning of Hippocrates and Galen failed to find . . . . The bone setter of the village Alekseevo is a cause for contention in all surgery. Kulibin and the mechanic Sobakin from Tver are two marvels in mechanics. . . . What the Russian cannot grasp will forever be unknown to men." [31]

As clearly as we shall ever find him described, we are here face to face with the Russian culture hero, the ideal that summarizes and represents the country which has given him birth. Neither the first nor the last of a type that has been taking shape for a century, he now steps forth with all his claims made explicit and uttered unmistakably on behalf of Russia. The rustic surgeon and the village pharmacist have as their direct ancestor the muzhik who made a straw hat for his lady as good as the one imported from London; and they are not unlike the peasant Zakharin whose feats as a public speaker Pavel Lvov held up to his countrymen who were overly impressed with the achievements of foreigners, or Novikov's strolling peasant actors. Down into the twentieth century, Plavilshchikov's heroes beget a numerous descent, each generation proving, whatever else it may be called upon to prove, that the untrained but richly endowed intelligence has a potential undreamed of in the philosophies of the West. Even the many Soviet claims to independent firsts in discovery and invention partake of the nature of this proof, as do Leskov's "Left-Handed Artificer from Tula" and the peasant inventor of the airplane.* In claiming for Russians such extraordinary capacities, Plavilshchikov was beset by certain doubts. He had not yet freed himself of the notion that men of all climes were endowed by their creator with reason and understanding, and he felt obliged to explain why he had abandoned it. The understanding which men of all nations enjoy is applied in the direction which most conforms to their nature. The Italians have had the greatest triumphs of their understanding in music, in art, and architecture, whereas they have had to yield superiority in commerce and industry to the Dutch. Inclination, habit, and custom guide and mold the native capacities, so that the Dutch can never become creators of fashion. The capacities being equally and fairly distributed do not then make the decisive difference, for, shaped by other factors, they may serve for one pursuit and fail in another. But instead of pursuing the logic of his argument and trying to determine for which endeavor custom and habit had inclined the national intelligence, Plavilshchikov concluded that unlike other nations, the Russians had no specialty in which they excelled, no determining principle of behavior: "With us the matter is quite different. The Russian is capable of understanding everything. . . . Can any other people boast of such qualities?" [32] Weakening by this demonstration of the universal excellence of Russians his own arguments for their rather special talents, he also denied them a national character. For a "national" character which combines all that is most admirable in every culture is too synthetic to be truly national.

* "Once (in a period of reaction, 1903–1914), when a practical joker let loose a report that an old peasant had flown several miles on a home-made aeroplane, this was taken to prove that a patriarchal system was not only the best, but also the cleverest." Bernard Pares, *Russia* (Washington, D. C. and New York, 1945), p. 75.

Russians of all classes and in every situation are without fear, truthful, and desirous of glory, yet modest, generous, and compassionate; they are of quick understanding in everything; religious without being superstitious, tolerant, and joyful. Their main characteristic, however, is that they are firm in all their undertakings. Nor do I want to deny certain weaknesses, perhaps even vices, but with the brilliance of these great virtues, they are hardly noticeable. . . . Their vices stem from their immoderate and often misapplied virtuousness.[33]

Though Plavilshchikov's panegyric to the national character could hardly be convincing to even the most uncritical patriot, it contained elements which were both credible and acceptable to his countrymen. Where he believed that the absence of formal learning, joined to a rich intelligence, held limitless promise for the future, others, before and after him, came to look upon the suffering of Russia's masses as an ennobling trait. It would not be long before *sancta simplicitas* and suffering came to be looked upon as the stuff of which a messianic people was made.

# Conclusion

National consciousness in eighteenth-century Russia was a phenomenon which differed in nature and extent from superficially similar attitudes which preceded and followed it. It was more articulate and less instinctive than mere xenophobia; it was less religious, more secular, and less isolationist than the official nationalism of Muscovy or that of the Old Believers; it was neither so comprehensive a world view nor so messianic a belief as were the nationalist theories of the nineteenth century. For the history of nationalism as for the history of Russian thought and society, the eighteenth century is first and foremost a transitional period, an age in which old thought patterns and ways of life slowly gave way to new beliefs and practices. Perhaps the single most important fact of Russian history in this period is the unprecedented receptivity to all that came from the West. This receptivity is basic to an understanding of national consciousness and its role in the intellectual history of Russia.

National consciousness, being neither the blind reaction of the masses, nor the religious seer's vision of divine election for his people, was particularly the product of the articulate, the educated, the literate portion of society—that is, its most highly Westernized sector. From the very start, this placed upon it a rather definite stamp, and explains why national consciousness did not, and in fact, could not, mean for the men of the eighteenth century a decisive turning away from contact with a world which they had just discovered. It was preeminently the search for national identity, for the bases of personal as well as national being, and it was stimulated by the intensity of Russia's relations with other cultures. This remained for most of the century the basic determinant in the development of national consciousness, and though it might seem tritely obvious, it requires restatement. For no abstract scheme of historical development can entirely supplant the elementary fact of the response made to the challenge of a more advanced civilization by the intellectual classes of a more backward one. Neither the concept of the striving of one class for the consolidation of a national market, nor that of the agitation of another for unity and democratic freedoms, takes sufficient account of the impact that a foreign culture has on the social and psychological life of a new member of the family of nations. Contemporary examples are all too abundant.

It is of great importance to note that far from being exclusively a matter of economic interest or political principle, the development of national consciousness is often motivated by psychological factors. In order not to feel inferior before the products and representatives of European culture, articulate Russians were forced to develop for themselves a national self in which they could take pride and with which they could identify. As far as Russia is concerned, the carriers of national consciousness were not a distinct social or economic group—such as the emergent middle-classes which Soviet historians profess to see—but an aristocracy of education and intellect which was shaped by the influence of the West. Its search for a national identity was not a rejection of Europe; it was itself another aspect of the Westernization of Russian society. The record of the eighteenth century certainly does not suggest a continuing, congenital hostility of Russian thought towards Europe.

Although the explanation for the development of national consciousness in Russia is not to be found in the growth of liberalism or middle-class aspirations, the wish to end the dominance of alien ways in Russian life did have certain social overtones. In the beginning of the century, until the accession of the Empress Elizabeth, a national reaction often went together with the social protest of those who felt themselves displaced from the sources of power by the rise of a new bureaucracy and governing class which they denounced as foreign. But this group lacked a definite class identity and was no more homogeneous in its social complexion and interests than the bureaucracy which it opposed was altogether foreign or dominated by foreign interests. The aristocratic oligarchs who tried to set limits to bureaucratic absolutism in the time of Anna were far from expressing the views of their entire class, nor did they consistently invoke national traditions against the monarch; and the opponents of arbitrary "foreign" rule under Biron willingly exchanged it for arbitrary native rule under Elizabeth. This early period did, however, leave an important legacy of hostility to government which was closely connected with the image of the state, its institutions and personnel as something essentially alien to Russia. For certain currents of Russian opinion, the power of the state, in the Westernized form in which Peter bequeathed it to his successors, never quite lost its stigma as something which was not native to the Russian soil, but was rather a foreign importation with purely repressive or exploitative aims.

In the second half of the century, and more particularly in the reign of Catherine, national consciousness frequently allied itself with a social protest made in the name of an oppressed class. The purely external Europeanization of an upper class no longer required to render service to the state, contrasted sharply with the condition of the peasantry which alone made this style of life possible. For men like Novikov and Radishchev the conclusion became inescapable that the immoral Westernism of the upper classes had not only separated them from the majority of the nation in a social, but also in a national sense. They implied that true morality, which tended to become synonymous with an unspoiled Russian way of life, was best preserved among the people. The point was not missed by later nationalists, and for many of them "the people" became the nation.

The eighteenth-century defenders of the people were far, however, from an apotheosis of the folk as the only true vessel of a national faith. They were as far from it as they were from an uncritical exaltation of the nation. They were not, in fact, nationalists, for they were primarily concerned with the discovery of their own character, their culture, and its values. When they discovered proof of national excellence or greatness in the records of their language, their literature, and their history they brought it forth to show that they were no worse than any other people and had as rich a cultural tradition as the nations of the West. For the most part, theirs was still a "compensatory nationalism" whose primary role was preparatory. Even in the search for a national character, for the determining and distinctive principle of national being which would distinguish Russians from all other peoples, the eighteenth century failed to speak with one voice. The formulation of a comprehensive theory of nationalism, the definition of Russia's unique contribution to universal history, was left to a later generation. Most men of the eighteenth century would have agreed with Chaadaev when he wrote in 1854 that they "were far from imagining that Russia represented some kind of abstract principle comprising the definite solution of the social problem, that she by herself constituted a whole world apart . . . that she had a special mission of absorbing all the Slav peoples in her bosom and thereby achieving the regeneration of mankind."

Yet periods in the history of thought are never so sharply divided as to make possible an absolute separation between the national consciousness of the eighteenth and the nationalism of the nineteenth century. The process by which Russian thought

arrived at the conviction that the time was near when Russia
would make her own mark in the history of mankind was a
cumulative and a continuous one. There was a gradual pro-
gression from an instinctive, almost brutal reaction against the
foreigner to a more reasoned evaluation of his role and culture.
It had the effect of turning Russian eyes inward, of stimulating
the search for an autonomy which imitation and dependence
had made difficult. In this way, the eighteenth century created
the necessary preconditions for the emergence of a full-blown
nationalist theory. It did all this without the benefit of philosophy, without having gone through the school of Schelling or
Hegel, by asserting first, that Russians were at least as good
as other Europeans; second, by discovering that in some ways
they were perhaps better, precisely because they were not as
good (i.e., as depraved by progress); and third, that since they
were making a fresh start, unencumbered by the weight of the
past, they might possibly go further than their teachers. But
they were still, in the eighteenth century, going in the direction
which their teachers had indicated.

A full-blown nationalist theory is never merely a blind
rejection of modes of life and thought that are foreign; it is an
attempt to prescribe for and to judge every aspect of life on
the basis of an ideal which is social and political, economic and
religious as much as it is purely national. The development of
national consciousness was an indispensable step for the elaboration of such a theory by later generations. The search for the
national virtues in the past and in the countryside, the antithesis between worldly skepticism and a naive but true faith, the
conviction of Russia's youth and freshness, of the rich intellectual endowment of even her lowliest citizens, furnished
nationalism with some of its central themes. When elaborated
and cherished, they turn into categories in which the individual
can find himself reflected, with which he can identify and
discover his personal "national character." Such categories,

slippery and cliché-like though they may be—one need only think of the broad Russian soul, the humble wisdom of the peasant, or the deep religiosity of the national character—gain a life of their own, and for all their lack of precision find a wide resonance.

BIBLIOGRAPHY

NOTES

INDEX

# Selected Bibliography

## PRIMARY SOURCES

Balukhatui, S. D., ed., *Russkie pisateli o literature.* 2 vols. Leningrad, 1939.

Bartenev, P., ed., *Osmnadtsaty vek, istoricheski sbornik.* 2nd ed. 4 vols. Moscow, 1869.

Berkov, P. N., ed., *Russkaya komediya i komicheskaya opera XVIII veka.* Moscow, 1950.

Bilyarski, P., ed., *Materialy dlya biografii Lomonosova.* St. Petersburg, 1865.

Bogdanovich, I. F., *Istoricheskoe izobrazhenie Rossii.* 2 vols. St. Petersburg, 1777.

—— *Russkiya Poslovitsy.* 2 vols. (in one). St. Petersburg, 1785.

—— *Sochineniya.* A. Smirdin, ed. 2 vols. St. Petersburg, 1848.

Bolotov, A. T., "Mysli i bespristrastnye suzhdeniya o romanakh," *Literaturnoe Nasledstvo,* nos. 9/10 (1933), pp. 194–218.

—— "Pismo k priyatelyu moemu S*** o petimetrakh," *ibid.*, pp. 182–189.

—— *Zhizn i priklyucheniya Andreya Bolotova, opisannyya samim im dlya svoikh potomkov, 1783–1793.* 4 vols. (in two). St. Petersburg, 1870–1873.

Boltin, I. N., *Kriticheskiya primechaniya general-maiora Boltina na pervy-vtoroi tom istorii knyazya Shcherbatova.* 2 vols. St. Petersburg, 1793–1794.

—— *Primechaniya na istoriyu drevniya i nyneshniya Rossii g. Leklerka, sochinennyya general-maiorom Ivanom Boltinym.* 2 vols. St. Petersburg, 1788.

Catherine II, Empress of Russia, *Documents of Catherine II.* W. F. Reddaway, ed. Cambridge, England, 1931.

—— *Sochineniya Imperatritsy Ekateriny II.* A. N. Pypin, ed. 12 vols. (in six). St. Petersburg, 1901–1907.

Chulkov, M. D., " 'Kak khochesh nazovi,' neizdannaya komediya Chulkova," N. Khardzhiev, ed., *Literaturnoe Nasledstvo,* nos. 9/10 (1933), pp. 222–242.

—— *Slovar russkikh sueveri.* St. Petersburg, 1782.

—— *Sobranie raznykh pesen* (*Sochineniya Mikhaila Dmitrievicha Chulkova*, I). Facsimile of the 1st ed., St. Petersburg, 1913.

Dashkova, E. R., *Memoirs of the Princess Daschkaw, Lady of Honour to Catherine II*. W. Bradford, ed. 2 vols. London, 1840.

Derzhavin, G. R., *Sochineniya*. A. Smirdin, ed. 2 vols. St. Petersburg, 1842.

Dmitriev, S. S. and Nechkina, M. V., eds., *Khrestomatiya po istorii SSSR*. 2 vols. Moscow, 1949.

Efremov, P. A., ed., *Materialy dlya istorii russkoi literatury*. St. Petersburg, 1867.

*Ezhemesyachnyya Sochineniya* (St. Petersburg) I, 1755.

Fonvizin, D. I., *Pervoe polnoe sobranie sochineni D. I. Fon-Vizina, kak originalnykh, tak i perevodnykh, 1761–1792*. Moscow, 1888.

Gukovski, G. A., ed., *Khrestomatiya po russkoi literature XVIII veka*. 3rd ed. Moscow, 1938.

Kantemir, A. D., *Sochineniya, pisma i izbrannye perevody knyazya Antiokha Dmitrievicha Kantemira*. P. A. Efremov, ed. 2 vols. St. Petersburg, 1867–1868.

Karamzin, N. M., *Istoriya Gosudarstva Rossiiskogo*. P. Einerling, ed. 5th ed. 3 vols. St. Petersburg, 1842–1843.

—— *Karamzin's Memoir on Ancient and Modern Russia*. R. Pipes, ed. and trans. Cambridge, Mass., 1959.

—— *Sochineniya Karamzina*. S. Selivanski, ed. 3rd ed. 9 vols. Moscow, 1820.

—— "Zapiska o drevnei i novoi Rossii," *Russki Arkhiv*, VIII (1870), 2224–2350.

Kheraskov, M. M., *Bakhariyana, ili neizvestny*. Moscow, 1803.

—— "Razsuzhdenie o rossiiskom stikhotvorstve," *Literaturnoe Nasledstvo*, nos. 9/10 (1933), pp. 290–294.

Knyazhnin, Ya. B., *Sochineniya Ya. B. Knyazhnina*. A. Smirdin, ed. 2 vols. St. Petersburg, 1848.

Kokorev, A. B., ed., *Khrestomatiya po russkoi literature XVIII veka*. Moscow, 1952.

Kozmin, P. B., ed., *Sbornik materialov k izucheniyu istorii russkoi zhurnalistiki*. Moscow, 1952.

Krylov, I. A., *Sochineniya*. Demyan Bedny, ed. 2 vols. Moscow, 1945–1946.

Lekhtblau, L. B., ed., *Russkie satiricheskie zhurnaly XVIII veka*. Moscow, 1940.

Lomonosov, M. V., *Rossiiskaya Grammatika*. St. Petersburg, 1775.

—— *Sochineniya*. A. Smirdin, ed. 3 vols. St. Petersburg, 1847–1850.

Lukin, V. I., *Sochineniya i perevody*. 2 vols. St. Petersburg, 1765.

Lvov, N. A., "Neizdannye stikhi N. A. Lvova," *Literaturnoe Nasledstvo*, nos. 9/10 (1933), pp. 264–286.

Manstein, C. H., *Zapiski Manshteina o Rossii, 1727–1744*. G. Pavlovsk, ed. St. Petersburg, 1875.

Minikh, B., *Zapiski feldmarshalla grafa Minikha*. S. N. Shubinski, ed. St. Petersburg, 1874.

Muennich, E., *Memoiren des Grafen Ernst von Muennich*. A. Juergensohn, ed. Stuttgart, 1896.

Novikov, N. I., *Izbrannye Sochineniya*. G. P. Makogonenko, ed. Moscow, 1951.

―――― *Opyt istoricheskago slovarya o rossiiskikh pisatelyakh*. St. Petersburg, 1772.

―――― *Satiricheskie zhurnaly N. I. Novikova*. P. N. Berkov, ed. Moscow-Leningrad, 1951.

―――― ed., *Drevnyaya rossiiskaya vivliofika*. 2nd ed. 20 vols. St. Petersburg, 1788–1791.

Obnorski, S. and Barkhudarov, S. G., eds., *Khrestomatiya po istorii russkogo yazyka*. 2 vols. Moscow, 1948–1949.

Pappadopoulo, M. L., ed. and trans., *Choix des meilleurs morceaux de la littérature russe*. Paris, 1800.

Plavilshchikov, P. A., "Nechto o vrozhdennom svoistve dush rossiiskikh," *Zritel* (St. Petersburg, 1792), no. 1, pp. 9–26; no. 3, pp. 163–181.

Pososhkov, I. T., *Kniga o skudosti i bogatstve*. B. B. Kafengauz, ed. Moscow, 1937.

Radishchev, A. N., *Izbrannye Sochineniya*. G. P. Makogonenko, ed. Moscow, 1952.

―――― *A Journey from St. Petersburg to Moscow*. L. Wiener, trans., with an introduction and notes by R. P. Thaler. Cambridge, 1958.

―――― *Polnoe sobranie sochineni*. 3 vols. I. K. Luppol, ed. Moscow-Leningrad, 1938–1952.

*Rossiiski Featr*. 43 vols. (in 23). St. Petersburg, 1786–1794.

*Russkaya Pravda*. 2nd ed. Edited with an introduction by I. N. Boltin and A. I. Musin-Pushkin. Moscow, 1799.

*Sammlung Russischer Geschichte*. 9 vols. St. Petersburg, 1732–1764. A historical journal edited by G. F. Mueller.

Semennikov, V. P., ed. *Materialy dlya istorii russkoi literatury*. St. Petersburg, 1914.

Schloezer, A. L., "Obshchestvennaya i chastnaya zhizn Avgusta Lyudviga Shletsera, im samim . . . ot 1761 do 1765 g.," V. Kenevich, trans., *Akademiya Nauk; sbornik otdeleniya russkogo yazyka i slovesnosti*, XIII (1875), 1–278.

———— *Oskold und Dir.* Goettingen-Gotha, 1773.

———— *Probe russischer Annalen.* Bremen-Goettingen, 1768.

———— "Russkaya grammatika; chast pervaya," *Akademiya Nauk; sbornik otdeleniya russkogo yazyka i slovesnosti,* XIII (1875), 419–515.

Shcherbatov, M. M., *Istoriya rossiiskaya ot drevneishikh vremen.* 3rd ed. 7 vols. (in 5). I. P. Khrushchov and A. G. Voronov, eds., St. Petersburg, 1901–1904.

———— *Neizdannye Sochineniya.* Edited with an introduction by P. Lyubomirov. Moscow, 1935.

———— *O povrezhdenii nravov v Rossii knyazya M. Shcherbatova, i puteshestvie A. Radishcheva.* Preface by Iskander (pseud: Alexander Herzen). London, 1858.

———— "Pismo k velmozham pravitelyam gosudarstva," *Russkaya Starina,* V (1875), 1–15.

———— "Raznye sochineniya knyazya M. M. Shcherbatova," *Chteniya v imperatorskom obshchestve istorii i drevnostei rossiiskikh pri Moskovskom universitete,* January–March 1860, pp. 1–140.

———— *Sochineniya knyazya M. M. Shcherbatova.* I. P. Khrushchov and A. G. Voronov, eds. vol. I, St. Petersburg, 1896; vol. II, St. Petersburg, 1898.

———— *Ueber die Sittenverderbnis in Russland von Fuerst M. Schterbatow.* Edited with an introduction by K. Staehlin. Berlin, 1925

Shchipanov, I. Ya., ed., *Izbrannye proizvedeniya russkikh myslitelei vtoroi poloviny XVIII veka.* 2 vols. Moscow, 1952.

Shishkov, A. S., *Razsuzhdenie o starom i novom sloge rossiiskago yazyka.* St. Petersburg, 1803.

*Smes* (St. Petersburg) 2nd ed. 1771. A satirical journal first published in 1769.

Staehlin, Jakob, "Zapiski Shtelina ob Imperatore Petre IIIm," *Chteniya v imperatorskom obshchestve istorii i drevnostei rossiiskikh pri Moskovskom universitete,* October–December, 1866, pp. 67–118.

Sumarokov, A. P., *Stikhotvoreniya.* A. S. Orlov, ed. Moscow, 1935.

———— *Théâtre Tragique.* M. L. Pappadopoulo, ed. and trans. Paris, 1801.

Tatishchev, V. N., *Istoriya Rossiiskaya.* 5 vols. Moscow, 1768–1848.

———— *Dukhovnaya Vasiliya Nikiticha Tatishcheva.* Leipzig, 1862.

Tredyakovski, V. K., *Sochineniya.* A. Smirdin, ed. St. Petersburg, 1849.

*Trudolyubivaya Pchela* (St. Petersburg) 2nd ed. 1780. A journal edited by Sumarokov; first published in 1759.

Vengerov, S. A., ed., *Russkaya Poeziya.* St. Petersburg, 1897.

Vockerodt, J. G., "Rossiya pri Petre Velikom," *Chteniya v imperatorskom obshchestve istorii i drevnostei rossiiskikh pri Moskovskom universitete,* April–June, 1874, pp. 1–120.

Zapadova, A. V. and Makogonenko, G. P., eds., *Russkaya proza XVIII veka.* 2 vols. Moscow-Leningrad, 1950.

SECONDARY WORKS

Adamczyk, A., *Tredjakovskij und die Reform.* Breslau, 1940.
Aksakov, Konstantin, *Lomonosov v istorii russkoi literatury i yazyka.* Moscow, 1846.
Alefirenko, P., "Ekonomicheskie vzglyady V. N. Tatishcheva," *Voprosy Istorii,* no. 12 (1948), pp. 89–97.
Aleksandrenko, V. N., *K biografii Kantemira.* Warsaw, 1896.
Anuchin, D. N., "Stoletie 'Pisem russkogo puteshestvennika'," *Russkaya Mysl,* (1891), VII, 1–31; VIII, 59–77.
Arkhangelski, A. S., *Imperatritsa Ekaterina II v istorii russkoi literatury i obrazovaniya.* Kazan, 1897.
—— *Russkaya literatura XVIII veka.* Kazan, 1911.
Bain, R. N., *The Daughter of Peter the Great.* New York and Westminster, 1900.
Bak, I. S., *Ekonomicheskie vozzreniya M. V. Lomonosova.* Moscow, 1946.
—— "Ya. P. Kozelski," *Voprosy Istorii,* no. 1 (1947), pp. 83–100.
Baranovich, A. I., et al., eds., *Ocherki istorii SSSR, XVIII v.; vtoraya chetvert.* Moscow, 1957.
—— *Ocherki istorii SSSR, XVIII v.; vtoraya polovina.* Moscow, 1956.
Berkov, P. N., *Istoriya russkoi zhurnalistiki XVIII veka.* Moscow, 1952.
—— "Lomonosov i folklor," *Lomonosov, sbornik statei i materialov.* A. I. Andreev and L. B. Mozdalevski, eds. Moscow, 1946, pp. 118–128.
—— *Lomonosov i literaturnaya polemika ego vremeni, 1750–1765.* Moscow, 1936.
—— *Vladimir Ignatevich Lukin, 1737–1794.* Moscow, 1950.
—— "Slavyanovedcheskie interesy Lomonosova," *Nauchny byulleten Leningradskogo gosudarstvennogo universiteta,* XI–XII (1946), 40–44.
—— *Aleksandr Petrovich Sumarokov, 1717–1777.* Leningrad-Moscow, 1949.
Bestuzhev-Ryumin, K. R., *Biografii i kharakteristiki.* St. Petersburg, 1882.
Blagoi, D. D., *Istoriya russkoi literatury XVIII veka.* 2nd ed. Moscow, 1951.
—— "Rol khudozhestvennoi literatury v formirovanii russkoi natsii," *Izvestiya Akademii Nauk; otdelenie literatury i yazyka,* XIII (1954), 22–36.

Bogumil, Aleksandr, *Nachalny period narodnichestva v russkoi khudozhestvennoi literature.* Kiev, 1907.

Brueckner, A. G., *Die Europaeisierung Russlands.* Gotha, 1888.

Bruford, W. H., *Germany in the Eighteenth Century.* Cambridge, England, 1935.

Bulakhovski, L. A., *Istoricheski kommentari k russkomu literaturnomu yazyku.* 5th ed. Kiev, 1958.

Bulich, S. K., *Ocherki istorii yazykoznaniya v Rossii.* St. Petersburg, 1904.

Cassirer, Ernst, *Die Philosophie der Aufklaerung.* Tuebingen, 1932.

Chadwick, H. M., *The Nationalities of Europe and the Growth of National Ideologies.* Cambridge, England, 1945.

Chechulin, N. D., *Russki sotsialny roman 180go veka: puteshestvie v zemlyu ofirskuyu knyazya M. M. Shcherbatova.* St. Petersburg, 1900.

Coleman, A. P., *Humor in the Russian Comedy from Catherine to Gogol.* New York, 1925.

Cross, S. H., "The Contribution of G. F. Mueller to Russian Historiography." Unpublished doctoral dissertation, Harvard University, 1916.

Desnitski, V. A., *Na literaturnye temy.* 2 vols. Leningrad, 1936.

Dmitriev, S., "Rabochi folklor XVIII veka," *Literaturnoe Nasledstvo,* nos. 19/21 (1935), pp. 1–15.

Falnes, O. J., *National Romanticism in Norway.* New York, 1933.

Firsov, N. N., *Vstuplenie na prestol Imperatritsy Elizavety Petrovny.* Kazan, 1887.

Florovski, Georgi, *Puti russkogo bogosloviya.* 2nd ed. Paris, 1951.

Fridberg, L., "Knigoizdatelskaya deyatelnost Novikova v Moskve (1779–1792)," *Voprosy Istorii,* no. 8 (1948), pp. 23–42.

Fursenko, V., "Shcherbatov," *Russki biograficheski slovar,* XXIV (1912), 104–124.

Grekov, B. D., "Lomonosov - istorik," *Istorik Marksist,* no. 11 (1940), pp. 18–34.

Gudzi, N. K., editor, *Problemy realizma v russkoi literature 180go veka.* Moscow, 1940.

Guenther, O. E., "Peter der Grosse im russischen Urteil des 18. Jahrhunderts," *Jahrbuecher fuer Kultur und Geschichte der Slawen.* N. F., X (1934), 529–557.

Gukovski, G. A., *Iz istorii russkoi ody 180go veka.* Leningrad, n. d.

—— *Ocherki po istorii russkoi literatury 180go veka; dvoryanskaya fronda v literature 1750–kh – 1760–kh godov.* Moscow, 1936.

—— *Ocherki po istorii russkoi literatury i obshchestvennoi mysli XVIII veka.* Leningrad, 1938.

—— *Russkaya literatura XVIII veka.* Moscow, 1939.

—— *Russkaya poeziya 180go veka.* Leningrad, 1927.

—— "Von Lomonosov bis Derzhavin," *Zeitschrift fuer slavische Philologie,* II (1925), 323–365.

Gukovski, G. A. and V. Orlov, "Podpolnaya poeziya 1770–1800–kh godov," *Literaturnoe Nasledstvo,* nos. 9/10 (1933), pp. 5–98.

Harkins, W. E., *The Russian Folk Epos in Czech Literature.* New York, 1953.

Haumant, E., *La culture française en Russie.* Paris, 1910.

—— *La Russie au XVIIIième siècle.* Paris, 1904.

Hayes, C. J. H., *Essays on Nationalism.* New York, 1926.

—— *The Historical Evolution of Modern Nationalism.* New York, 1931.

—— "Two Varieties of Nationalism: 'Original' and 'Derived'," *Proceedings of the Association of History Teachers of the Middle States and Maryland,* 26 (1928), 71–83.

Hertz, Friedrich, *Nationalgeist und Politik.* Zuerich, 1937.

Hinz, W., "Peters des Grossen Anteil an der wissenschaftlichen und kuenstlerischen Kultur seiner Zeit," *Jahrbuecher fuer Kultur und Geschichte der Slawen.* N. F., VIII (1932), 347–447.

Huizinga, Johan, *Im Bann der Geschichte.* Basel, 1943.

Ikonnikov, V., "Boltin," *Russki biograficheski slovar,* III (1908), 186–204.

Ivanov-Razumnik, R. V., *Istoriya russkoi obshchestvennoi mysli.* 2 vols. St. Petersburg, 1914.

Ivanov, I. I., *Istoriya russkoi kritiki.* 2 vols. St. Petersburg, 1898–1900.

Jakobson, R. O., "The Puzzles of the Igor Tale," *Speculum,* XXVII (1952), 43–66.

Kizevetter, A. A., *Istoricheskie Ocherki.* Moscow, 1912.

Klyuchevski, V. O., *Kurs russkoi istorii.* vol. IV, Moscow, 1910; vol. V, Moscow, 1921.

—— *Ocherki i rechi.* Moscow, 1918.

Kohn, Hans, *The Idea of Nationalism.* 3rd ed. New York, 1946.

—— *The Mind of Modern Russia.* New Brunswick, New Jersey, 1955.

—— *Nationalism: Its Meaning and History.* New York, 1955.

Koyalovich, M. O., *Istoriya russkogo samosoznaniya.* 3rd ed. St. Petersburg, 1901.

Korsakov, D. A., "Artemi Petrovich Volynskoi i ego 'konfidenty'," *Russkaya Starina,* XV (1885), 17–54.

—— *Iz zhizni russkikh deyatelei XVIII veka.* Kazan, 1891.

—— *Votsarenie Imperatritsy Anny Ioannovny.* Kazan, 1880.

Kovalevski, P. I., *Istoriya Rossii s natsionalnoi tochki zreniya.* St. Petersburg, 1912.

Koyré, Alexandre, *Etudes sur l'histoire de la pensée philosophique en Russie.* Paris, 1950.

Kulakova, I. I., *Yakov Borisovich Knyazhnin, 1742–1791.* Moscow, 1951.

——— *Petr Alekseevich Plavilshchikov, 1760–1812.* Moscow, 1952.

Lang, D. M., "Boileau and Sumarokov, the Manifesto of Russian Classicism," *Modern Language Review,* XLIII (1948), 500–506.

——— *The First Russian Radical: Alexander Radishchev, 1749–1802.* London, 1959.

Lemberg, Eugen, *Geschichte des Nationalismus in Europa.* Stuttgart, 1950.

Likhachev, D. S., *Russkie Letopisi.* Moscow-Leningrad, 1947.

Lipski, Alexander, "A Re-examination of the 'Dark Era' of Anna Ioannovna," *The American Slavic and East European Review,* 15 (1956), 477–488.

Loboda, A. M., *Lektsii po istorii novoi russkoi literatury.* Kiev, 1913.

Maikov, L. N., *Ocherki iz istorii russkoi literatury XVII i XVIII vv.* St. Petersburg, 1889.

Makogonenko, G. P., *Novikov.* Moscow, 1953.

Martel, Antoine, *Michel Lomonosov et la langue littéraire russe.* Leningrad, Bibliotheque de l'Institut français, 1933.

Mazour, A. G., *Modern Russian Historiography.* Princeton, New Jersey, 1958.

Mediger, Walther, *Moskaus Weg nach Europa.* Braunschweig, 1952.

Melgunov, S. P., *Religiozno-obshchestvennye dvizheniya XVII - XVIII vekov v Rossii.* Moscow, 1922.

Melgunova-Stepanova, P. E., *Russki byt po vospominaniyam sovremennikov XVIII veka.* 2 vols. Moscow, 1914–1918.

Menshutkin, B. N., "Lomonosov," *Russki biograficheski slovar,* X (1914), 593–628.

Milyukov, P. N., *Glavnye techeniya russkoi istoricheskoi mysli.* Moscow, 1897.

——— *Iz istorii russkoi intelligentsii.* 2nd ed. St. Petersburg, 1903.

——— *Ocherki po istorii russkoi kultury.* Jubilee ed. 3 vols. Paris, 1937.

——— *Russia and Its Crisis.* Chicago and London, 1905.

Nezelenov, A. I., *Literatura pri Ekaterine.* St. Petersburg, 1889.

——— *Literaturnye napravleniya v Ekaterininskuyu epokhu.* St. Petersburg, 1889.

——— *Nikolai Ivanovich Novikov; izdatel zhurnalov.* St. Petersburg, 1875.

Orlov, A. S., editor, *Vosemnadtsaty Vek.* Moscow-Leningrad, 1935.

Pascal, R., *The German Sturm und Drang.* Manchester, England, 1953.

——— *Shakespeare in Germany.* Cambridge, England, 1937.

Pekarski, P. P., *Istoriya Imperatorskoi Akademii Nauk v Peterburge*. 2 vols. St. Petersburg, 1870–1873.

—— *Nauka i literatura v Rossii pri Petre Velikom*. 2 vols. St. Petersburg, 1862.

—— *Novyya izvestiya o V. N. Tatishcheve*. St. Petersburg, 1864.

Pokrovski, V. I., *Shchegoli v satiricheskoi literature XVIII veka*. Moscow, 1903.

—— *Shchegolikhi v satiricheskoi literature XVIII veka*. Moscow, 1903.

—— *Aleksandr Petrovich Sumarokov*. Moscow, 1911.

—— ed., *Sokrashchennaya istoricheskaya khrestomatiya*. 3rd ed., vol. III. Moscow, 1911.

Popov, A. N., *V. N. Tatishchev i ego vremya*. Moscow, 1861.

Preuss, U., "Katharina II von Russland und ihre auswaertige Politik im Urteile der deutschen Zeitgenossen," *Jahrbuecher fuer Kultur und Geschichte der Slawen*. N. F., V (1929), 1–56, 169–227.

Pushkarev, Ivan, *Istoriya imperatorskoi Rossiiskoi gvardii*. St. Petersburg, 1844.

Pypin, A. N., *Istoriya russkoi etnografii*. 4 vols. St. Petersburg, 1890–1892.

—— *Istoriya russkoi literatury*. 4 vols. St. Petersburg, 1898–1899.

—— "Russkaya nauka i natsionalny vopros v XVIII veke," *Vestnik Evropy*, III (1884), 212–256, 548–600 and IV (1884), 72–117.

Rabinovich, A. S., *Russkaya opera do Glinki*. Moscow, 1948.

Rammelmeyer, A., "Studien zur Geschichte der russischen Fabel des 18. Jahrhunderts," *Veroeffentlichungen des Slawistischen Instituts Berlin*. no. 21. Leipzig, 1938.

Recke, Walter, "Die Verfassungsplaene der russischen Oligarchen im Jahre 1730 und die Thronbesteigung der Kaiserin Anna Iwanowna," *Zeitschrift fuer Osteuropaeische Geschichte*, II (1911–1912), 11–64, 161–203.

Riasanovsky, N. V., *Russia and the West in the Teaching of the Slavophiles*. Cambridge, Mass., 1952.

Richter, Liselotte, *Leibniz und sein Russlandbild*. Berlin, 1946.

Rozanov, I. N., *Pesni russkikh poetov*. Moscow, 1936.

—— *Russkaya Pesnya*. Moscow, 1944.

Rubinshtein, N. L., *Russkaya Istoriografiya*. Moscow, 1941.

Sakulin, P. N., *Istoriya novoi russkoi literatury; epokha klassitsizma*. Moscow, 1918.

—— *Russkaya literatura; sotsiologo-sinteticheski obzor literaturnykh stilei*. Moscow, 1928.

Semevski, V. I., "Iz istorii obshchestvennykh techeni v Rossii v XVIII i pervoi polovine XIX veka," *Istoricheskoe Obozrenie*, IX (1897), 244–290.

—— *Krestianski vopros v Rossii v XVIII i pervoi polovine XIX veka.* 2 vols (in one). St. Petersburg, 1888.

Shchegolev, S. A., "Neizvestnaya drama o smerti Petra I," *Akademiya Nauk; trudy otdela drevnerusskoi literatury,* VI (1948), 376–404.

Shchipanov, I. Ya., ed., *Iz istorii russkoi filosofii, sbornik statei.* Moscow, 1949.

Shklovski, V. B., *Chulkov i Levshin.* Leningrad, 1933.

—— *Matvei Komarov.* Leningrad, 1929.

Shmurlo, E. F., "Petr Veliki v otsenke sovremennikov i potomstva," *Zhurnal Ministerstva Narodnogo Prosveshcheniya,* October 1911, pp. 315–340; November-December 1911, pp. 1–37, 201–273; May-June 1912, pp. 1–40, 193–259.

Simmons, E. J., *English Literature and Culture in Russia (1553–1840).* Cambridge, Mass., 1935.

Sipovski, V. V., *Istoriya russkoi slovesnosti.* 2 vols. St. Petersburg, 1908.

—— *Iz istorii russkogo romana i povesti.* 2nd ed. 2 vols. St. Petersburg, 1903.

—— "Iz istorii russkoi mysli XVIII stoletiya," *Zhurnal Ministerstva Narodnogo Prosveshcheniya,* March-April 1917, pp. 78–117.

—— "Iz istorii samosoznaniya russkogo obshchestva XVIII veka," *Akademiya Nauk; izvestiya otdeleniya russkogo yazyka i slovesnosti,* XVIII (1913), 248–272.

—— *N. M. Karamzin.* St. Petersburg, 1899.

—— *Ocherki iz istorii russkogo romana.* 2 vols. St. Petersburg, 1909–1910.

—— "Vliyanie 'Vertera' na russki roman XVIII veka," *Zhurnal Ministerstva Narodnogo Prosveshcheniya,* January 1906, pp. 52–106.

Sivkov, K. V., "Podpolnaya politicheskaya literatura v kontse XVIII veka," *Istoricheskie Zapiski,* no. 19 (1946), pp. 63–101.

Sokolov, Y. M., *Russian Folklore.* C. R. Smith, trans. New York, 1950.

Solovev, S. M., *Istoriya Rossii s drevneishikh vremen.* 29 parts. St. Petersburg, 1893–1896.

—— "Pisateli russkoi istorii XVIII veka," *Sobranie Sochineni,* V, 1317–1388. St. Petersburg, 1900.

Staehlin, Karl, *Geschichte Russlands.* 4 vols. Berlin and Koenigsberg, 1930.

Stieda, W., "Die Anfaenge der kaiserlichen Akademie der Wissenschaften in St. Petersburg," *Jahrbuecher fuer Kultur und Geschichte der Slawen,* II (1925), 152–163.

Strakhov, N. N., *Borba s zapadom v nashei literature.* 2 vols. St. Petersburg, 1887–1890.

Stupperich, Robert, *Staatsgedanke und Religionsphilosophie Peters des Grossen*. Koenigsberg, 1936.
Sukhomlinov, M. I., "Istoriya rossiiskoi Akademii," *Akademiya Nauk; sbornik otdeleniya russkogo yazyka i slovesnosti*, XI (no. 2), XIV, XVI, XIX (no. 1), XXII (no. 1), XXXI (no. 3), XXXV, XXXVII, XLIII (no. 4), 1875–1888.
Sulzbach, Walter, *National Consciousness*. Washington, D. C., 1943.
Tikhomirov, I., "Deyatelnost M. V. Lomonosova v oblasti geografii Rossii," *Zhurnal Ministerstva Narodnogo Prosveshcheniya*, January 1915, pp. 26–57 and April 1915, pp. 264–281.
—— "O trudakh M. V. Lomonosova po politicheskoi ekonomii," *ibid.*, February 1914, pp. 249–264.
—— "O trudakh M. V. Lomonosova po russkoi istorii," *ibid.*, September 1912, pp. 41–64.
—— "O trudakh M. V. Lomonosova po statistike Rossii," *ibid.*, February 1915, pp. 390–394.
Tikhomirov, M., "Russkaya istoriografiya XVIII veka," *Voprosy Istorii*, no. 2 (1948), pp. 94–99.
—— "V. N. Tatishchev," *Istorik Marksist*, no. 6 (1940), pp. 43–56.
Tolstoy, D. A., *Das Unterrichtswesen Russlands im 18. Jahrhundert*. St. Petersburg, 1885.
Tomashevski, B. V., *Iroi-komicheskaya poema*. Leningrad, 1933.
Trubitsyn, N. N., *O narodnoi poezii v obshchestvennom i literaturnom obikhode pervoi treti XIX veka*. St. Petersburg, 1912.
Van Tieghem, P., *Le mouvement romantique*. 3rd ed. Paris, 1940.
—— *Le préromantisme*. 3 vols. Paris, 1947.
Vernadski, G. V., *N. I. Novikov*. Petrograd, 1918.
Veselovski, A. N., *Prosvetitelny vek i Aleksandrovskaya pora*. Moscow, 1916.
Vinogradov, V. V., *Ocherki po istorii russkogo literaturnogo yazyka XVII–XIX vv*. Leiden, 1949.
Vinokur, Grigorij, *Die russische Sprache*. Leipzig, 1944.
Waliszewski, Kazimierz, *La dernière des Romanov, Elizabeth Ière, 1741–1762*. Paris, 1902.
—— *Paul the First of Russia*. London, 1913.
Zamotin, I. I., *Romantism 20–kh godov XIX stoletiya v russkoi literature*. 2nd ed. 2 vols. St. Petersburg, 1911–1913.
Zenkovski, V. V., *Russkie mysliteli i Evropa*. Paris, 1925.
Zhitetski, P. I., "K istorii literaturnoi russkoi rechi v XVIII veke," *Akademiya Nauk; izvestiya otdeleniya russkogo yazyka i slovesnosti*, VIII (1903), 1–51.

# Notes

## INTRODUCTION

1. Boyd C. Shafer, *Nationalism: Myth and Reality* (New York, 1955), p. 5.
2. A. G. Mazour, *Russia Past and Present* (New York, 1951), p. 29: "Real Russian nationalism, however, did not emerge until the nineteenth century, coming with the romantic movement of that time."
3. Paul Milyukov, *Russia and Its Crisis* (Chicago and London, 1905), p. 48 ff. See also Hans Kohn, *The Mind of Modern Russia* (New Brunswick, New Jersey, 1955), p. viii: "From the moment that they crossed the Elbe and the Rhine and entered Paris, the Russians debated the relationship between Russia and the West and their common or opposite destiny"; and Georg von Rauch, *A History of Soviet Russia* (New York, 1957), p. 4: "The Napoleonic wars and the problematic relationship between Russia and Europe led to the development of Russian national consciousness."
4. C. J. H. Hayes, "Two Varieties of Nationalism: 'Original' and 'Derived'," *Proceedings of the Association of History Teachers of the Middle States and Maryland*, 26 (1928), 71.
5. Hans Kohn, *Nationalism: Its Meaning and History* (New York, 1955), p. 17.
6. Royal Institute of International Affairs, *Nationalism* (London, 1939), p. 65.
7. Kohn, *Nationalism*, p. 9.
8. Otto Bauer, *Die Nationalitaetenfrage und die Sozialdemokratie* (Wien, 1924), p. 44.
9. See Eugen Lemberg, *Geschichte des Nationalismus in Europa* (Stuttgart, 1950), pp. 123-127.
10. Roy Pascal, *The German Sturm und Drang* (Manchester, England, 1953), p. 43.
11. W. H. Bruford, *Germany in the Eighteenth Century* (Cambridge, England, 1935), p. 297.
12. Cf. Johan Huizinga, *Im Bann der Geschichte* (Basel, 1943), p. 132, and Bauer, *Die Nationalitaetenfrage*, p. 138, who takes a knowledge of foreign ways to be the precondition of all national consciousness. Walter Sulzbach, *National Consciousness* (Washington, D. C., 1943), p. 71, writes: "In speaking of definitions, Spinoza states: 'Omnis determinatio negatio.' It is the same with nations. The German, insofar as he is nationally conscious, is non-French, non-Polish, non-English; the Spaniard is non-French, non-Italian"; Friedrich Hertz, *Nationalgeist und Politik* (Zuerich, 1937), p. 310, states: "Von grundlegender Bedeutung fuer die Ausbildung der nationalen Stroemungen bei den Slawen wurde ihr Gegensatz zu anderen Nationen."

The point was made with special relevance to Russia by Alexandre Koyré in the preface to his *Etudes sur l'histoire de la pensée philosophique en Russie* (Paris, 1950): "On ne se pose qu'en s'opposant et ne se détermine qu'en se distinguant . . . ."

CHAPTER I: THE GOVERNMENT OF FOREIGNERS

1. E. F. Shmurlo, "Petr Veliki v otsenke sovremennikov i potomstva," *Zhurnal Ministerstva Narodnogo Prosveshcheniya*, October 1911, p. 316 ff.; S. P. Melgunov, *Religiozno-obshchestvennye dvizheniya XVII–XVIII vekov v Rossii* (Moscow, 1922), pp. 115–119.

2. Konstantin Aksakov, *Lomonosov v istorii russkoi literatury i yazyka* (Moscow, 1846), pp. 6 and 45; cf. Ivan Aksakov: "St. Petersburg as the embodiment of a negative moment of history cannot create anything positive in the Russian sense. According to a well-known dialectical law it is possible to return to the *positive* only through a *negation of the negation itself*, in other words, through a negation of St. Petersburg as a political *principle* which guided Russian life for almost two centuries. The result will be a Russian nation freed from exclusiveness, and called into the arena of world history. Is that clear?" quoted by N. V. Riasanovsky, *Russia and the West in the Teaching of the Slavophiles* (Cambridge, Mass., 1952), p. 66.

3. Ernst Herrmann, *Zeitgenoessische Berichte zur Geschichte Russlands* (Leipzig, 1872–1880), II, 144.

4. I. A. Golubtsev, "Dvoryane," in A. I. Baranovich et al., eds., *Ocherki istorii SSSR, XVIII v.; vtoraya chetvert* (Moscow, 1957), p. 84.

5. Dispatch of the Saxon envoy Lefort of March 4, 1730, cited in *Ueber die Sittenverderbnis in Russland von Fuerst M. Schterbatow*, Karl Staehlin, ed. (Berlin, 1925), pp. 146–147.

6. N. A. Popov, *V. N. Tatishchev i ego vremya* (Moscow, 1861), p. 97 and D. A. Korsakov, *Votsarenie Imperatritsy Anny Ioannovny* (Kazan, 1880), p. 179.

7. J. G. Vockerodt, "Rossiya pri Petre Velikom," *Chteniya v imperatorskom obshchestve istorii i drevnostei rossiiskikh pri Moskovskom universitete*, April–June 1874, p. 97.

8. *Ibid.*, p. 97.

9. Letter of Edward Finch to Lord Harrington, June 2, 1741 in *Sbornik imperatorskogo russkogo istoricheskogo obshchestva*, XCI (1894), 107–108.

10. Quoted by Popov, *Tatishchev*, p. 94.

11. *Polnoe Sobranie Zakonov Rossiiskoi Imperii*, VIII (St. Petersburg, 1830), nos. 5862 and 5905.

12. For the decree on the foundation of Moscow University, see *Ezhemesyachnye Sochineniya*, I (1755), 98–104.

13. "Puteshestvie v zemlyu Ofirskuyu g-na S . . . shvetskago dvoryanina," *Sochineniya knyazya M. M. Shcherbatova*, I. P. Khrushchov and A. G. Voronov, eds. (St. Petersburg, 1896–1898), I, 748–1059. The work is discussed by N. D. Chechulin, *Russki sotsialny roman 18ogo veka* (St. Petersburg, 1900).

14. Shcherbatov, *Sochineniya*, I, 792.

15. *Ibid.*, I, 793–795.

16. In his "Corruption of Morals in Russia" Shcherbatov sympathetically characterized the conditions which the upper nobility tried to impose on the Empress Anna in 1730 as an attempt "to formulate basic law for the state and to limit the power of the ruler by a Senate or Parliament" ("O povrezhdenii nravov v Rossii," *Sochineniya*, II, 182). Like some of the contemporaries to the event, he was however suspicious of the motives for such a step and elsewhere spoke with approval of Anna's resumption of full autocratic power. ("Proshenie Moskvy o zabvenii eya," *Sochineniya*, II, 59.) In an interesting anticipation of the reign of Alexander I and Arakcheev, he also suggested the establishment of permanent military settlements to feed and furnish the country's military forces. Presumably this was to ease the burdens of military service for the landed nobility.

17. "Moskva," *Bolshaya sovetskaya entsiklopediya*, XL (1938), 314.

18. "O Vremya!," *Sochineniya Imperatritsy Ekateriny II*, A. N. Pypin, ed. (St. Petersburg, 1901), I, 1–42.

19. *Ibid.*, XII, 641–643.

20. *Ibid.*, XII, 642.

21. *Primechaniya na istoriyu drevniya i nyneshniya Rossii g. Leklerka, sochinennyya general-maiorom Ivanom Boltinym* (St. Petersburg, 1788), I, 549.

22. N. M. Karamzin, "Zapiska o drevnei i novoi Rossii," *Russki Arkhiv*, VIII (1870), 2258.

23. *Ibid.*, 2258.

24. *Ibid.*, 2253.

25. For the events surrounding Anna's elevation to the throne see, in addition to Korsakov's *Votsarenie*, P. N. Milyukov, "Verkhovniki i shlyakhetstvo," in his *Iz istorii russkoi intelligentsii* (2nd ed., St. Petersburg, 1903), pp. 1–51 and W. Recke, "Die Verfassungsplaene der russischen Oligarchen im Jahre 1730," *Zeitschrift fuer Osteuropaeische Geschichte*, II (1911–1912), 44 ff.

26. What the bulk of Russia's upper classes, outside of the *verkhovniki*, were interested in was not so much a fundamental reorganization of the government—their interest in political theory was slight—as a guarantee of their rights vis-à-vis the state and the nonprivileged classes. V. O. Klyuchevski, *Kurs russkoi istorii*, IV (Moscow, 1910), 370, quotes the Prussian Ambassador Mardefeld to the effect that all Russians (i.e. the upper classes) wish their liberties, only they cannot agree on their extent and the degree of limitation of absolutism. See also Korsakov, *Votsarenie*, p. 146 ff. and the project of Prince A. M. Cherkasski in S. S. Dmitriev and M. V. Nechkina, eds., *Khrestomatiya po istorii SSSR* (Moscow, 1949), II, 149.

27. *Polnoe Sobranie Zakonov*, VIII, nos. 5623, 5664, 5883; Karl Staehlin, *Geschichte Russlands* (Berlin und Koenigsberg, 1930), II, 222; *Zapiski feldmarshalla grafa Minikha*, S. N. Shubinski, ed., (St. Petersburg, 1874), p. 70.

28. Ivan Pushkarev, *Istoriya imperatorskoi rossiiskoi gvardii* (St. Petersburg, 1844), I, 149, 151, 174, 199.

29. The secretary of the English consul, Ward, reported on January 4, 1731 to Lord Hampton that the "old-Russian party looked with great dis-

turbance on the course of national affairs," and that its disturbance was in large measure caused by the favorites who surrounded the Empress. *Stoletie voennogo ministerstva* (St. Petersburg, n.d.), I, 104.

30. From Mardefeld's reports, quoted by Staehlin, *Geschichte*, II, 223; see also *Zapiski Minikha*, pp. 62-63.

31. Shcherbatov's comments in this connection are revealing: "Insofar as Russia is concerned, he [Biron] never tried to enrich himself during the life of the Empress Anna; and although he supplied Courland with Russian treasure, he knew . . . that he could retain the Duchy only with the protective strength of Russia, and therefore subordinated its welfare to the welfare of Russia. . . . Although the whole court trembled, although there was not a single courtier who did not fear Biron's malice, the people were well ruled. They were not oppressed by taxes, the laws were clearly formulated and fully executed." Shcherbatov, *Sochineniya*, II, 189, 191.

32. *Memoiren des Grafen Ernst von Muennich*, A. Juergensohn, ed. (Stuttgart, 1896), p. 198.

33. Staehlin, *Geschichte*, II, 250.

34. "Unzufriedenheit mit dem Regiment der Auslaender," *Sbornik imperatorskogo russkogo istoricheskogo obshchestva*, V (1870), 464-465.

35. Shcherbatov, *Sochineniya*, II, 190; D. A. Korsakov, *Iz zhizni russkikh deyatelei XVIII veka* (Kazan, 1891), pp. 107 ff., 252-253.

36. Georgi Florovski, *Puti russkogo bogosloviya* (Paris, 1951), pp. 95-96; Popov, *Tatishchev*, p. 198; Staehlin, *Geschichte*, II, 227-228.

37. This account of Volynski's activities and plans is based on D. A. Korsakov, "Artemi Petrovich Volynskoi i ego 'konfidenty'," *Russkaya Starina*, XV (1885), 17-54; the article was reprinted in the same author's *Iz zhizni russkikh deyatelei*, pp. 285-330. Volynski is also discussed in the following: S. M. Solovev, *Istoriya Rossii s drevneishikh vremen* (St. Petersburg, 1896), XVIII, 654-673; XX, 1615-1634 and Baranovich, *Ocherki . . . vtoraya chetvert*, pp. 260-264.

38. Korsakov, in *Russkaya Starina*, XV, 19. On the initiative of the historian M. I. Semevski, then editor of this journal, a monument to Volynski and two of his fellow conspirators was erected in St. Petersburg in 1885, the 145th anniversary of their execution.

39. Quoted by Staehlin, *Geschichte*, II, 214. Doubt has been expressed about the accuracy of this ascription (Korsakov, *Votsarenie*, p. 265) but as recent a work as Baranovich, *Ocherki . . . vtoraya chetvert* repeats it (p. 262).

40. Popov, *Tatishchev*, p. 149. In his "Testament" Tatishchev warned his son never to make common cause with those who "praise the liberties of other states and seek to diminish the power of the monarch," citing the events of 1730 to prove the folly of such a step. *Dukhovnaya Vasiliya Tatishcheva* (Leipzig, 1862), pp. 27-28.

41. The project itself has not been preserved. What is known of it derives chiefly from the records of the inquiry into Volynski's activities by the Secret Chancery. See Korsakov, *Iz zhizni*, p. 308.

42. Korsakov, in *Russkaya Starina*, XV, 48.

43. *Klyuchevski*, IV, 348-350; Baranovich, *Ocherki . . . vtoraya chetvert*, pp. 264-266.

44. Alexander Brueckner, *Die Europaeisierung Russlands* (1st ed.; Gotha, 1888), p. 334.
45. Quoted by Solovev, *Istoriya*, XXI, 150.
46. *Ibid.*
47. *Ibid.*, XXI, 150–151.
48. Brueckner, pp. 336–338.
49. N. N. Firsov, *Vstuplenie na prestol Imperatritsy Elizavety Petrovny* (Kazan, 1887), p. 160.
50. Quoted by P. E. Melgunova-Stepanova, *Russki byt po vospominaniyam sovremennikov XVIII veka* (Moscow, 1914–1918), I, 292.
51. M. V. Lomonosov, *Sochineniya*, A. Smirdin, ed. (St. Petersburg, 1847–1850), I, 60, 79, 557, 558, 576, 581–582. See also V. K. Tredyakovski, *Sochineniya*, A. Smirdin, ed. (St. Petersburg, 1849), I, 158, 293–300.
52. Quoted by Shmurlo in *Zhurnal Ministerstva Narodnogo Prosveshcheniya*, May–June 1912, p. 209. Cf. Alexander Sumarokov's second ode in S. A. Vengerov, ed., *Russkaya Poeziya* (St. Petersburg, 1897), I, 171–172.
53. Kazimierz Waliszewski, *La dernière des Romanov* (Paris, 1902), pp. 23, 28.
54. See *Zhizn i priklyucheniya Andreya Bolotova* (St. Petersburg, 1871), II, 163–175, 270–277.
55. Solovev, *Istoriya*, XXV, 1296.
56. *Ibid.*, 1301 and Staehlin, *Geschichte*, II, 417.
57. Bolotov, *Zhizn i priklyucheniya*, II, 172–173.
58. Klyuchevski, IV, 461.
59. *Memoirs of the Princess Daschkaw*, W. Bradford, ed. (London, 1840), I, 82, 94.
60. *Ibid.*, I, 109.
61. The texts of both manifestoes in P. I. Bartenev, ed., *Osmnadtsaty Vek* (Moscow, 1869), IV, 216–224.
62. Solovev, *Istoriya*, XXV, 1371–1373.
63. Vengerov, *Russkaya Poeziya*, I, 174.
64. Lomonosov, *Sochineniya*, I, 175.
65. Shcherbatov, *Sochineniya*, II, 226.
66. M. M. Shcherbatov, "O supruzhestve rossiiskikh knyazei," in *Neizdannye Sochineniya* (Moscow, 1935), pp. 100–111.
67. Shcherbatov, *Sochineniya*, II, 268.
68. A. V. Zapadova and G. P. Makogonenko, eds., *Russkaya proza XVIII veka* (Moscow-Leningrad, 1950), I, 252.
69. "Plach krepostnykh kholopov," in Dmitriev, *Khrestomatiya*, II, 227–229. D. D. Blagoi, *Istoriya russkoi literatury XVIII veka* (2nd ed.; Moscow, 1951), places the poem in the years 1767–1768.
70. K. V. Sivkov, "Podpolnaya politicheskaya literatura v kontse XVIII veka," *Istoricheskie Zapiski*, no. 19 (1946), pp. 63–101.
71. G. A. Gukovski and V. Orlov, "Podpolnaya poeziya 1770–1800-kh godov,"*Literaturnoe Nasledstvo*, nos. 9/10 (1933), p. 53.

CHAPTER II: MANNERS AND MORALS

1. Waliszewski, *La dernière des Romanov*, p. 29; Firsov, *Vstuplenie*, p. 160.

2. This attitude is revealed in the very title of Bakunin's "L'Empire Knouto-Germanique et la Revolution sociale" and his characterization of Nicholas I as "this Genghis-Khan Germanized or rather this German prince mongolized, [who] realized . . . the sublime ideal of the absolute sovereign." *Oeuvres* (Paris, 1907), II, 397.

3. Klyuchevski, V, 118 ff.

4. Shcherbatov, *Neizdannye Sochineniya*, p. 126.

5. Quoted by Emile Haumant, *La culture française en Russie* (Paris, 1910), pp. 95–96.

6. Klyuchevski, V, 147.

7. Vockerodt had already noted that considerations of honor were of little avail in convincing the Russian noble of the necessity of service, military service in particular. "If one speaks to them of the example of other European nations, where the nobility views it as a great honor to distinguish itself in military service, they answer as a rule: examples of this kind only prove that there are more fools than wise men in the world. If you foreigners have sufficient to live, and you expose yourselves nonetheless for vain honor, at risk of health and life, in the possession of which alone you can enjoy such honor, then you must show us a more reasonable cause for your conduct," in *Chteniya v imperatorskom obshchestve istorii i drevnostei rossiiskikh*, April–June 1874, pp. 106–107.

8. *Sochineniya, pisma i izbrannye perevody knyazya Antiokha Dmitrievicha Kantemira*, P. A. Efremov, ed. (St. Petersburg, 1867–1868), I, 17–18, 50.

9. Tredyakovski, *Sochineniya*, III, 585.

10. Quoted by P. N. Milyukov, *Ocherki po istorii russkoi kultury* (Paris, 1937), III, 361–362.

11. *Ibid.*

12. "Chudovishchi," in *Rossiiski Featr*, XVI (St. Petersburg, 1787), 17.

13. "Ssora u muzha s zhenoyu," in P. N. Berkov, ed., *Russkaya komediya XVIII veka* (Moscow-Leningrad, 1950), pp. 76–77.

14. A. P. Sumarokov, *Stikhotvoreniya*, A. S. Orlov, ed. (Moscow, 1935), p. 195.

15. "La première et la principale révolte des Strelitz," in M. L. Pappadopoulo, tr., *Choix des meilleurs morceaux de la littérature russe* (Paris, 1800), p. 83.

16. *Ibid.*

17. Shcherbatov, *Sochineniya*, II, 20.

18. *Ibid.*, II, 28.

19. *Ibid.*, II, 167–168.

20. *Ibid.*, II, 244.

21. I. P. Elagin's *Russkoi-frantsuz*, performed in 1764–1765. See Berkov, *Russkaya Komediya*, p. 13.

22. *Ibid.*, pp. 12–14.

23. V. I. Lukin, *Sochineniya* (St. Petersburg, 1765), I, 1–150.

24. "Shchepetilnik," in *Russkaya komediya*, pp. 85–121.

25. "Samolyubivoi stikhotvorets," in *Rossiiski Featr*, XV, 31.

26. *Smes*, 2nd ed. (1771), pp. 102–104; see also A. I. Klushin's comedy "Smekh i gore," where Vetron (Windbag) is compared to a machine which is animated by a spring.

27. Nikolev, "Samolyubivoi stikhotvorets," in *Rossiiski Featr*, XV, 119–120.

28. "Neschastie ot karety," in *Sochineniya Ya. B. Knyazhnina*, A. Smirdin, ed. (St. Petersburg, 1848), I, 109–138.

29. This is particularly pronounced in Krylov's journal *Pochta Dukhov* ("The Spirit Post.") "Our store alone," says the owner of a French shop in St. Petersburg, "can ruin up to 100,000 peasants a year, and these peasants enjoy less respect here than one Frenchman who deals in hats, pomade, and steel buttons," or: "In this manner, the rich landowner converts his grain and his peasants into fashionable goods. . . ." I. A. Krylov, *Sochineniya*, Demyan Bedny, ed. (Moscow, 1945), I, 209–214, 240.

30. Knyazhnin, *Sochineniya*, II, 117.

31. *Ibid.*, II, 131.

32. *Ibid.*, II, 136.

33. *Satiricheskie zhurnaly N. I. Novikova*, P. N. Berkov, ed. (Moscow-Leningrad, 1951), p. 142.

34. Knyazhnin, *Sochineniya*, II, 119; see also Novikov's journal *Zhivopisets* ("The Painter"), no. 3 (1772) in *Satiricheskie zhurnaly N. I. Novikova*, p. 290: "A badly educated, illiterate officer, living in retirement on his estate, tyrannizes his serfs. These he treats like the foreign enemies against whom he fought in former years. Then he battled the infidels, and now he lashes and tortures the faithful. Then he gave no quarter to his enemies, and now shows no mercy to his peasants . . . [and] would not hesitate to put them before a firing squad."

35. Knyazhnin, *Sochineniya*, II, 133 ff. The same theme is treated in two other plays of Knyazhnin's, *Chudaki* ("Odd People") and *Khvastun* ("The Braggart"), but they lack the impact of "The Carriage." (*Sochineniya*, I, 453–720.)

36. A. T. Bolotov, "Pismo k priyatelyu moemu S . . . o petimetrakh," *Literaturnoe Nasledstvo*, nos. 9/10 (1933), pp. 182–189.

37. P. N. Berkov, *Istoriya russkoi zhurnalistiki XVIII veka* (Moscow-Leningrad, 1952), p. 213 and V. V. Sipovski, *Ocherki iz istorii russkogo romana* (St. Petersburg, 1909–1910), I, part II, 627.

38. "Nenavistnik," in *Rossiiski Featr*, X, 66.

39. "Russkoi Parizhanets," *ibid.*, XV, 194–195.

40. *Ibid.*, 196.

41. Sipovski, *Ocherki*, I, part I, 189–190.

42. V. I. Pokrovski, *Shchegoli v satiricheskoi literature XVIII veka* (Moscow, 1903), pp. 4–5.

43. Boltin, *Primechaniya na Leklerka*, II, 104, 152–153.

44. In V. P. Semennikov, ed., *Materialy dlya istorii russkoi literatury* (St. Petersburg, 1914), p. 34.

45. Milyukov, *Ocherki*, III, 479–486; A. Ya. Kucherov, "Frantsuzskaya revolyutsiya i russkaya literatura 18-ogo veka," in A. S. Orlov, ed., *Vosemnadtsaty Vek* (Moscow-Leningrad, 1935), pp. 259–307.

46. Quoted by Milyukov, *Ocherki*, III, 359.

47. *Truten, Zhivopisets, Koshelek, Pustomelya.*

48. *Satiricheskie zhurnaly Novikova*, pp. 62–63, 299, 327–329.

49. *Ibid.*, p. 106.

50. *Ibid.*, pp. 477–495.
51. *Ibid.*, p. 488.
52. "Brigadir" and "Nedorosl" in *Pervoe polnoe sobranie sochineni D. I. Fonvizina* (St. Petersburg and Moscow, 1888), pp. 61–102, 103–156.
53. *Ibid.*, pp. 121–122.
54. *Ibid.*, p. 963.
55. P. A. Vyazemski, *Polnoe sobranie sochineni* (St. Petersburg, 1880), V, 87 ff.; cf. Zhdanov, "Ocherk zhizni i literaturnoi deyatelnosti Fonvizina," in V. I. Pokrovski, ed., *Sokrashchennaya istoricheskaya khrestomatiya* (3rd ed.; Moscow, 1911), II, 742.
56. Fonvizin, *Pervoe polnoe sobranie sochineni*, p. 963.
57. *Ibid.*, p. 895.
58. *Ibid.*, p. 907.
59. *Ibid.*, p. 896.
60. *Ibid.*, pp. 901–906, 960.
61. *Ibid.*, p. 969.
62. *Ibid.*, pp. 902, 963.
63. "Chistoserdechnoe priznanie," *ibid.*, p. 851 ff.
64. Letter to Ya. I. Bulgakov, *ibid.*, p. 914.

CHAPTER III: TOWARDS A NATIONAL LANGUAGE

1. *Herders Saemmtliche Werke*, B. Suphan, ed. (Berlin, 1887), XIII, 37–38.
2. L. A. Bulakhovski, *Istoricheski kommentari k russkomu literaturnomu yazyku* (5th ed.; Kiev, 1958), p. 18 ff.; P. I. Zhitetski, "K istorii literaturnoi russkoi rechi v XVIII veke," *Akademiya Nauk; izvestiya otdeleniya russkogo yazyka i slovesnosti*, VIII (1903), 1–51; V. V. Vinogradov, *Ocherki po istorii russkogo literaturnogo yazyka XVII–XIX vv.* (Leiden, 1949), chs. i and ii.
3. Vinogradov, *Ocherki*, p. 72.
4. *Ibid.*, p. 73.
5. S. Obnorski and S. G. Barkhudarov, eds., *Khrestomatiya po istorii russkogo yazyka* (Moscow, 1949), II, part I, 150.
6. A. S. Arkhangelski, *Russkaya literatura XVIII veka* (Kazan, 1911), p. 44; I. Ya. Shchipanov, ed., *Izbrannye proizvedeniya russkikh myslitelei vtoroi poloviny XVIII veka* (Moscow, 1952), I, 113; Zhitetski in *Izvestiya*, VIII, 19–21.
7. Letter to Rudakovski, quoted by Vinogradov, p. 60.
8. Blagoi, *Istoriya russkoi literatury*, p. 60.
9. V. N. Tatishchev, *Istoriya Rossiiskaya*, I, (Moscow, 1768), part I, xxv; part II, 495–496.
10. M. T. Sukhomlinov, "Istoriya rossiiskoi Akademii," *Akademiya Nauk; sbornik otdeleniya russkogo yazyka i slovesnosti*, XI (1875), 5.
11. Popov, *Tatischev*, pp. 149, 201; P. P. Pekarski, *Novyya izvestiya o V. N. Tatishcheve* (St. Petersburg, 1864), p. 31.
12. D. A. Tolstoy, *Das Unterrichtswesen Russlands im 18. Jahrhundert* (St. Petersburg, 1884), p. 37.
13. Letter to Tredyakovski in Zapadova, *Russkaya Proza*, I, 10.

14. Tatishchev, *Istoriya*, I, part I, 1–5; part II, 493–497.

15. Tredyakovski, *Sochineniya*, III, 649–650.

16. *Ibid.*, I, 266.

17. Antoine Martel, *Michel Lomonosov et la langue littéraire russe* (Leningrad, 1933), p. 18.

18. Excerpts of the 1735 version in Obnorski, *Khrestomatiya*, II, no. 1, 163–168. The version in Tredyakovski, *Sochineniya*, I, 121–178 is dated 1752.

19. A. Adamczyk, *Tredjakovskij und die Reform* (Breslau, 1940), pp. 16–17, 44; W. E. Harkins, *The Russian Folk Epos in Czech Literature* (New York, 1953), pp. 3–4.

20. Tredyakovski, *Sochineniya*, III, 571–581; Martel, p. 42.

21. "O pervenstve slovenskago yazyka pred tevtonicheskim," *Sochineniya*, III, 319–369.

22. *Ibid.*, III, 332, 337, 369.

23. F.e., S. K. Bulich, *Ocherki istorii yazykoznaniya v Rossii* (St. Petersburg, 1904), I, 205.

24. Vinogradov, *Ocherki*, pp. 88–90.

25. "O pravilakh rossiiskogo stikhotvorstva," *Sochineniya*, I, 537.

26. "O polze knig tserkovnykh v rossiiskom yazyke," *Sochineniya*, I, 527–535.

27. *Ibid.*, I, 532.

28. *Ibid.*, III, 249–250.

29. P. P. Pekarski, *Istoriya Imperatorskoi Akademii Nauk v Peterburge* (St. Petersburg, 1870–1873), II, 685.

30. Sumarokov, *Stikhotvoreniya*, pp. 78, 344–354, 381.

31. Quoted by Vinogradov, *Ocherki*, p. 133.

32. Sumarokov, *Stikhotvoreniya*, p. 380.

33. *Ibid.*, p. 205.

34. *Ibid.*, p. 365.

35. Martel, *Michel Lomonosov*, p. 23; Bulich, *Ocherki*, I, 211–212.

36. Dashkova, I, pp. 4, 14.

37. "Pisma russkogo puteshestvennika," in Zapadova, *Russkaya Proza*, II, 534.

38. N. N. Popovski, "Rech govorennaya v nachatii filosoficheskikh lektsi," in Shchipanov, *Izbrannye proizvedeniya*, I, 90–91.

39. Sukhomlinov, in *Akademiya Nauk; sbornik otdeleniya russkogo yazyka i slovesnosti*, XLII, 54–55.

40. Blagoi, *Istoriya*, p. 435. The "Discourse," written in 1772, had been requested by Kheraskov's French translator. The original is in French, "Discours sur la poesie russe." It was first published in Russian, under the title "Rassuzhdenie o rossiiskom stikhotvorstve," in *Literaturnoe Nasledstvo*, nos. 9/10 (1933), pp. 290–294.

41. Fonvizin, *Pervoe polnoe sobranie sochineni*, p. 837.

42. *Ibid.*, p. 854.

43. P. N. Berkov, "Materialy dlya istorii russkoi literatury XVIII v.," in Orlov, *Vosemnadtsaty Vek*, p. 367.

44. Boltin, *Primechaniya na Leklerka*, II, 32.

45. "Zapiski kasatelno rossiiskoi istorii," *Sochineniya*, VIII, 55–56.

46. Dashkova, I, 374; 96.

47. A. S. Orlov, "Telemakhida V. K. Tredyakovskogo," in Orlov, *Vosemnadtsaty Vek*, p. 23.

48. *Sochineniya Imperatritsy Ekateriny*, V, 104–105; Zhitetski in *Akademiya Nauk; izvestiya otdeleniya russkogo yazyka i slovesnosti*, VIII, 49–50.

49. Sukhomlinov in *Akademiya Nauk; sbornik otdeleniya russkogo yazyka i slovesnosti*, XI, 6–7.

50. *Ibid.*, XI, 9, 308; a second edition of the Dictionary appeared in 1792.

51. Quoted by A. N. Pypin, *Istoriya russkoi etnografii* (St. Petersburg, 1890), I, 172.

52. Quoted by Vinogradov, *Ocherki*, pp. 156–157.

53. Dashkova, I, 318.

54. *Ibid.*, I, 144–147.

55. Bulich, *Ocherki*, pp. 240–244.

56. *Ibid.*, pp. 233–237; Blagoi, *Istoriya*, p. 474; G. A. Gukovski, *Russkaya literatura XVIII veka* (Moscow, 1939), p. 220.

57. *Sochineniya Karamzina* (3rd ed., Moscow, 1820), IX, 306–307.

58. *Ibid.*, IX, 314.

59. Quoted by Vinogradov, *Ocherki*, p. 158.

60. A. S. Shishkov, *Razsuzhdenie o starom i novom sloge rossiiskago yazyka* (St. Petersburg, 1803), p. 8.

61. *Ibid.*, p. 205.

CHAPTER IV: THE DISCOVERY OF THE FOLK

1. *The Poetical Works of William Cowper* (London, n.d.), p. 236.

2. J. J. Rousseau, *The Social Contract*, Charles Frankel, ed. (New York, 1947), pp. 40–41.

3. Herder, XIII, 339.

4. "Pismo o krasote prirody," *Trudolyubivaya Pchela* (2nd ed., 1780), pp. 312–314, originally published in May 1759.

5. G. A. Gukovski, *Ocherki po istorii russkoi literatury i obshchestvennoi mysli XVIII veka* (Leningrad, 1938), pp. 94–96.

6. Blagoi, *Istoriya*, p. 436.

7. *Satiricheskie zhurnaly Novikova*, pp. 66–67, 286–287 and Krylov, *Sochineniya*, I, 367–374.

8. *Ibid.*, I, 213.

9. Quoted by Berkov, *Istoriya russkoi zhurnalistiki*, p. 472.

10. Knyazhnin, *Sochineniya*, II, 113; similar sentiments are expressed in N. P. Nikolev's "Rozana and Lyubim" and A. D. Kopiev's "Converted Misanthrope" in Berkov, *Russkaya komediya*, pp. 207, 498–499; see also V. V. Sipovski, "Iz istorii russkoi mysli XVIII stoletiya," *Zhurnal Ministerstva Narodnogo Prosveshcheniya*, March–April 1917, pp. 113–114.

11. A. N. Radishchev, *Izbrannye Sochineniya*, G. P. Makogonenko, ed. (Moscow, 1952), pp. 124–125.

12. *Ibid.*, p. 128.

13. I. F. Bogdanovich, *Sochineniya*, A. Smirdin, ed. (St. Petersburg, 1848), II, 37.

14. *Ibid.*, II, 53–54.

15. Cited by Kucherov, in Orlov, *Vosemnadtsaty Vek*, p. 273. The

pamphlet was a translation from the French and printed at the government printing house in 1793.

16. "Derevnya," *Sochineniya Karamzina*, VII, 117–125.

17. "Natalya, boyarskaya doch," *ibid.*, VI, 100, 107, 109.

18. N. N. Strakhov, *Borba s zapadom v nashei literature* (St. Petersburg, 1887–1890), II, 37 and N. G. Chernyshevski, *Literaturno-kriticheskie stati* (Moscow, 1939), p. 6.

19. Paul van Tieghem, *Le mouvement romantique* (3rd ed.; Paris, 1940), p. 79.

20. L. Fridberg, "Knigoizdatelskaya deyatelnost Novikova v Moskve," *Voprosy Istorii*, no. 8 (1948), p. 31.

21. E. J. Simmons, *English Literature and Culture in Russia* (Cambridge, Mass., 1935), passim; Gukovski, *Ocherki po istorii russkoi literatury i obshchestvennoi mysli*, p. 235 ff.; N. Trubitsyn, *O narodnoi poezii v obshchestvennom i literaturnom obikhode pervoi treti XIX veka* (St. Petersburg, 1912), p. 128 gives the date of the first Ossian translation as 1788.

22. Trubitsyn, p. 9; P. N. Sakulin, *Istoriya novoi russkoi literatury; epokha klassitsizma* (Moscow, 1918), p. 60; G. A. Gukovski, *Ocherki po istorii russkoi literatury 18ogo veka; dvoryanskaya fronda v literature 1750–kh–1760–kh godov* (Moscow, 1936), p. 14; V. V. Sipovski, *Istoriya russkoi slovesnosti* (St. Petersburg, 1908), II, 180–181.

23. Quoted by Sipovski, *Istoriya russkoi slovesnosti*, II, 72.

24. "O stikhotvorstve," in Vengerov, *Russkaya Poeziya*, pp. 166–168.

25. Lukin, *Sochineniya*, II, 116.

26. Quoted by N. Khardzhiev, "'Kak khochesh nazovi,' neizdannaya komediya Chulkova," *Literaturnoe Nasledstvo*, nos. 9/10 (1933), p. 223.

27. Lukin, *Sochineniya*, II, 116.

28. *Ibid.*, I, 154.

29. "Predislovie k 'Shchepetilniku'," in Berkov, *Russkaya komediya*, p. 92.

30. Lukin, *Sochineniya*, I, xxiii, xv.

31. No complete Russian version of Sumarokov's "Reflections" has been available. A full French version, together with Voltaire's letter, is contained in Pappadopoulo, *Choix des meilleurs morceaux*, pp. 199–207. Extensive Russian excerpts are found in V. B. Shklovski, *Chulkov i Levshin* (Leningrad, 1933), p. 189.

32. P. A. Plavilshchikov, "Teatr," in A. B. Kokorev, ed., *Khrestomatiya po russkoi literature XVIII veka* (Moscow, 1952), p. 502.

33. Quoted by Blagoi, *Istoriya*, pp. 409–410.

34. Quoted by Berkov, *Istoriya zhurnalistiki*, p. 467.

35. In G. A. Gukovski, ed., *Khrestomatiya po russkoi literature XVIII veka* (3rd ed.; Moscow, 1938), pp. 360–375.

36. "Melnik—Koldun, obmanshchik i svat," in Berkov, *Russkaya komediya*, pp. 217–262.

37. For conflicting views see Blagoi, *Istoriya*, p. 374 and A. I. Nezelenov, *Literaturnye napravleniya v ekaterininskuyu epokhu* (St. Petersburg, 1889), p. 68.

38. *Sochineniya Imperatritsy Ekateriny*, II, 219–409.

39. B. V. Tomashevski, *Iroi-komicheskaya poema* (Leningrad, 1933), passim; V. A. Desnitski, *Na literaturnye temy* (Leningrad, 1936), II, 101–103.

40. A. I. Bolotov, "Mysli i bespristrastnye suzhdeniya o romanakh," *Literaturnoe Nasledstvo*, nos. 9/10 (1933), p. 127.
41. A. N. Pypin, *Istoriya russkoi etnografii* (St. Petersburg, 1890–1892), I, 73.
42. M. M. Kheraskov, *Bakhariyana ili neizvestny* (Moscow, 1803), p. 127.
43. Vengerov, *Russkaya Poeziya*, part 7, 95.
44. Quoted by Sipovski, *Istoriya . . . slovesnosti*, II, 128–129.
45. O. J. Falnes, *National Romanticism in Norway* (New York, 1933), p. 250.
46. Aksakov, *Lomonosov*, pp. 27, 37.
47. Herder, *Werke*, IX, 538 ff.
48. Radishchev, *Izbrannye Sochineniya*, p. 184.
49. Dashkova, I, 336–337.
50. Y. M. Sokolov, *Russian Folklore*, C. R. Smith, tr. (New York, 1950), p. 44; S. Dmitriev, "Rabochi folklor XVIII veka," *Literaturnoe Nasledstvo*, nos. 19/21 (1935), p. 7; Blagoi, *Istoriya*, p. 471.
51. Tredyakovski, *Sochineniya*, I, 194; see also his "O drevnem, srednem i novom stikhotvorenii rossiiskom," *ibid.*, I, 759–762.
52. Cf. P. N. Berkov, "Lomonosov i folklor," in A. I. Andreev and L. B. Mozdalevski, eds., *Lomonosov; sbornik statei i materialov* (Moscow, 1946), II, 118–128.
53. I. N. Rozanov, *Russkaya Pesnya* (Moscow, 1944), preface, and *Pesni russkikh poetov* (Moscow, 1936), pp. 18–19; Trubitsyn, *O narodnoi poezii*, pp. 3–5, 38–39; Harkins, *Russian Folk Epos*, p. 11.
54. Sokolov, *Russian Folklore*, p. 46.
55. I. N. Rozanov, "Pesni o gostinom syne," in Orlov, *Vosemnadtsaty Vek*, pp. 219–221.
56. *Sochineniya M. D. Chulkova*, facsimile of the 1st edition (St. Petersburg, 1913), I, 7.
57. Trubitsyn, *O narodnoi poezii*, pp. 44, 63–65, 236.
58. *Pypin, Istoriya . . . etnografii*, I, 108–110. Chulkov, for example, included material from Krasheninnikov in his "Dictionary of Russian Superstitions" (1782).
59. Shklovski, *Chulkov i Levshin*, pp. 74–75; Aleksandr Bogumil, *Nachalny period narodnichestva v russkoi khudozhestvennoi literature* (Kiev, 1907), p. 260; Berkov, *Istoriya . . . zhurnalistiki*, p. 266; G. P. Makogonenko, *Novikov* (Moscow, 1953), p. 463.
60. From "Sobesednik lyubitelei rossiiskogo slova" (1783), in P. B. Kozmin, ed., *Sbornik materialov k izucheniyu istorii russkoi zhurnalistiki* (Moscow, 1952), I, 71.
61. Bogdanovich, *Sochineniya*, I, 377–378.
62. Shklovski, *Chulkov i Levshin*, p. 96.
63. Quoted by Sipovski, *Istoriya . . . slovesnosti*, II, 187. Although Sipovski ascribes this passage to Chulkov's "Scoffer," the portions which appear in Zapadova, *Russkaya Proza*, I, 89–156, including a preface ("Iz sbornika 'Peresmeshnik ili slavenskie skazki' "), are taken from the first edition and do not contain the preface quoted by Sipovski. It is possible that this was a preface to a second edition (1783–1789) or even to a third and last one (1789). Sipovski may of course have erred in thinking Chulkov the author

of the preface as, according to later researches (Shklovski, Harkins), he as well as Pypin erred in believing that Chulkov was the author of Levshin's "Russian Tales." I have not been able to examine the original texts, but do not think that the question of authorship affects the general line of the argument.

64. Shklovski, *Chulkov i Levshin*, p. 97 et passim.
65. Pypin, *Istoriya . . . etnografii*, I, 69-73.
66. M. D. Chulkov, *Slovar russkikh sueveri* (St. Petersburg, 1782), preface.
67. Sipovski, *Ocherki*, II, 217. See also Shklovski, *Chulkov i Levshin*, p. 162; Sokolov, *Russian Folklore*, p. 47, and Harkins, *Russian Folk Epos*, p. 12.
68. Trubitsyn, *O narodnoi poezii*, p. 197.
69. Gukovski, *Russkaya literatura*, p. 11.
70. Bogumil, *Nachalny period*, pp. 47 and 169.
71. I. T. Pososhkov, *Kniga o skudosti i bogatstve*, B. B. Kafengauz, ed. (Moscow, 1937), pp. 254 and 259.
72. "Mnenie deputata Korobina," in Zapadova, *Russkaya Proza*, I, 210.
73. See V. I. Semevski, *Krestyanski vopros v Rossii v XVIII i pervoi polovine XIX veka* (St. Petersburg, 1888), I, 82-88; Chulkov's "Peresmeshnik," in Zapadova, *Russkaya Proza*, I, 145, and the sermon of P. A. Slovtsov in Shchipanov, *Izbrannye proizvedeniya*, I, 402-403 which bears a striking resemblance in some of its passages to the famous pamphlet of the Abbé Siéyès, "What is the Third Estate?".
74. Kantemir, *Sochineniya*, I, 54.
75. *Tryudolyubivaya Pchela* (2nd ed., 1780), pp. 738-747.
76. A. P. Sumarokov, "Drugoi khor ko prevratnomu svetu," in Vengerov, *Russkaya Poeziya*, I, 262-263.
77. Shcherbatov, *Sochineniya*, II, 269-290.
78. V. I. Maikov, *Derevenski Prazdnik*, quoted by L. N. Maikov, *Ocherki po istorii russkoi literatury XVII i XVIII vv.* (St. Petersburg, 1889), p. 284.
79. *Smes*, no. 25 (1769), in L. B. Lekhtblau, ed., *Russkie satiricheskie zhurnaly XVIII veka* (Moscow, 1940), p. 84.
80. Novikov, *Satiricheskie zhurnaly*, pp. 56, 130, 295.
81. "Opyt rossiiskogo soslovnika," in Kozmin, *Sbornik*, I, 68. See also Lekhtblau, pp. 31-33, 286 and Berkov, *Istoriya . . . zhurnalistiki*, p. 448. See also Radishchev, *Polnoe sobranie sochineni*, I. K. Luppol, ed., I, (Moscow-Leningrad, 1938), pp. 215-223, 278, 322.
82. N. P. Nikolev, "Rozana i Lyubim," in Berkov, *Russkaya komediya*, p. 194.
83. P. A. Plavilshchikov, "Bobyl," *Ibid.*, p. 449.
84. Karamzin, "Bednaya Liza," in Zapadova, *Russkaya Proza*, II, 237-249.
85. Karamzin, "Frol Silin, blagodetelnoi chelovek," *Sochineniya*, A. Smirdin, ed. (St. Petersburg, 1848), III, 661-665.
86. Sipovski, *Ocherki*, II, 740.
87. *Ibid.*, II, 424, 494 and Sipovski, *Iz istorii russkogo romana*, I, 225-226.

CHAPTER V: THE USES OF HISTORY

1. Ernst Cassirer, *Die Philosophie der Aufklaerung* (Tuebingen, 1932), ch. v.

310						Notes to Chapter V

2. Karamzin, *Sochineniya*, IV, 189.
3. Walter Hinz, "Peters des Grossen Anteil an der wissenschaftlichen und kuenstlerischen Kultur seiner Zeit," *Jahrbuecher fuer Kultur und Geschichte der Slawen*, VIII (1932), 395–400.
4. P. P. Pekarski, *Nauka i literatura v Rossii pri Petre Velikom* (St. Petersburg, 1862), I, 317–318; see also D. S. Likhachev, *Russkie Letopisi* (Moscow-Leningrad, 1947), p. 433.
5. S. M. Solovev, "Pisateli russkoi istorii XVIII veka," *Sobranie Sochineni* (St. Petersburg, 1900), V, 1317–1328; M. O. Koyalovich, *Istoriya russkogo samosoznaniya* (3rd ed.; St. Petersburg, 1901), p. 90.
6. N. L. Rubinshtein, *Russkaya Istoriografiya* (Moscow, 1941), p. 64; Blagoi, *Istoriya*, p. 91.
7. Tatishchev, *Istoriya*, I, part I, xvi.
8. *Ibid.*, I, part I, vi. In a later passage Tatishchev somewhat softened his censure of foreign historians; they were not altogether guilty of misrepresentation, since Russians themselves did not know their history and geography.
9. Rubinshtein, *Russkaya Istoriografiya*, p. 70; P. N. Milyukov, *Glavnye techeniya russkoi istoricheskoi mysli* (Moscow, 1897), p. 24.
10. Tatishchev, *Istoriya*, I, part II, 42.
11. *Ibid.*, I, part II, 541–545.
12. *Ibid.*, I, part I, 2–3; see also 6 and 52.
13. *Ibid.*, I, part I, 9.
14. Solovev, *Sobranie Sochineni*, V, 1331.
15. For the biographical data on Mueller, see Pekarski, *Istoriya*, I, 308–430 and S. H. Cross, "The Contribution of G. F. Mueller to Russian Historiography," (Unpublished dissertation, Harvard University, 1916).
16. Koyalovich, p. 99 and M. Tikhomirov, "Russkaya istoriografiya XVIII veka," *Voprosy Istorii*, no. 2 (1948), pp. 94–96.
17. Pekarski, *Istoriya*, I, 332–342.
18. *Ibid.*, I, 33 ff. and W. Stieda, "Die Anfaenge der kaiserlichen Akademie der Wissenschaften in St. Petersburg," *Jahrbuecher fuer Kultur und Geschichte der Slawen*, II (1925), 152–163. The last president, Karl Brevern, a protégé of Biron's, fell together with his protector in 1741.
19. Pekarski, *Istoriya*, I, 345–347.
20. *Ibid.*, I, 360.
21. Letter of Teplov to Razumovski, September 15, 1749, quoted by Cross, pp. 145–146.
22. Pekarski, *Istoriya*, I, 361–365 and II, 144–145, 423–440. Tredyakovski's was the only dissenting voice. Though he did not share Mueller's views, he held them to have been the result of honest and conscientious effort.
23. *Sammlung Russischer Geschichte*, V (1760), 385.
24. Pekarski, *Istoriya*, II, 906–907.
25. "Versuch einer neueren Geschichte Russlands," *Sammlung Russischer Geschichte*, V (1760), 1–2.
26. Report of Lomonosov to Razumovski, in P. Bilyarski, ed., *Materialy dlya biografii Lomonosova* (St. Petersburg, 1865), pp. 491–492.
27. Milyukov, *Glavnye techeniya*, pp. 69, 99.
28. Lavrovski, "Lomonosov v Marburge," in Pokrovski, *Sokrashchennaya . . . khrestomatiya*, II, 243.

29. *Sochineniya,* I, 696 and 750–752.

30. *Ibid.,* I, 728–735 and Bilyarski, pp. 211, 323. Voltaire's project, submitted to the Empress Elizabeth as far back as 1745, was finally approved in 1757. From the start, there were misgivings about entrusting such a task to a non-Russian. When the first portion of Voltaire's manuscript arrived in St. Petersburg, it met with a cool reception by those charged with its examination. Taubert, Mueller, and Lomonosov criticized it sharply, the latter primarily on patriotic grounds. It was not true, Lomonosov said among other things, that Peter had been afraid to cross water as a child; inappropriate to describe his table manners in such detail as M. Voltaire had done; Moscow should not simply be called a town, but a large town; Sheremetev and Shein were not of Prussian origin and Lefort was assigned too great an importance (Shmurlo, in *Zhurnal Ministerstva Narodnogo Prosveshcheniya,* February 1912, pp. 224–228; Milyukov, *Glavnye techeniya,* p. 29; Pekarski, *Istoriya,* II, 760).

31. "Drevnyaya rossiiskaya istoriya," *Sochineniya,* III, 74–76.

32. *Ibid.,* III, 89.

33. *Ibid.,* III, 132.

34. "Kratki rossiiski letopisets," *ibid.,* III, 1–69.

35. See, for example, "Petr Veliki . . . ," *ibid.,* I, 301–354; "Slovo pokhvalnoe . . . ." *ibid.,* I, 579–616; the second ode to Elizabeth, *ibid.,* I, 45, et al.

36. *Ibid.,* I, 763–765; Bilyarski, p. 702; Milyukov, *Glavnye techeniya,* pp. 80–81. Schloezer's own version of his quarrels with Lomonosov, who was in this instance supported by Mueller, is contained in his memoirs of his Russian stay: "Obshchestvennaya i chastnaya zhizn Avgusta Lyudviga Shletsera, im samim opisannaya," *Akademiya Nauk; sbornik otdeleniya russkogo yazyka i slovesnosti,* XIII (1875), 193–202.

37. See note 16, above; K. N. Bestuzhev-Ryumin, *Biografii i kharakteristiki* (St. Petersburg, 1882), p. 202; Milyukov, *Glavnye techeniya,* pp. 125–126 and Rubinshtein, p. 165.

38. *Nestor,* I, 418–419, quoted by Koyalovich, p. 116.

39. *Nestor,* I, 388–390, cited by Milyukov, *Glavnye techeniya,* p. 124.

40. *Nestor,* II, 178–180, quoted by Koyalovich, p. 116.

41. Schloezer's *Probe russischer Annalen* (Bremen-Goettingen, 1768) is generally moderate in tone and points out that the history of Russia in the tenth and eleventh centuries was no more barbaric than that of other European nations (p. 164). At the same time, he rejected attempts to link the Slavs to Troy or Babel and the "Roxolani" theory of the Russian name (pp. 67–70, 82). See also his favorable comments on Russia in his memoirs (note 36 above), p. 68.

42. *Ibid.,* p. 70.

43. Quoted by Milyukov, *Glavnye techeniya,* p. 110.

44. M. M. Shcherbatov, *Istoriya rossiiskaya ot drevneishikh vremen* (3rd ed.; St. Petersburg, 1901), I, 8–12, 161–162, 264–265, 270.

45. *Ibid.,* I, 367–372.

46. Quoted by Milyukov, *Glavnye techeniya,* p. 121 from the second edition, I, p. 11. I have been unable to find this passage in the edition available to me.

47. Shcherbatov, *Istoriya,* I, 330.

48. V. Fursenko in *Russki biograficheski slovar* s. v. "Shcherbatov, M. M."

49. Sukhomlinov in *Akademiya Nauk; sbornik otdeleniya russkogo yazyka i slovesnosti*, XXXV (1880–1881), 110–128.

50. Quoted by V. O. Klyuchevski, *Ocherki i rechi* (Moscow, 1918), p. 170.

51. Boltin, *Primechaniya na Leklerka*, I, i.

52. *Ibid.*, I, 268, 278; II, 7, 120–121, and *Kriticheskiya primechaniya general-maiora Boltina na pervy-vtoroi tom istorii knyazya Shcherbatova* (St. Petersburg, 1793–1794), I, 308–309; II, 35, 295, 375.

53. Boltin, *Primechaniya na Leklerka*, I, 6, 316.

54. Boltin, *Kriticheskiya primechaniya*, II, 82–87.

55. Boltin, *Primechaniya na Leklerka*, II, 152.

56. Sukhomlinov (see note 49, above) reprints the speech (pp. 383–390) and notes that some academicians objected to its being printed as delivered. As a result of the examination which was ordered, the speech, except for a brief excerpt, was not published.

57. Boltin, *Primechaniya na Leklerka*, I, 75.

58. *Russkaya Pravda* (2nd ed.; Moscow, 1799), pp. iii–9.

59. Boltin, *Primechaniya na Leklerka*, II, 308.

60. *Ibid.*, II, 248 and 254–258, 288; see also I, 124 ff. and 146.

61. *Ibid.*, I, 85–86, 272–275; II, 265, 294.

62. *Ibid.*, I, 35–36, 57–59, 80–82; *Kriticheskiya primechaniya*, I, 61–62.

63. *Primechaniya na Leklerka*, II, 295.

64. *Ibid.*, II, 250.

65. *Ibid.*, II, 349, 355, 362–364.

66. *Ibid.*, II, 252–254.

67. *Ibid.*, II, 369–370.

68. On Emin and Elagin, whose works have not been available, see Solovev, *Sochineniya*, V, 1381–1386; Koyalovich, pp. 132–134; Rubinshtein, pp. 93–95; Milyukov, *Glavnye techeniya*, pp. 30–32; Blagoi, *Istoriya*, p. 453.

69. "Zapiski kasatelno rossiiskoi istorii," *Sochineniya Imperatritsy Ekateriny*, VIII, 5.

70. *Ibid.*, XI, 523, 578.

71. *Drevnyaya rossiiskaya vivliofika*, I (1787), i–ii.

72. Sukhomlinov in *Akademiya Nauk; sbornik otdeleniya russkogo yazyka i slovesnosti*, XI (1875), 134.

73. Musin-Pushkin's preface to the *Dukhovnaya*, quoted by Sukhomlinov, *ibid.*, pp. 98–99. Mention must also be made of the revival of interest in the collection and publication of chronicles. In 1778, Peter's decree ordering their deposition in the Holy Synod was renewed. Beginning with the Nikon chronicle in 1762, at least ten others were made available in print (Likhachev, pp. 427–475).

74. Dashkova, I, 259.

75. Quoted by Shmurlo, in *Zhurnal Ministerstva Narodnogo Prosveshcheniya*, May–June 1912, p. 11.

76. *Sochineniya Karamzina*, IV, 187–189.

77. *Ibid.*, IV, 191.

78. Cited by Rubinshtein, *Russkaya Istoriografiya*, p. 186.

79. "Zapiska o novoi i drevnei Rossii," *Russki Arkhiv*, VIII (1870), 2231, 2238–2239, 2249.

80. *Ibid.*, VIII, 2250–2251.

The Search for a National Character 313

81. *Ibid.*, VIII, 2258.
82. "O lyubvi k otechestvu i narodnoi gordosti," *Sochineniya*, VII, 135.
83. *Istoriya Gosudarstva Rossiiskogo*, P. Einerling, ed. (5th ed.; St. Petersburg, 1842), I, ix.

CHAPTER VI: THE SEARCH FOR A NATIONAL CHARACTER

1. Dashkova, I, 152–154.
2. "Akademiya Nauk," *Entsiklopedicheski Slovar*, I (1890), 264; Blagoi, *Istoriya*, p. 43.
3. *Ibid.*, p. 92; see also Feofan Prokopovich's sermon on the fleet in Zapadova, *Russkaya Proza*, I, 18–19.
4. Quoted by Shmurlo, in *Zhurnal Ministerstva Narodnogo Prosveshcheniya*, October 1911, p. 322 and November–December 1911, p. 206.
5. *Ibid.*, November-December 1911, pp. 202, 238, 267.
6. "Gistoriya o rossiiskom matrose Vasilii Koriotskom i o prekrasnoi korolevne Iraklii florenskoi zemli," in Zapadova, *Russkaya Proza*, I, 22–38.
7. S. E. Desnitski, "Slovo . . . ," in Shchipanov, *Izbrannye proizvedeniya*, I, 189.
8. Lomonosov, "Kratkoe opysanie raznykh puteshestvi," in Zapadova, *Russkaya Proza*, I, 46; *Sochineniya*, I, 143–151, 165, 334.
9. N. I. Novikov, *Opyt istoricheskago slovarya o rossiiskikh pisatelyakh* (St. Petersburg, 1772), p. 122.
10. V. V. Sipovski, *N. M. Karamzin* (St. Petersburg, 1899), appendix, p. 35.
11. See, for example, T. Alefirenko, "Ekonomicheskie vzglyady V. N. Tatishcheva," *Voprosy Istorii*, no. 3 (1948), pp. 89–97.
12. Quoted by Gukovski, *Russkaya literatura*, p. 23.
13. I. Bak, "Ya. P. Kozelski," *Voprosy Istorii*, no. 1 (1947), pp. 83–100 and Blagoi, *Istoriya*, p. 36.
14. *Satiricheskie zhurnaly Novikova*, p. 410.
15. Sipovski, *Iz istorii russkogo romana*, II, 865.
16. Shcherbatov, "Zamechaniya na bolshoi nakaz," *Neizdannye Sochineniya*, p. 18.
17. In Bartenev, *Osmnadtsaty vek*, IV, 229–230, 239, 289–290.
18. *Ibid.*, IV, 246–260, 328.
19. Boltin, *Primechaniya na Leklerka*, II, 236.
20. Quoted by Hans Kohn, *The Idea of Nationalism* (3rd ed.; New York, 1946), p. 350.
21. "Nakaz Imperatritsy Ekateriny II," *Pamyatniki russkogo zakonodatelstva 1649–1832 gg.*, no. 2 (St. Petersburg, 1907), p. 10.
22. Fonvizin, *Pervoe polnoe sobranie sochineni*, p. 814.
23. *Satiricheskie zhurnaly Novikova*, p. 477.
24. Berkov, *Istoriya . . . zhurnalistiki*, p. 484.
25. Quoted by Trubitsyn, *O narodnoi poezii*, p. 217.
26. "Neizdannye stikhi N. A. Lvova," *Literaturnoe Nasledstvo*, nos. 9/10 (1933), p. 275.
27. "Nechto o vrozhdennom svoistve dush rossiiskikh," *Zritel* (St. Petersburg, 1792), no. 1, pp. 9–26 and no. 3, pp. 163–181.
28. *Ibid.*, no. 1, p. 9.

29. *Ibid.*, no. 1, p. 10.
30. *Ibid.*, no. 3, p. 173.
31. *Ibid.*
32. *Ibid.*, no. 3, p. 175.
33. *Ibid.*, no. 3, p. 181.

# Index

# Russian Research Center Studies

\* Out of print.
† Publications of the Harvard Project on the Soviet Social System.
‡ Published jointly with the Center for International Affairs, Harvard University.